Short Histories are authoritative and elegantly written introductory texts which offer fresh perspectives on the way history is taught and understood in the twenty-first century. Designed to have strong appeal to university students and their teachers, as well as to general readers and history enthusiasts, *Short Histories* comprise novel attempts to bring informed interpretation, as well as factual reportage, to historical debates. Addressing key subjects and topics in the fields of history, the history of ideas, religion, classical studies, politics, philosophy and Middle East studies, these texts move beyond the bland, neutral 'introductions' that so often serve as the primary undergraduate teaching tool. While always providing students and generalists with the core facts that they need to get to grips with, *Short Histories* go further. They offer new insights into how a topic has been understood in the past, and what different social and cultural factors might have been at work. They bring original perspectives to bear on current interpretations. They raise questions and – with extensive bibliographies – point the reader to further study, even as they suggest answers. Each text addresses a variety of subjects in a greater degree of depth than is often found in comparable series, yet at the same time in a concise and compact handbook form. *Short Histories* aim to be 'introductions with an edge'. In combining questioning and searching analysis with informed historical writing, they bring history up-to-date for an increasingly complex and globalized digital age.

For more information about titles and authors in the series, please visit: https://www.bloomsbury.com/series/short-histories/

A Short History of . . .

the American Civil War	Paul Anderson, Clemson University, USA
the American Revolutionary War	Stephen Conway, University College London, UK
Ancient Greece	P J Rhodes, Emeritus, Durham University, UK
the Anglo-Saxons	Henrietta Leyser, University of Oxford, UK
Babylon	Karen Radner, University of Munich, Germany
the Byzantine Empire: Revised Edition	Dionysios Stathakopoulos, University of Cyprus, Cyprus
Christian Spirituality	Edward Howells, University of Roehampton, UK
Communism	Kevin Morgan, University of Manchester, UK
the Crimean War	Trudi Tate, University of Cambridge, UK
English Renaissance Drama	Helen Hackett, University College London, UK
the English Revolution and the Civil Wars	David J Appleby, Nottingham University, UK
the Etruscans	Corinna Riva, University of Erfurt, Germany
Florence and the Florentine Republic	Brian J Maxson, East Tennessee State University, USA
the Hundred Years War	Michael Prestwich, Emeritus, Durham University, UK
Judaism and the Jewish People	Steven Jacobs, The University of Alabama, USA
Medieval Christianity	G R Evans, Emertius, University of Cambridge, UK
the Minoans	John Bennet, British School of Athens, Greece
the Mongols	George Lane, University of London, UK

A Short History of the Weimar Republic

Revised Edition

COLIN STORER

BLOOMSBURY ACADEMIC
LONDON • NEW YORK • OXFORD • NEW DELHI • SYDNEY

BLOOMSBURY ACADEMIC
Bloomsbury Publishing Plc
50 Bedford Square, London, WC1B 3DP, UK
1385 Broadway, New York, NY 10018, USA
29 Earlsfort Terrace, Dublin 2, Ireland

BLOOMSBURY, BLOOMSBURY ACADEMIC and the Diana logo are
trademarks of Bloomsbury Publishing Plc

First published in Great Britain by I.B. Tauris 2013
Rebranded edition published by Bloomsbury Academic 2019
Reprinted 2019, 2020, 2021, 2023 (twice)
This revised edition first published in Great Britain 2024

A catalogue record for this book is available from the British Library.

Library of Congress Cataloging-in-Publication Data
Names: Storer, Colin, author.
Title: A short history of the Weimar Republic / Colin Storer.
Description: Revised edition. | London ; New York : Bloomsbury Academic, 2024. |
Series: Short histories ; vol. 31 | Includes bibliographical references and index.
Identifiers: LCCN 2023041946 (print) | LCCN 2023041947 (ebook)
| ISBN 9781350172357 (hb) | ISBN 9781350172364 (pb) |
ISBN 9781350172388 (epdf) | ISBN 9781350172371 (ebook)
Subjects: LCSH: Germany–History–1918–1933.
Classification: LCC DD237 .S765 2024 (print) | LCC DD237 (ebook) |
DDC 943.085–dc23/eng/20231205
LC record available at https://lccn.loc.gov/2023041946
LC ebook record available at https://lccn.loc.gov/2023041947

ISBN:	HB:	978-1-3501-7235-7
	PB:	978-1-3501-7236-4
	ePDF:	978-1-3501-7238-8
	eBook:	978-1-3501-7237-1

Series: Short Histories

Typeset by Integra Software Services Pvt. Ltd.
Printed and bound in Great Britain

To find out more about our authors and books visit www.bloomsbury.com
and sign up for our newsletters.

To Jenny, with love.

Contents

Illustrations

Illustrations

---

* Note to the reader: The captions for Pahl's photographs have been translated and abridged by the author. For full captions, please follow Wikimedia Commons links.

Figures

Tables

Map

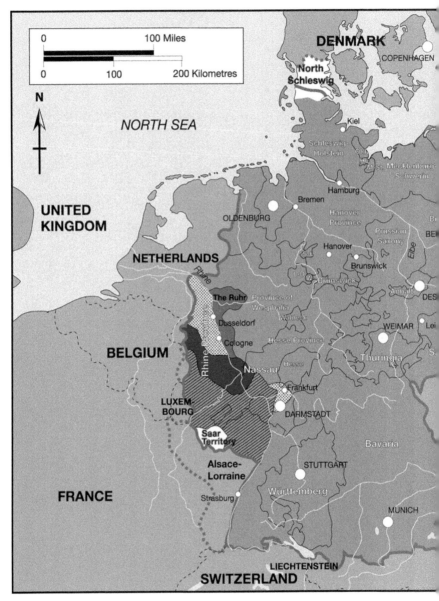

Weimar Germany

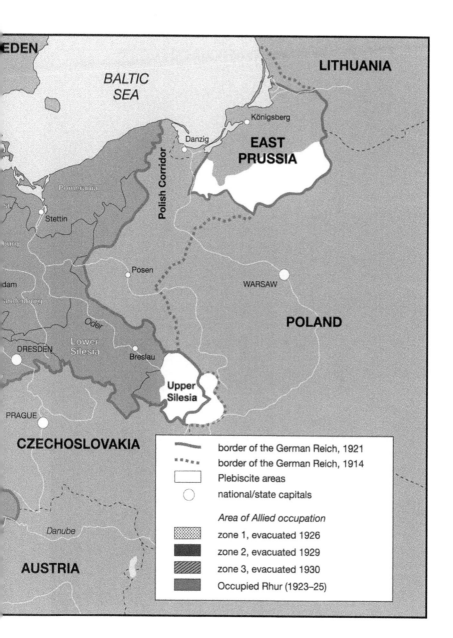

EDEN

LITHUANIA

BALTIC SEA

Königsberg

Danzig

EAST PRUSSIA

Polish Corridor

Pomerania

Stettin

St

burg

Posen

WARSAW

dam

anderburg

POLAND

Oder

Lower Silesia

DRESDEN

Breslau

Upper Silesia

PRAGUE

CZECHOSLOVAKIA

	border of the German Reich, 1921
	border of the German Reich, 1914
	Plebiscite areas
◯	national/state capitals
	Area of Allied occupation
	zone 1, evacuated 1926
	zone 2, evacuated 1929
	zone 3, evacuated 1930
	Occupied Rhur (1923–25)

Danube

AUSTRIA

Acknowledgements

This was not an easy book to write, and in some ways it was an even harder book to revise. Much has changed in the decade since the first edition was published. 2019 saw the centenary of the founding of the republic and many of the events covered in the first chapters of this book now seem firmly in the past. Yet with the rise of political populism in Europe and the United States, challenges to Western democratic norms, a global pandemic, inflation and industrial unrest, the present perhaps no longer seems as stable and certain as it did a decade ago and the Weimar Republic can seem eerily near at hand. Perhaps because of this, the flow of academic and popular discussion of the period has shown little sign of slackening. So much has already been written about the topic that condensing it all into a short history seemed a mammoth task back in 2013. It was even more daunting in 2022. I hope that I have both done the subject, and the diverse range of people who lived through the period, justice and managed to produce a coherent narrative and analysis that can be followed by students and general readers alike.

Like most authors I owe many debts of gratitude, too many to acknowledge in full here. I would like to thank Jo Godfrey who first suggested the project and who provided much useful input and advice during the writing of the first edition. I would also like to thank Emily Drewe who commissioned this revised edition and Abigail Lane and Megan Harris for their support and boundless patience in the face of my delays during the preparation of the manuscript. Thanks are due to my academic colleagues and students at the University of Warwick, and to the staff at the various libraries I consulted while working on the book. Finally, thanks, as ever, to all my friends and family – and especially to my wife Jenny – who have been unfailing in their encouragement and support throughout the writing of this book.

Timeline

1918

28 January	Beginning of a week-long nationwide series of strikes.
21 March	Beginning of German spring offensive on the Western Front.
18 July	Allied counter-attack begins.
8 August	'The Black Day of the German Army': British forces break through German lines.
29 September	Army High Command calls for an immediate armistice and formation of a civilian government.
3 October	New government under Prince Max von Baden formed. Armistice negotiations opened with President Wilson of the USA.
3 November	Austria–Hungary surrenders. Naval mutiny in Kiel.
9 November	Proclamation of the Republic. A new government under Friedrich Ebert formed.
10 November	Ebert–Groener Pact by which the army promises to defend the government against the threat from the extreme left in return for political autonomy.
11 November	Armistice comes into effect on the Western Front.
15 November	Stinnes–Legien Agreement between big business and trade unions.

16–21 December	Congress of Workers' and Soldiers' Councils.
29 December	Independent Social Democratic Party (USPD) withdraw from the Council of People's Representatives.
30 December– 1 January 1919	Founding congress of the German Communist Party (KPD).

1919

5 January	The German Workers' Party (DAP) founded in Munich.
5–12 January	Spartacist Uprising in Berlin.
19 January	Elections for the National Assembly.
6 February	National Assembly opened in Weimar.
13 February	Dissolution of the Council of People's Representatives. Philipp Scheidemann becomes Chancellor. Ebert elected Reich President by the National Assembly.
21 February	Bavarian Prime Minister Kurt Eisner assassinated.
3–10 March	'Bloody Week' in Berlin as second wave of left-wing unrest crushed.
7 April–1 May	Short-lived Soviet Republic in Bavaria.
21 June	Scheidemann government resigns to be replaced by a new administration under Gustav Bauer.
28 June	Treaty of Versailles signed.
11 August	Weimar Constitution ratified by the National Assembly.

1920

24 February	The DAP is renamed the National Socialist German Workers' Party (NSDAP).
13–17 March	Kapp Putsch in Berlin.

March–April	Communist uprisings in Central Germany and the Ruhr defeated by government troops.
6 June	Reichstag elections result in losses for the German Democratic Party (DDP) and an upsurge in support for right-wing parties.
21 June	A 'bourgeois' coalition under Konstantin Fehrenbach formed.
4 December	Split in the USPD. The 40,000-strong left-wing of the party votes to merge with the KPD.

1921

23 March	Beginning of Communist 'March Action'.
29 July	Hitler becomes chairman of the NSDAP.
26 August	Matthias Erzberger assassinated.
4 November	*Sturmabteilung* (SA) established.

1922

21 January	Walther Rathenau becomes Germany's first Jewish foreign minister.
16 April	Treaty of Rappallo signed with the USSR.
24 June	Rathenau assassinated.
18 July	Law for the Protection of the Republic is ratified by the Reichstag.
24 September	The right-wing of the USPD merges with the Social Democratic Party (SPD).
22 November	Shipping magnate Wilhelm Cuno becomes Chancellor.

Timeline

1923

11–16 January	Franco–Belgian invasion of the Ruhr.
13 August	Resignation of the Cuno government. Gustav Stresemann becomes Chancellor.
26 September	'Passive resistance' called off. A state of emergency declared.
21–23 October	Communist uprisings in Hamburg, Saxony and the Rhineland.
29 October	Elected governments of Saxony and Thuringia deposed.
3 November	The SPD withdraw from the government.
9 November	Attempted 'Beer Hall Putsch' in Munich.
15 November	Introduction of the Rentenmark.
30 November	Stresemann steps down as Chancellor and is replaced by Wilhelm Marx.

1924

26 February– 1 April	Hitler/Ludendorff 'Beer Hall Putsch' trial.
4 May	Reichstag elections result in a swing away from the moderate parties to the Communists and Nationalists.
1 September	The Dawes Plan is introduced.
7 December	Fresh Reichstag elections provide modest gains for the government parties and the SPD. The period of 'relative stabilization' begins.
20 December	Hitler released from Landsberg Prison, having served only nine months of his five-year sentence.

1925

15 January	The German National People's Party (DNVP) joins the government for the first time.
24 February	The NSDAP is refounded.
28 February	President Ebert dies.
26 April	Paul von Hindenburg is elected Reich President.
August	French troops withdraw from the Ruhr.
15–16 October	Locarno Treaties signed.

1926

24 April	Treaty of Berlin signed with the Soviet Union.
17 May	Wilhelm Marx becomes chancellor.
8 September	Germany joins the League of Nations.
9 October	Hans von Seeckt forced to resign as head of the Reichswehr.
10 December	Stresemann is awarded the Nobel Peace Prize.
18 December	The Law for the Protection of Youth Against Trashy and Filthy Literature is passed.

1927

29 January	The DNVP joins the government for the second time.
16 July	New law providing universal unemployment insurance is passed.

1928

20 May	Reichstag elections result in a swing from the DNVP to the SPD.
29 June	Formation of the 'Grand Coalition' under Hermann Müller.

20 October   Alfred Hugenberg becomes leader of the DNVP.

1929

1–3 May   'Bloody May' riots in Berlin between communist demonstrators and SPD-controlled police.

7 June   Publication of the Young Plan.

3 October   Death of Gustav Stresemann.

28–29 October   Wall Street Crash.

22 December   Referendum on the Young Plan.

1930

12 March   Reichstag ratifies the Young Plan.

27 March   Fall of the Grand Coalition and appointment of Heinrich Brüning as Chancellor.

30 June   Withdrawal of Allied troops from the Rhineland.

16 July   The Reichstag dissolved by presidential decree.

14 September   Reichstag elections result in Nazi electoral breakthrough.

1931

July   Banking crisis in Germany.

11 October   Formation of the Harzburg Front.

1932

10 April   Hindenburg re-elected in the second round of the presidential elections.

13 April   Ban on the SA introduced.

12 May   Wilhelm Groener resigns as defence minister.

30 May	Resignation of Heinrich Brüning, Franz von Papen becomes leader of a 'government of national concentration'.
4 June	Reichstag dissolved.
16 June	Ban on the SA lifted.
20 July	Illegal dissolution of the elected government of Prussia.
31 July	Reichstag elections see the NSDAP become the largest party.
13 August	Meeting between Hindenburg and Hitler. Hitler refuses the offer of the vice-chancellorship and demands to be appointed chancellor.
12 September	Reichstag dissolved following a vote of no confidence in Papen.
6 November	Reichstag elections see the NSDAP lose 2 million votes but remain the largest party.
2 December	Papen resigns. General Kurt von Schleicher becomes chancellor.

1933

4 January	Secret meeting between Papen and Hitler.
28 January	Schleicher resigns.
30 January	Hitler is appointed chancellor.
1 February	Reichstag is dissolved.
27–28 February	Reichstag Fire. The Law for the Protection of People and State suspends civil liberties and effectively bans the KPD.
5 March	Reichstag elections return a narrow majority for the NSDAP–DNVP coalition.
23 March	Enabling Act grants the new government sweeping emergency powers.

INTRODUCTION

On 30 December 2020, just days before supporters of President Donald Trump stormed the US Capitol, American news website *The Daily Best* published an article with the title 'Is America About to Suffer its Weimar Moment?'[1] This may have seemed prescient given the events of 6 January 2021, but it was also just the latest example of at least four years of media commentary in Britain and the United States that periodically evoked the spectre of Germany's first, 'failed' democracy as – to borrow the title of Laurence Rees's 1997 television documentary – 'a warning from history.'[2]

This reflects a widespread tendency to use Weimar Germany as a negative benchmark against which a society or a democracy can measure itself. Since Hitler's 'seizure of power' in January 1933 the republic that he subverted and destroyed has become a byword for economic collapse, political instability and democratic failure. At the same time, a sheen of glamour and decadence clings to the image of the republic in the popular imagination. Thanks to the novels of Christopher Isherwood, the musical *Cabaret* and, more recently, German television's adaptation of Volker Kutscher's Gereon Rath novels (as *Babylon Berlin*), the Weimar Republic has come to be associated with what often seem like surprisingly modern attitudes to female emancipation and gay rights.

Perhaps this is why the republic has been so endlessly fascinating to subsequent generations. Put simply, there is something for everyone. For those whose interest is primarily in politics, there was revolution and unrest, uniformed paramilitaries and violence in the streets. For those interested in the history of modern art, there was Dadaist poetry, Expressionist drama and Bauhaus architecture and design. For others, it is the sleazy cabarets and glitzy department stores that fascinate. The Weimar Republic was the home of new ideas about sex and sexuality and a vocal gay rights movement; of new rights and opportunities for women and a sometimes violent backlash against these. It saw the development of new scientific ideas and cutting-edge technology at the same time as widespread belief in alternative therapies and the occult. Its legacy is manifold and still with us today.

HISTORIANS AND THE WEIMAR REPUBLIC

History, unlike the past, is mutable and ever-changing. The reality of the past is unknowable – none of us can really experience what it was like – so it is the task of the historian to try to make sense of the evidence we have and construct a story that gives us a flavour of, in the words of the founder of modern Western historiography Leopold von Ranke, 'how essentially, things happened' (*wie es eigentlich gewesen*).[3] We are often told that we cannot rewrite history, but this is precisely what historians do. As new information and sources come to light, as we move further away in time from events, or as new perspectives are brought to bear, our understanding of the past changes and develops. Each generation brings its own values and outlook on life to the study of a period or event and establishes a consensus – or generates a debate – about how that piece of the past should be interpreted.

This is as true for the Weimar Republic as it is for any other period or event. Over time different facets of the republic have attracted historians and our understanding of the period has changed accordingly. For a long time, Weimar was regarded by historians and laymen alike as little more than the precursor of Hitler. This is hardly surprising considering that for a generation of Germans and, to a lesser extent, Anglo-American historians, the experience of dictatorship, world war and the Holocaust were the seminal traumas of their lives. To those refugees from Nazism who helped to shape our perception of interwar Germany, and for a generation of historians who sought to explain how the barbarity of the 1940s could have happened, the Weimar Republic was a weak and inherently flawed experiment, unloved by its people and doomed almost from the beginning by the circumstances of its birth.

Later, for many historians of the 1960s the republic came to be seen as a missed opportunity, a chance to forge a Marxist middle-way between soulless consumer capitalism and Stalinist totalitarian tyranny that was squandered or betrayed by moderate Social Democrats and 'bourgeois' politicians. Such negative and deterministic perspectives continued to pervade the historiography of Weimar into the 1980s and 1990s. These interpretations have cast a long shadow over our understanding of the period and contemporary accounts continue to focus on the problematic notion of the 'crisis' of the republic.[4] Even the title of Eric Weitz's generally more up-beat 2007 study, *Weimar Germany: Promise and Tragedy*, has a melancholy and elegiac air, redolent of missed opportunities and hopes betrayed, which only underlines this sense of fragility and doom.

Nevertheless, recent research has to some extent proved a corrective to this pessimistic perspective on Germany's first democratic republic. The 'cultural turn' in Weimar historiography which was begun by Peter Gay and Walter Laqueur in the 1960s and 1970s has both broadened and deepened our understanding of the Weimar Republic and begun to open it up from the narrow historical discourse that saw it as little more than a prelude to the Third Reich. More recently a new generation of historians have shone a light onto previously neglected areas such as gender relations and popular culture to better understand how the traumas and trials of the Weimar period related to everyday life. In so doing they have not only often given voices to those who have for too long been overlooked by scholars interested in politics and the 'failure' of the republic, but also challenged older narratives of an embattled polity unloved by its citizens.

The centenary of the Weimar Republic, as well as a sense that Western liberal democracy is facing a resurgence of populist extremism, have in recent years led to a resurgence of interest in the period. Since 2015 there have been new studies and reinterpretations of the November Revolution of 1918 and the events surrounding the foundation of the republic, while new attention has also been paid to political extremism (particularly on the right) and the collapse of German democracy. At the same time, a new generation of scholars have again reinvigorated the study of the Weimar by pointing out the gendered and heteronormative nature of many older studies and interpretations and arguing that we need to view the republic from a broader perspective that includes those who have often been overlooked in the literature for reasons of race, gender or sexuality.

The primary aim of this book is to bring together some of this research, both old and new, and to provide those who are unfamiliar with this fascinating period of modern German history with an accessible introduction to the history of the Weimar Republic. To this end, it will examine both the politics and culture (broadly defined) of

Weimar Germany and seek to place them in their wider historical and international context. In this way it is hoped that the reader will be presented with a more rounded portrait of the first German democracy, one which assesses it on its own merits and finds that while it may not have endured in the face of extraordinary pressures it still left a legacy of which it could be proud.

WEIMAR GERMANY IN CONTEXT

Historians tend to like their history to come in small, bite-size pieces, divided neatly by period or country, all the better to structure school or university curricula or books like this. Yet all such divisions are inherently artificial and arbitrary. History, as lived by its participants, is not episodic or clear-cut. In a sense the study of history is all about context. We can examine people, events, nations or whole time periods in exhaustive detail, but we can never fully understand their significance unless we appreciate their place in the bigger picture. Just as 'no man is an island', no historical event operates in isolation; every occurrence is just part of a larger whole and it is only when we take a step back and view all the separate pieces in relation to each other that we get a full understanding of them.

This is perhaps particularly true in the case of Germany. Two of the central historical debates within the study of modern German history have been the extent to which continuities and common threads can be identified running through the development of successive regimes, and the degree to which the German journey towards becoming a modern liberal democracy took a 'special path' (*Sonderweg*) that diverged from the more 'normal' road taken in countries like Britain and France. Although the *Sonderweg* theory is not nowadays as influential as it once was, it is still important to us as students of the Weimar Republic because it sees Germany's political and social development in a wider historical and international context.

Briefly, the theory goes that the failure of liberal unification movements in the nineteenth century meant that a pre-modern aristocratic elite were able to maintain their hold on power and Germany was thus prevented from developing the kind of civil society and political institutions that ensured the creation of stable democracies in Western Europe. The continuing influence of these old elites and lack of strong democratic traditions and institutions are often cited as key reasons why democracy did not take root in Germany during the interwar period, so this theory has particular relevance to our examination of the Weimar Republic. But to assess the merits of the *Sonderweg* thesis we need to look back into German history and to draw comparisons with developments in other nations.

This is equally true of many other explanations for the apparent 'failure' of the republic. One of the chief difficulties with much of Weimar historiography is that it tends to view developments in Germany in isolation from those taking place elsewhere in Europe. Again, this is a particular problem when looking at Germany. Internally divided and situated in the centre of the continent, Germany was for centuries Europe's battleground. Surrounded by powerful neighbours and with an economy dependent on exports, Germany was perhaps more at the mercy of international developments than any other European state. This became particularly apparent after the First World War when the peace settlement imposed on it hampered Germany's freedom of movement on the world stage. Furthermore, when viewed by itself or merely in comparison to older, established democracies like Britain or the United States, Weimar Germany might seem weak and unstable. But when compared to some of its close neighbours in the same period it begins to look much more robust. Similarly, when one considers Germany's path towards modernity in relation to the nations of Southern and Central Europe it begins to seem much less unique than it does if Britain or France are the benchmark.

ABOUT THIS BOOK

The first edition of this *Short History of the Weimar Republic* took a largely thematic approach to the subject, with each chapter dealing with a particular aspect of the history of Germany in the 1920s (political culture, the economy, foreign policy, society, etc.). For this edition the text has been extensively revised to present the material in a more straightforwardly chronological way. The first three chapters therefore aim to tell the story of the republic from its origins in Germany's defeat in the First World War to the end of the so-called 'Golden Twenties' in 1929. These chapters focus mainly on the political and economic history of the republic. Chapters 4 and 5, in contrast, step out of the narrative to look in more detail at the society and culture of Weimar Germany respectively. Finally, in Chapter 6 we return to the chronological approach to bring the story of the Weimar Republic to its conclusion with an examination of the republic's final economic and political crisis and the rise of the Nazis. It is hoped that this will aid the understanding of those readers who are coming to the subject for the first time and give a better sense of how events unfolded and how developments in various areas connected with one another.

As the title suggests, this is a *short* history of Weimar Germany. As such it aims to present a clear and *concise* introduction to the subject to both students and general readers. It makes no claims to completeness and readers will find that some aspects of life in the Weimar Republic receive more attention than others. Some readers will no doubt regret that some topics that they are particularly interested in are covered in less detail – or not at all – while others that they find less compelling are treated in more detail. For them, and for those who after reading this book would like to know more about Weimar Germany or to continue their study of its history a guide to further reading has been provided.

Just as it makes no claims to be a comprehensive history of Weimar Germany, this book is emphatically not the last word on the subject. The opinions expressed in this book reflect the author's current understanding of the subject and represent just one interpretation of the history of the republic. As has been noted above, much research continues to be undertaken on all aspects of German politics, society and culture in the 1920s and the available literature on Weimar continues to grow year by year. For now, though, it is hoped that this book will provide a concise and accessible introduction to the complex and nuanced history of the first German republic that will bring together some of the latest thinking on this fascinating period of German history that continues to have much to tell us about our own times.

1

WAR AND REVOLUTION: THE BIRTH OF THE REPUBLIC

Considering what came afterwards, it is perhaps significant that the Weimar Republic came into being almost by accident. The proclamation of the republic on 9 November 1918 was not the result of a detailed political programme or a long hard-fought campaign, but a reaction to events and an attempt to divert the people's energies from a more radical course. Yet the fact that democracy was thrust upon the German people should not mislead us into thinking that the Weimar Republic emerged out of nowhere, or that the revolution that brought it about was a failure. In fact, it represented the coming together of trends and traditions, some of them contradictory, that had long been present in Germany. Most of all it was the culmination and fulfilment of forces that had been unleashed by the brutal and traumatic experience of four years of mass industrialized warfare.

The Great War cast a long shadow over the Weimar Republic. Such was the scale of the conflict that few families were left untouched by it or by the social and economic changes that it brought about. Its effects were felt in the absence of loved ones who never came home or in the absence of limbs for some of those who did. But the war also led to lasting changes at a more abstract level. The demands of 'total war' changed the ways in which the German state and economy were run, changes that outlasted the war itself and which helped to shape the institutions of the Weimar Republic. It also unleashed forces that had long been held in check by the German Empire, accelerated the pace of social change and led to a shift in the gender dynamics of the German population.

GERMANY BEFORE THE FIRST WORLD WAR

It is easy to forget that at the time of the First World War, Germany was still a comparatively young nation. Unlike Britain, France, Spain and Portugal, that had evolved into unitary nation states by the end of the seventeenth century, Germany remained 'only a geographical expression'[1] for another two hundred years. Although the people who occupied the area shared a common language and culture, as well as a sense of 'Germanness', political power was divided between numerous autonomous kingdoms, principalities, dukedoms, bishoprics and free cities. There were 234 distinct states and 51 self-governing Imperial Cities in 1648 but these had been reduced through annexation and amalgamation to 39 by 1815. Although they nominally owed allegiance to some form of higher 'German' authority – the Holy Roman Empire until 1806, Napoleon's Confederation of the Rhine between 1806 and 1813, the German Confederation (*Deutscher Bund*) after 1815 – in reality the rulers of these states jealously guarded their independence, powers and privileges. These included the right to impose their religious beliefs on their subjects and following the Protestant Reformation of the sixteenth century, political disunion was deepened by a roughly north–south confessional split between Protestants and Catholics.

These disparate German states were finally 'hammered together by war and crafted with shrewd diplomacy'[2] into a nation state through the policies of Otto von Bismarck. He saw in German unification not the culmination of the yearning of all German people to come together under one flag, but rather an opportunity to increase the power and prestige (not to mention the territory) of the state of which he was Minister President, Prussia. By orchestrating three Wars of Unification against Denmark (1864), Austria (1866) and France (1870–1), Bismarck brought the north German states under Prussian control, decisively excluded Prussia's chief rival Austria from German affairs, and finally united the German states in opposition to the old enemy, France. With nationalist sentiment at an all-time high and fearing a backlash from their own subjects if they did not, the rulers of the south German states reluctantly consented to political union with Prussia. On 18 January 1871, the German Empire was proclaimed in the Hall of Mirrors at the Palace of Versailles.

The Germany that emerged from the Wars of Unification was a somewhat ambiguous polity. The Constitution of the German Empire defined it not as a unitary nation state like Britain or France, but as 'an eternal alliance for the protection of the territory of the Confederation' and 'the promotion of the welfare of the German people'.[3] It was made up of four kingdoms (Prussia, Bavaria, Württemberg and Saxony), six grand duchies, five duchies, seven principalities, three free cities (Hamburg, Bremen and Lübeck) and the *Reichsland* (imperial territory) of Alsace-Lorraine. The Imperial government was responsible for foreign policy, civil and criminal law, foreign trade and military affairs, but the individual states retained considerable powers over areas such as direct taxation, education and public health. Imperial Germany also combined contrasting and conflicting political traditions. On the one hand, the traditions of Prussia's authoritarian military monarchy were reflected in the extensive powers given to the Kaiser (Emperor), a hereditary office that was always to be held by the Kings of Prussia. On the other, Germany's tradition of constitutionalism and parliamentarism was represented in the establishment of a bicameral federal parliament, the lower house of which, the Reichstag, was elected by universal male suffrage. This was one of the most democratic franchises in the world at the time, more so than those operating in Britain and the United States, and led to the development of a sophisticated system of party politics and democratic culture. Although the powers of parliament continued to be limited – the Reichstag could approve or reject, but not initiate legislation and the government and military were not subject to direct parliamentary oversight – as time went on it became clear that Germany had entered into a period of mass politics in which the cooperation of the political parties (and by extension the electorate) was necessary for the smooth functioning of the state and the maintenance of the rule of law.

With 41 million citizens in 1871, rising to 50 million in 1890, Imperial Germany was the most populous nation in Western Europe. It was also one of the best educated. Compulsory elementary education had been commonplace in the German states since the late eighteenth century and by 1900 fewer than 0.05 per cent of the population were unable to read and write.[4] German universities were widely considered to be the best in the world and German academics produced groundbreaking research in disciplines as diverse as philosophy and physics, theology and chemistry. This huge, well-educated labour force, together with the establishment of a single currency (the *Goldmark*) in 1873 and the foundation of a central bank (the Reichsbank) in 1875, laid the foundations for an unprecedented period of industrial expansion, especially in emerging sectors such as chemicals and electrical and mechanical engineering. Between 1895 and

1911 German industry grew by an average of between 2 and 5 per cent per year, inflation was low (less than 1 per cent) and there was almost no unemployment. Between 1880 and 1914 Germany's share of world manufacturing surpassed that of Britain and its steel production was double that of the United Kingdom. By 1914 German gross domestic product (GDP) was larger than Britain's and nearly double that of France.

As the twentieth century dawned, Germany seemed to be at the height of its power. But beneath the surface Imperial Germany was a society that was ill at ease with itself. Germany's history of political fragmentation and the circumstances in which unification had been achieved left the new state with significant problems. All the constituent territories of the Empire had long-established and differing traditions and identities, not to mention political institutions, religious practices, ethnic makeups and, in some cases, languages. In this environment old loyalties – regional, social or confessional – endured. Campaigns against those who the government branded '*Reichsfeinde*' (enemies of the Empire) in the 1870s ultimately only served to solidify the separate identities of Catholics and the working classes and provided a guaranteed constituency to the political parties that represented their interests: the Catholic *Zentrumpartei* (Centre Party) and the Social Democratic Party of Germany (*Sozialdemokratische Partei Deutschlands* [SPD]). Both parties were to play a key role in the formation of the Weimar Republic, but the consequent identification of the republic with these groups which within living memory had been regarded as fundamentally 'un-German' only added fuel to the sense that the post-war democracy was an alien imposition.

Bismarck's dismissal as Chancellor in 1890 and the determination of the young Kaiser Wilhelm II to rule as well as reign did nothing to smooth over the divisions within German society. While the conservative and authoritarian traditional elites – the aristocracy, the army, big business – sought to maintain their grip on political power, there were significant forces at work in *fin de siècle* Germany that threatened to change the economic and social fabric of the nation forever. Industrialization and urbanization had a transformative effect on population distribution and social relations within the Reich, while new class tensions between the emerging working class, the expanding bourgeoisie and the nobility only exacerbated existing confessional, ethnic and regional divisions. At the same time demands for rights for women, rebelliousness amongst the young and avant-garde cultural experiments were all interpreted as acute threats to the existing order. Most commentators came to believe that modern capitalism was undermining the very fabric of society and as international tension rose the German people began to feel increasingly uncertain and embattled.

'THE SPIRIT OF 1914'

Many of the great turning points of German history have come as the result of conflict. The Thirty Years War helped shape the modern European state system; Frederick the Great's wars in the eighteenth century transformed Prussia into a European Power; the wars against Napoleon stimulated German nationalism; and the Wars of Unification united Germany under Prussian leadership. But if war was responsible for creating the German Empire, it also brought about its destruction. Following Bismarck's fall the feeling grew that Germany was being denied its legitimate rights as a Great Power by jealous rivals who sought to contain it in continental Europe. At the same time, the delicate system of alliances developed by Bismarck to avoid the nightmare scenario of Germany being surrounded by hostile powers began to break down, and by 1907 Europe was divided into two mutually hostile camps and riven by rivalry and distrust.

It was in this poisonous atmosphere of international suspicion and increasing tension that the heir to the throne of the Austro–Hungarian Empire, the Archduke Franz Ferdinand, was assassinated during a state visit to Sarajevo on 28 June 1914. The murder of the heir to the throne of one of Europe's Great Powers shocked the world and offered an opportunity for Austria–Hungary to put an end to the simmering nationalist discontent that neighbouring Serbia was thought to be fermenting within the multi-ethnic empire. Having first secured Germany's backing (the so-called 'blank cheque') the Austrians issued an ultimatum to Serbia and, when its terms were not met, declared war on 28 July. But Serbia was not without allies. Russia was pledged to support and protect the Serbs and duly mobilized its armies against Austria. In response, Austria's ally Germany declared war on Russia and, two days later, on Russia's ally France as well. The next day, 4 August, German troops crossed the Belgian frontier on their way to France and in response Great Britain declared war on Germany. Within days what had initially seemed to be a regional crisis had escalated into a general European conflict and the First World War had begun.

News of the declaration of war was greeted by large crowds in towns and cities throughout Germany, but those who welcomed it with patriotic demonstrations were a small minority who were 'youthful, middle-class and mostly, though not exclusively, male.'[5] At the other extreme, an equally small number of people openly opposed the war and around 750,000 people took part in nearly three hundred anti-war demonstrations between 28 and 30 July 1914. Most of the German population entered the conflict anxious but resigned to do their duty. Nevertheless, there were those who saw the war as a chance to settle old scores, to challenge the status quo, and to escape the monotony of modern life and win fame and glory on the battlefield. Moreover, the war was seen as an opportunity to suspend, if not transcend, social divisions and to finally complete the work of 1871 by creating a genuinely unified *Volksgemeinschaft* (national community). On 4 August Wilhelm II addressed the crowds from the balcony of the royal palace in Berlin, declaring that he no longer recognized parties, only Germans. Such sentiments were mirrored in the Reichstag, where the party leaders responded to the Kaiser's rhetoric by declaring a political truce, the *Burgfriede*, for the duration of hostilities. War credits necessary to finance the conflict were passed unanimously, and even the SPD joined in the patriotic fervour and declared their support for the war, much to the surprise of the military leadership who had been ready to impose press censorship and institute mass arrests in order to quell socialist 'defeatism'. The search to recreate this (largely imagined) 'spirit of 1914' and the national unity it implied was to be the holy grail of politicians on both left and right during the Weimar period and after.

Once war had been declared, it was essential that Germany acted quickly to get its troops in to the field. Facing enemies in both the east and the west, Germany put its faith in the so-called Schlieffen plan which envisioned a massive assault through Belgium into northern France that would encircle Paris and defeat France in six weeks. The German armies would then be free to turn and face Russian forces which, it was assumed, would be slower to mobilize due to the Russian Empire's vast size. But in the event, the attack into northern France was held up by stiffer than expected resistance and the German advance stalled in the face of an Anglo-French counter-attack along the river Marne in September 1914. There then began a 'race to the sea', as the Allies and the Germans each sought to outflank one another, leading to the construction of a four hundred-mile-long line of trenches and fortifications that stretched from the border with Switzerland to the North Sea. By December the Western

Front had stagnated into a war of attrition. Germany was confronted with precisely what it had tried to avoid, a war on two fronts for which it was not prepared militarily, let alone socially and economically.

Meanwhile, the war in the east was not proceeding according to plan either. The Russians had mobilized more quickly than expected and launched twin offensives into Austrian Galicia and East Prussia in August 1914. Panicked by the invasion, and under pressure from the East Prussian nobility, the German High Command transferred a further two army corps to the east to stem the Russian advance. These forces were under the command of the 67-year-old Paul von Hindenburg, who had been called out of retirement at the outbreak of hostilities. Together with his chief of staff Erich Ludendorff, Hindenburg annihilated the invaders at the Battle of Tannenberg. The Russians lost over 250,000 men, while German losses were about a tenth of that number. Hindenburg became a popular hero and was rewarded with promotion to the rank of Field Marshal and command of the entire Eastern Front.

With the failure of the Schlieffen plan and with it any hope of a quick victory, it soon became apparent that modern mechanized warfare would impinge on the lives of those left at home to an unprecedented extent. From the start, war production and the Allied blockade put huge strains on the German economy. Banks and export industries were badly disrupted, while Germany's ability to import essential raw materials and food stuffs was severely curtailed. Consequently, the state was required to step in at an early stage in order to ensure that the troops at the Front continued to be supplied with sufficient quantities of ammunition. As the war continued more and more elements of the peacetime economic and political order were subordinated to military needs, and the power and influence of the General Staff grew. By the time that the popular heroes of the Eastern Front Hindenburg and Ludendorff were appointed heads of the General Staff in 1916, Germany was effectively being governed by the 'silent dictatorship' of the *Oberste Heeresleitung* (Army Supreme Command [OHL]) which increasingly used their influence on the Kaiser to exert control of the appointment of ministers, veto reform and introduce legislation to militarize society.

As the war dragged on, rising casualties and the falling standard of living led to an increasing feeling of disillusionment and war-weariness. Under pressure from their constituents, the liberal and leftist parties began to press for a negotiated peace, while repeated attempts to break the stalemate on the Western Front met with failure. Ultimately the attempt to starve and terrorize the enemy into capitulation through a strategy of unrestricted submarine warfare only served to draw the United States into the conflict in April 1917, a development that more than offset the collapse of Tsarist Russia the same year and doomed Germany to defeat. In March 1918 the High Command made their last desperate throw of the dice by transferring troops from the east to launch a massive offensive against the British and French in the hope of bringing an end to the war before the Americans could arrive in any numbers. Despite an unprecedented 40-mile advance that saw Paris menaced for the first time since August 1914, the spring offensive had ground to a halt by July. Lack of reserves and equipment meant that the Germans were unable to withstand the Allied counter-attack which began on 18 July. Under pressure from the better equipped and better fed Allies, worn out by four years of warfare and facing fresh American troops in many sections of the Front, the German defensive line buckled and then broke. By the end of September, the Germans were in full retreat and the deteriorating military situation, combined with growing unrest at home, convinced the High Command that the war was effectively lost.

On 7 November a fleet of cars bearing large white flags and carrying German plenipotentiaries, led by Matthias Erzberger, crossed the Western Front. They were met by Allied troops and taken through the ruined landscape of northern France to a railway siding in the forest of Compiègne, where they were confronted by the representatives of the Allies. Given the stark choice between agreeing the Allied terms or seeing Germany invaded, Erzberger and his companions had no choice but to sign an armistice at 5 am on 11 November 1918. Six hours later the guns fell silent, and the war was at an end. But by the time the armistice was signed the German Empire that Bismarck had brought into being almost half a century before had already been consigned to history.

THE CRUCIBLE OF WAR

Together the Central Powers lost over 4 million men during the hostilities. Of the 13 million Germans who marched off to war between 1914 and 1918 around 2 million never came home at all, while of those who did return, 4.2 million did so bearing the physical wounds of their wartime experience. More than 24,000 German soldiers lost at least one arm and 48,000 at least one leg. Even those who escaped physical harm carried psychological scars and few returned from the Front unaffected by what they had seen and done. Roughly 19 per cent of the adult male population were direct casualties of the war.[6] As more and more men were thrown into the meat-grinder of the trenches, as quantities of rations and quality of equipment deteriorated and news of wartime shortages on the Home Front filtered through to the fighting men, morale began to suffer. While discipline amongst soldiers at the Front mostly remained strong, behind the lines it was a different matter. One in ten men transferred from the Eastern Front in 1917 deserted while in transit and by September the Berlin police estimated that there were around 50,000 deserters in the capital alone. By the summer of the following year as many as 100,000 men had deserted, while mutinies broke out in Ingolstadt, Munich and Würzberg.[7]

These ominous signs of military unrest were mirrored by growing dissatisfaction on the Home Front. Before the war Germany had imported around one third of its food, and with the Allied blockade in place no amount of rationing or *Ersatz* ('substitute') foods could solve the problem of shortages and high prices. The nutritional value of the German diet plummeted, and cases of malnutrition and rickets soared, especially amongst children. During the so-called 'turnip winter' of 1916–17 an early frost destroyed most of the potato crop, forcing much of the population to survive on a diet of turnips. Few Germans starved to death, but many were desperately hungry and the search for food and fuel became a full-time occupation for many older women. In this the Germans were more fortunate than their allies. By 1918 the Austro–Hungarian food supply had broken down completely and famine had gripped the Empire. Starvation accounted for between 7 and 11 per cent of civilian deaths in Vienna, where people dropped dead in the streets.[8] In both Vienna and Berlin a flourishing black market only increased public anger and exacerbated existing social tensions. The middle classes viewed those who relied on state and charitable assistance as freeloaders, while the poor resented this attitude and felt humiliated by their dependence on handouts. Both groups reserved their greatest anger for those in authority whose lifestyle seemed unaffected by the war. In many cases complaints about 'profiteers' took on an ugly, anti-Semitic, tone as people looked for someone to blame for their hardships and the Nationalist right were only too happy to fan the flames of prejudice.

All this had a radicalizing effect on the German population, leaving both men and women more independent, less deferential, and determined to challenge social convention and live life to the full. With men mostly away at the Front women and adolescents increasingly moved into the labour force, creating a huge new pool of unskilled workers who laboured in poor conditions for low pay and had little to lose from striking. Who they should look to for help in improving their conditions and articulating their political demands was far from certain, though. Already deeply divided between reformist and revolutionary wings, the SPD split in April 1917 and 42 break-away Reichstag deputies formed the *Unabhängige Sozialdemokratische Partei Deutschlands* (Independent Social Democratic Party [USPD]) which demanded an immediate end to the war and a radical programme of social and political reform. This schism was further widened by the Russian Revolution which seemed to offer a model of radical action to those on the left of the labour movement. At the same time, the Centre Party responded to the mood of their constituents and took up the popular cause of a negotiated peace, while the embattled bourgeoisie, fearful of defeat and revolution, retreated to the right and adopted even more extreme positions in the face of widespread opposition and uncertainty.

These developments created a dangerous and highly combustible mood within Germany that threatened to explode at any moment. A year before the end of the war there was a dramatic indication of the growing public hostility towards the Imperial regime when between two and three thousand Berliners went out on strike in protest over cuts in the bread ration and the regime's vague promises of domestic reform after the war. The unrest quickly spread throughout the country and was largely orchestrated not by the official trade unions, but by radical elements within the labour movement such as the Revolutionary Shop Stewards (*Revolutionäre Obleute*) in Berlin and unaffiliated radicals in other industrial cities. The demands of the strikers were both economic and political: lower food prices and higher wages, but also an end to the war, the restoration of civil liberties, and domestic political reform. In this instance the trade unions and Majority Social Democrats (MSPD) were able to reassert their authority and bring about a peaceful end to the strikes, but this was only a temporary truce in the struggle between government and workers.

Industrial unrest flared up again in January 1918 when a week-long strike broke out following similar disturbances in Vienna and Budapest. Up to 1 million German workers downed tools, with around 500,000 striking in Berlin and many more coming out in sympathy in Cologne, Hamburg, Danzig, Leipzig, Nuremburg and Munich. The strikers called for solidarity with workers elsewhere in Central and Eastern Europe which sounded dangerously like the kind of rhetoric used by the Russian Bolsheviks. Furthermore, this time the MSPD found themselves unable to rein in the strikers, and, in a foreshadowing of events at the end of the year, they were forced to ride the tide of popular dissatisfaction and place themselves at the head of the movement for fear of losing the support of the working class once and for all. The government hit back, imposing martial law, placing factories under military control, declaring a state of siege in Berlin, and banning the Social Democratic newspaper *Vorwärts*. Nevertheless, a strike on this scale and for this duration was an ominous indication of the public mood and contained clear signs that the social changes wrought by the war would have a significant impact on political events.

REVOLUTION FROM ABOVE AND BELOW

This was the situation when on 29 September the OHL informed the Kaiser that the war was to all intents and purposes lost. The failure of the German spring offensive, the Allied breakthrough on the Western Front on 8 August 1918 – Ludendorff's 'black day of the German Army'[9] – and the collapse of Bulgarian and Austro–Hungarian forces in September, brought home to the High Command that their final gamble had failed and that an immediate surrender was essential to prevent invasion and social collapse. On 1 October Ludendorff told the General Staff that 'a total defeat could probably no longer be averted' and that 'Our own army was unfortunately already badly infected with the poison of Spartacist-socialist ideas' to the extent that 'One could no longer rely on the troops.' In a display of staggering hypocrisy or self-delusion, he also announced that the High Command had dropped their opposition to domestic political reform, saying that 'I have ... asked His Majesty to include in the government those circles who are largely responsible for things having developed as they have ... Let them be the ones to sign the peace treaty that must now be negotiated. Let them clean up the mess they got us into.'[10]

To this end, the moderate Prince Max von Baden was appointed Chancellor on 3 October and for the first time two Social Democrats – the co-chairman of the MSPD Philipp Scheidemann as minister without portfolio and the trade unionist Gustav Bauer as labour minister – were included in the cabinet. There followed three weeks of frantic attempts at reform that have been characterized as a 'revolution from above'. It was announced that henceforth the Chancellor and the government would be accountable to parliament and the personal prerogatives of the

Kaiser (and in particular his powers to appoint ministers) were curtailed. However, the practical effects of the reforms were limited by the fact that they were not widely publicized and that the Reichstag almost immediately adjourned pending new elections. For most people there would be little change in their daily lives. Furthermore, the proposed reforms did not go far enough to appease those who had come to see the Kaiser himself as the problem, while at the same time alienating those who believed that a hard line should be taken with the malcontents.

By the end of October Germany was a powder keg just waiting to explode. The spark that lit the fuse of revolution was the decision by right-wing officers amongst the High Seas Fleet (which had played little part in the war aside from the indecisive Battle of Jutland in 1916) to order the *Kriegsmarine* to be put to sea for a final suicidal confrontation with the Royal Navy. When news of this impending *Todeskampf* ('suicide offensive') leaked out it led to a mutiny at the naval base at the Baltic port of Kiel, and on Sunday 3 November more than 20,000 sailors and dockworkers gathered at a local park in a show of solidarity with the mutineers. The demonstration was met with force and seven people were killed and 29 injured when military police opened fire on the protestors. However, this only served to further radicalize the sailors, and the next day the whole of the Third Squadron of the fleet mutinied. Armed sailors then marched ashore and occupied the military prison, freed their comrades, and then took over other strategic buildings. By 6 November, the disturbances had escalated with dockworkers and soldiers joining the rebels and the establishment of Workers' and Soldiers' Councils along the lines of those set up during the Russian Revolution of 1917.

This was at first more of a spontaneous protest movement than a revolution. As the playwright and revolutionary Ernst Toller recalled, 'No leader had arranged this uprising. The revolutionary leaders at the factories had reckoned for a later day. The Social Democratic Deputies were surprised and dismayed.'[11] The Kiel mutineers were not trying to topple the government – if anything they saw themselves as defending it against reactionary elements within the officer corps. Nevertheless, once news of the disturbances at Kiel and the initial heavy-handed attempts to crush it leaked out, the discontent that had simmered beneath the surface for so long exploded into a full-blown revolution that quickly spread throughout the Reich. As far afield as Hanover, Stuttgart and Frankfurt strikes were held, mass demonstrations staged, and Workers' and Soldiers' Councils established. This was followed by the occupation of public buildings and freeing of political prisoners, but there was little

Anti-war demonstrations at Kiel, 4 November 1918 (Bundesarchiv, Bild 183-R72520/ CC-BY-SA 3.0).

bloodshed: in most cases the authorities lost their nerve at the first sign of unrest and either fled or handed power to the councils. In Bavaria anti-war demonstrations so alarmed King Ludwig III that he and his family fled Munich on 7 November. That night a new 'Revolutionary Parliament' nominated the left-wing journalist Kurt Eisner as Prime Minister. Within 24 hours and without a shot being fired the old regime in Germany's second largest state had collapsed and power was in the hands of a scruffy-looking intellectual who claimed to represent the interests of the working classes.

One of the things that set the November Revolution in Germany apart from other moments of major political upheaval such as the French Revolutions of 1789, the revolutions of 1848 or the Russian Revolutions of 1917, is that it began not in the national capital, but in the provinces. The Anglo-German aristocrat and patron of the arts Harry Kessler described it in his diary as a 'Viking strategy', the 'progressive encroachment, as by a patch of oil, by the mutinous sailors from the coast to the interior'.[12] There was little coordination and events 'unfolded in a highly regionalized way'.[13] Although mutinous sailors from Kiel acted as 'rail-borne revolutionary evangelists', spreading the word of their revolt to towns and cities throughout northern Germany, places like Munich and Frankfurt experienced their own revolutions that were motivated by dissatisfaction with the general conditions that prevailed in the country, but also by very local concerns, and in some ways only tangentially linked to the Kiel mutiny.[14] This reflected the tradition of regional political autonomy that had been carried over into the federal structure of the German Empire and the spontaneous nature of the revolution. It also meant that it was difficult both for the forces of the old regime to stem the tide of the revolution and for any of the organizations of the political left (the MSPD, the USPD, the trades unions, etc.) to control its course and outcome.

Another notable feature of the revolution that, until recently, has not been fully appreciated by historians, was the leading role played by women in the upheavals of 1918–19. Although women were denied the vote under the German Empire, in the years before 1914 they participated in politics in large numbers as members of political parties, activists and campaigners. Some of the leading theorists of the German labour movement were women – Clara Zetkin, Luise Zeitz and Rosa Luxemburg are the most famous – and votes for women had been part of the SPD's programme since 1890. In 1906 women made up 1.7 per cent of the membership of the Social Democrats, rising to 16.1 per cent at the beginning of the war and 20.4 per cent in 1919. During the war women had been at the forefront of anti-war protests. As early as 1915 women had gathered in their hundreds in Berlin to protest about high food prices and to demand an end to the war, but as more women entered the workplace and as conditions deteriorated on the Home Front many were further politicized and radicalized. In 1916, 62 per cent of all striking workers in Germany were women, rising to 75 per cent in 1917. Female membership of the SPD nearly doubled (from 107,336 to 206,354) between 1916 and 1919 and 500,000 women were members of a trade union in 1918. In Hanover, women outnumbered men in strike committees during the labour unrest of January 1918.

Women were well-represented in the crowds and marches that spearheaded the revolution throughout Germany and played leading roles in the establishment of the USPD, the Spartacist League and the Communist Party of Germany. They volunteered to assist the Councils (mostly in clerical and administrative capacities) in their thousands and took part (albeit usually in a supporting role) in the fighting during the second, bloodier, stage of the revolution in the first half of 1919. The declaration that 'All elections to public bodies shall henceforth be conducted according to equal, secret, general voting rights on the basis of a proportional election system for all male and female persons of at least twenty years of age'[15] on 12 November 1918 (four days after equal suffrage had been announced in Bavaria) unleashed a new wave of mass mobilization as women seized the opportunity to participate fully in the political process. The enfranchisement of women ushered in debates about the role of women in politics and society that were to run throughout the Weimar period and beyond, while the role played by women in the political upheavals of 1918–19 also generated a violent backlash from the political right. It is notable, and an indication of how threatening some men found the changes taking place in gender relations, that the revolution itself was denounced as 'feminine' by its opponents and that women were especially targeted during the counter-revolutionary violence of 1919.[16]

By 7 November, the revolution was closing in on the capital and the military governor, General Alexander von Lisingen, responded by locking down Berlin, banning mass gatherings and ordering more troops into the city. But filling the capital with troops who were supposedly reliable but were also bored, hungry and dissatisfied only stoked tensions further. MSPD chairman Friedrich Ebert warned Prince Max that 'Unless the Kaiser abdicates, the Social Revolution is inevitable'[17] and later that day Scheidemann told the cabinet that 'We have done all we could to influence the masses' but 'it ought to be stated frankly that it is the Kaiser who must shoulder the heaviest responsibility of all ... Already he is generally regarded as having been to blame for the war ... It is our conviction that Germany will suffer a revolutionary break-down unless the Kaiser abdicates at once.'[18]

Early in the morning of 9 November workers gathered in their factories before setting off to join various protest marches that made their way through Berlin to converge on the city centre. This was a well-planned and co-ordinated event, though not one over which the MSPD had much control. Soldiers and police either joined the revolutionaries or stood by and let the demonstrations pass. After frantic attempts to contact the Kaiser who was at military headquarters in Spa, Belgium, had no result, Prince Max felt that he had no choice but to act on his own initiative and issued a proclamation announcing that 'the Kaiser and King has resolved to *renounce the throne*' and the formation of a regency.[19] Thirty-five minutes later a delegation of the SPD executive arrived at the Chancellery to demand that they take over the government 'for the avoidance of bloodshed'.[20] Prince Max was only too happy to comply and willingly handed power to Ebert, whose first act as Chancellor was to call on the protestors to leave the streets.

However, this appeal, like the declaration of the Kaiser's abdication, was too little too late. By this time, 'a perfect avalanche of humanity'[21] had reached the city centre and early in the afternoon Karl Liebknecht and members of the far-left Spartacus League occupied the Imperial Palace, hauled down the Imperial standard and replaced it with the red flag. Liebknecht then appeared before the dense crowds milling about between the Palace and the Reichstag and delivered a fiery speech in which he proclaimed the formation of a Soviet Republic. At roughly the same time Philipp Scheidemann addressed the crowd in the hope of persuading them to disperse. Speaking from a window in the Reichstag, he announced the formation of a 'Labour Government to which all Socialist Parties will belong', exhorted the masses to 'stand loyal and united' and ended his oration with the words 'Long live the German Republic!'[22]

Scheidemann believed that this was a decisive moment in the revolution, the point at which the crowds turned away from radicalism and the idea of a democratic republic became 'a thing of life in the brains and heart of the masses'.[23] Yet this assessment smacks of wishful thinking. The republic still had a long way to go before it became a reality. That Ebert recognized the precarious nature of his position is evidenced by the precautions that he proceeded to take to ensure that having gone this far, the revolution went no further. Even as the MSPD entered feverish negotiations with the Independent Socialists in order to deliver the promised 'Labour Government', he never formally relinquished the title of Imperial Chancellor and as such remained head of the traditional organs of the state.

After much internal debate the USPD agreed to enter a coalition with the MSPD on the condition that only socialists be included in the cabinet (thus dashing Ebert's hopes of a cross-party government of national unity), that the government declare that all power resided with the Councils, and that elections to a National Assembly be postponed until the revolution had been consolidated. Reluctantly, Ebert agreed, and on 10 November the Council of Peoples' Representatives (*Rat der Volksbeauftragten*) was formed. This was in effect a new government outside the traditional power structure of the Imperial state and was made up of three representatives of the MSPD – Ebert, Scheidemann and Otto Landsberg (an SPD Reichstag deputy from Magdeburg) – and three members of the USPD – Hugo Haase, Wilhelm Dittmann and the Revolutionary Shop Steward Emil Barth – with Ebert and Haase as co-chairmen.

For the next eight weeks the Council of Peoples' Representatives and the Workers' and Soldiers' Councils on one hand, and the more

Scheidemann proclaims the German Republic from the window of the Reichstag (Bundesarchiv, Bild 175-01448/CC-BY-SA 3.0).

traditional apparatus of the state (the civil service, the army, etc.) on the other, governed Germany in tandem. Ebert maintained that the council was merely a caretaker government and that all decisions relating to the long-term constitutional settlement would be put off until after elections to National Assembly could be held. At the same time, he used his position as Chancellor to try and establish a functioning relationship with the middle-class parties and civil service to ensure the orderly demobilization of the army, continuation of food supplies and a smooth transition to a peacetime economy. All this was contrary to the USPD's insistence that the Councils were the embodiment of the revolutionary will of the people and as such had a mandate to implement a radical social programme including the nationalization of industry, the break-up of the landed estates and the radical democratization of the army, civil service and judiciary. The scene was set for a clash between the radically different visions of state and society espoused by the two wings of the labour movement.

Ebert's ability to impose his authority on the country was enhanced when on the evening of 10 November, he received a telephone call from General Groener at Army Headquarters in Spa. Groener offered the new Chancellor the army's support in return for his cooperation in 'combating Bolshevism' and 'maintaining order and discipline within the army'.[24] Ebert's agreement to this suggestion has been seen as a betrayal of the revolution, and it is true that the so-called Ebert–Groener Pact ensured that the army, particularly the officer corps, would retain a degree of their former power and independence from the civilian authorities during the Weimar period. Yet while Ebert's decision to do a deal with the army has often been roundly attacked by historians on the left,[25] to interpret it as a betrayal is to fundamentally misunderstand the nature of the November Revolution. Ebert's authority and legitimacy were shaky – his assumption of the Chancellorship was unconstitutional (Article 15 of the Imperial Constitution stated that the Chancellor was directly appointed by the Emperor and therefore Prince Max had no right to confer the title on Ebert) and the Council of People's Representatives' claim to speak for the council movement nationwide was 'at best, tenuous'[26] – and he had little means of imposing his will on a truculent and potentially violent populace beyond asking nicely. Under the circumstances the deal with Groener seems like 'a pragmatic agreement'[27] born of 'clear-sighted realism'.[28]

Ebert and his Social Democratic colleagues never desired a complete transformation of German society – indeed, the Chancellor was heard to comment that he hated the revolution 'like sin'[29] – and once the monarchy had been toppled they consistently sought to guide Germany along a moderate course. Nor was there much appetite amongst the population in general for the radicalism of the far-left – the mass of soldiers, sailors and workmen's demands were for peace, bread and democratization, not social revolution. While it is true that on the whole the middle classes and the moderate Socialists exaggerated the threat from the left – there was, after all, no disciplined revolutionary party like Lenin's Bolsheviks in Germany, only the small band of intellectuals who made up the Spartacists – it is also true that historians have had a tendency to exaggerate the degree to which the new government's accommodation with Groener signalled a shift to the right. Ebert's government was not pernicious in intent. When one considers that they lacked any other means to impose their fragile authority on the capital, let alone the country as a whole, Ebert's compromise with Groener begins to look less like a betrayal of the revolution and more like 'a reasonable precaution to protect his government against violence from the extreme left'.[30]

Ebert's position was further strengthened by two events. Firstly, on 15 November, the trade unions under Karl Legien came to an agreement with employers, represented by the industrialist Hugo Stinnes. The so-called Stinnes-Legien Agreement saw the employers' associations recognize the legitimacy of the unions and agree to the introduction of an eight-hour working day, in return for an agreement to abandon calls for the wholesale nationalization of industry. This did much to satisfy the long-held grievances of the working classes and dampened enthusiasm for a more radical socio-economic programme. At the same time, elections to the Councils produced a victory for the moderates who favoured Western-style parliamentary democracy over Soviet Communism. When over 500 delegates (299 for the SPD, 101 USPD, 25 liberals and 75 without party affiliation) representing Workers' and Soldiers Councils from all over Germany met at Berlin's Busch Theatre on 16–21 December 1918 they were easily persuaded that any momentous decisions about Germany's future should be put off until after the election of a National Assembly. Despite some fiery rhetoric about the nationalization of key industries and the democratization of the army, on 19 December the Congress of Workers' and Soldiers' Councils voted in favour of the proposal that all power should be left in the hands of Ebert's government until elections on 19 January 1919.

THE CHALLENGE FROM THE LEFT

By December 1918 it looked as though the revolutionary energies of the proletariat had been channelled along the moderate liberal-democratic course favoured by Ebert and the MSPD leadership. However, events over the Christmas period proved that the revolution was far from over. On 23 December the People's Naval Division (*Volksmarinedivision*), 500 sailors from Kiel who had come to Berlin to defend the revolution, took MSPD commandant of Berlin, Otto Wels, hostage and barricaded themselves in the royal stables. On Christmas Eve government troops bombarded the palace with artillery, but the sailors stayed put. The next day the government, fearful of a widespread reaction against their hard-line tactics, backed down, while a crowd of Spartacists briefly occupied the *Vorwärts* offices. This skirmish brought to a head the tensions between the USPD and MSPD members of the Council of People's Representatives, and on 29 December Haase, Dittmann and Barth resigned from the government.

The withdrawal of the USPD from the Council also provided the MSPD's spokesman on military and colonial matters, Gustav Noske, with an opportunity to play the role of strong man. Noske accepted the post of Minister for National Defence with the words 'You can count on me to re-establish order in Berlin. Someone must be the bloodhound. I am not afraid of the responsibility.'[31] His first move was to appoint the aristocratic reactionary General Walther von Lüttwitz as Commander-in-Chief of Berlin and to provide the government with a better means of defending itself. Whatever Groener might have promised Ebert on 10 November, the regular military establishment was 'almost completely incapable of taking action to suppress unrest within Germany'.[32] Once it became clear that the war was over, the overriding concern of most soldiers was to get back home as quickly as possible. Despite appeals from Hindenburg for troops to be patient and remain with their units until formally demobilized, most soldiers gave in to a powerful *Drang nach Hause* (drive to get home) and simply left their units without waiting for their discharge papers, 50-marks and free civilian suit. By January 1919, only 1 million of the 6 million troops of the wartime army remained at their posts. Of the 3 million men returning from the Western Front, about 1 million left the army without being officially discharged.[33] Those soldiers who did stay with their units, especially those who had been stationed behind the lines, became a menace to the public, stealing food and equipment and selling them on the black market, refusing to obey orders, intimidating the local population, and getting involved in violent clashes with fellow soldiers returning from the Front.

Under these circumstances Ebert's government turned to irregular paramilitary forces to maintain any sort of order and defend itself from the radical left. This idea has been attributed to General Groener's adjutant, the future Chancellor and *éminence grise* of late Weimar Germany, Colonel (later General) Kurt von Schleicher, but some such voluntary paramilitary detachments had already come into being. After the November Revolution a wave of volunteerism and 'self-help' flooded across the country, resulting in the formation of a variety of ad hoc paramilitary groups ranging from revolutionary 'Red Guards' to republican 'self-defence regiments' and middle-class *Einwohnerwehren* (Home Guards). Among the first was the 1,500 strong *Eiserne Brigade* ('Iron Brigade') under Colonel von Roden, raised by Noske in November 1918 from loyal naval officers in Kiel. Independently and on his own initiative, General Ludwig von Maercker formed the *Freiwillige Landesjägerkorps* (Volunteer Rifleman's Corps) which was led by experienced officers and non-commissioned officers (NCOs) who had seen front-line service and was open to any man who had completed basic training but rejected overtly political (i.e. anti-republican) volunteers and required all members to take an oath of allegiance to the Ebert government. Other units sprang up, phoenix-like, from the ashes of the regular army in the winter of 1918–19: General von Hoffmann brought a division of Horse Guards, General Held formed a unit from the 17th Infantry Division, while General von Hulsen raised an 11,000-strong force in Potsdam. All these followed the precedent set by Maercker, with an officer (sometimes a General, but more often a Colonel, Major or Captain) announcing his intention to form a *Korps* to like-minded colleagues who then occupied a barracks or similar building to use as a base and began recruitment and training. Recruitment was initially by word of mouth, but soon newspaper advertisements and lurid recruiting posters began to appear, appealing to Germans to stand up and defend their country from Bolshevism.

These volunteer units quickly became collectively known as *Freikorps*, after the irregular volunteer formations that had joined the Prussian Army during the Wars of Liberation against Napoleon. This title was at once descriptive – the volunteer units were 'Free Companies' of irregular troops outside the normal military hierarchy – and a political statement. By adopting the mantle of the *Freikorps* the volunteers were positioning themselves as defenders of the Fatherland against foreign encroachment – be that in the form of French or Polish invasion or in the form of the 'alien' ideology of Communism.

The rapid proliferation of these units and the zeal with which they went about their work have often been seen as evidence of the brutalizing effects of war that bequeathed a culture of political violence to Weimar Germany. The writer Ernst von Salomon, who fought with the *Freikorps* in Germany and the Baltic and later served five years in prison for his part in the murder of Walter Rathenau, described the volunteers as men who:

> had not yet got over the war. War had moulded them; it had given meaning to their lives and a reason for their existence. They were unruly and untamed, beings apart who gathered themselves into little companies animated by a desire to fight ... They had realised that this peace was a delusion – they would have no part in it.[34]

As such they had much in common with men throughout Europe who struggled to re-adjust to civilian life following the First World War. The *Freikorps* were just one part of 'a fairly homogeneous transnational milieu of predominantly middle- and upper-class political radicals characterized by youth and war-induced militancy', who shared a common experience of war, revolution, unfulfilled personal and national ambitions, opposition to Western democracy and a fear and loathing of the Slavonic world (which was seen as being the origins of almost everything they despised) that bordered on the pathological.[35] In places as far afield as Ireland and Turkey, Finland and Italy the war had unleashed a tide of nationalist and economic discontent and 1919 saw a global wave of strikes, demonstrations and uprisings against the established order. There was a very real fear amongst Western leaders that the foundations of capitalism and liberal democracy were being shaken and might give way. The political violence that was unleashed upon the German population in the years between 1918 and 1923 was far from being unique and can indeed be seen as conforming to a wider regional, European and even global, trend towards violence and unrest.[36]

With his troops in place, Noske attempted to dismiss Berlin's Police President, the left-wing USPD member Emil Eichhorn (who was widely suspected of having helped the Peoples' Naval Division during their confrontation with the government). Although the events that followed are known to history as the Spartacist Revolt, the initial response to Eichhorn's dismissal was organized by the USPD and the Revolutionary Shop Stewards who interpreted the move as a 'counter-revolutionary' bid to roll back the gains of the November Revolution. The Spartacists, who had merged with other left-wing groups to form the Communist Party of Germany (*Kommunistische Partei Deutschlands* [KPD]) at a Congress held between 30 December 1918 and 1 January 1919, felt compelled to act to take leadership of what seemed like the beginnings of a workers revolt. Following protest marches and the seizure of Berlin's newspaper district on 5 January a revolutionary committee was formed and proclamations issued denouncing the 'Judases in the government' as 'miserable underlings of capitalist intrigue' who were 'stained with the blood of their brothers' and calling on the masses to 'Get out, out of the factories and into the streets' and to 'Take up arms! Use your weapons against your deadly enemies, the Eberts and the Scheidemanns!'[37]

The government responded by unleashing the *Freikorps* upon the insurgents. On 10 January a detachment of soldiers was sent to secure the suburb of Spandau where the Spartacists threatened to take the local munitions works. The following day, 1,200 young officers, cadets and students attacked the Belle–Alliance Platz (Berlin's publishing district) with overwhelming force, using flame throwers, machine guns and artillery to drive the Spartacists out of their positions behind makeshift barricades. By Wednesday 15 January the revolt was all but over and the Communist leaders had gone into hiding. However, this did not save them from vicious reprisals. On 16 January it was reported in the *Berliner Zeitung* that Karl Liebknecht and Rosa Luxemburg had been arrested and taken to the Eden Hotel, headquarters of the Garde Kavalrie Division. There they had been beaten and interrogated before being bundled into separate cars. Liebknecht, already bleeding profusely from a head wound, was taken to the Tiergarten, told to get out of the car and then shot in the back. Luxemburg was clubbed over the head before being shot and dumped into the Landwehr canal.

But this was not an end to the violence. On 6 February the United Worker's Council for the Ruhr, fearing that the government would move against them after an earlier clash over the expropriation of the region's coal mines, ordered a general strike. When *Freikorps* moved in an autonomous republic was proclaimed and coal shipments to the rest of Germany suspended. On 3 March the KPD published an appeal for a general strike in Berlin, signalling 'Bloody Week', a second wave of revolutionary unrest in the capital which left up to 15,000 people dead and 12,000 injured after nine days of savage street-fighting. This was followed by a series of violent confrontations in Gotha, Halle, Dresden,

Brunswick and Leipzig between March and May 1919 as General von Maercker was dispatched to 'pacify' central Germany.

Meanwhile, the assassination of Kurt Eisner and wounding of his Social Democrat rival for leadership of the revolution, Erhard Auer, on 21 February 1919 had thrown Bavaria into turmoil. With the two dominant personalities in Bavarian Social Democracy out of action, the state descended into anarchy. The newly elected Provincial Assembly broke up in disorder, what was left of the cabinet fled to Bamburg and a general strike was called in Munich. The power vacuum was filled on 7 April by an unlikely group of anarchists and intellectuals led by the essayist and poet Erich Mühsam and the playwright Ernst Toller. The stated aim of this new Council Republic (*Räterrepublik*) was the creation of 'a truly socialist community' and 'a just socialist-communist economy'.[38] It also rejected 'any cooperation with the despicable government of Ebert' and declared that 'there will be no union between socialist Bavaria and the imperial Germany, no matter its republican façade.'[39] However, its leaders lacked practical experience of politics and the short-lived experiment was marked with chaos and eccentricity. The Minister of Finance, Silvio Gesell, wanted to abolish money, and the Foreign Minister Franz Lipp (who had recently been released from a psychiatric hospital) declared war on Switzerland and telegraphed Lenin complaining that his predecessor had absconded with the key to the ministry toilet.[40] The regime quickly managed to alienate both the Bavarian middle class and the more orthodox left, and after only six days the Council Republic collapsed in the face of an attempted putsch by Republican Guards. The Russian Communist, Eugene Leviné, who had been dispatched to Munich by Liebknecht and Luxemburg to set up a Bavarian Communist Party, seized control of Munich and managed to recruit a 10,000–strong Red Army which immediately began requisitioning food, property and cash and rounding up political opponents.

Initial attempts to retake the state capital by the SPD-led government in Bamburg were met with humiliating failure and Prime Minister Johannes Hoffmann was reluctantly forced to appeal to Berlin for military assistance. Noske was only too happy to oblige and on 27 April a 30,000 strong force of *Freikorps* entered Bavarian territory. Dachau was taken two days later, and on 1 May government troops entered Munich virtually unopposed. Opposition to 'Bolshevism' had already taken on a distinctly extreme and anti-Semitic tone. As the Jewish academic and diarist Victor Klemperer recalled, around this time 'the Jew became a convenient, all-purpose enemy'[41] and for many on the right, there was little distinction drawn between Jews and Communists. This was made manifest in the indiscriminate violence of the week-long 'White Terror' that followed. Estimates vary as to how many were killed, but official statistics record around 600 deaths in the first week of May alone and a further 2,200 'Reds' subsequently sentenced to death or long periods of imprisonment.[42] Amongst those killed were Leviné and the anarchist Gustav Landauer, both summarily executed by *Freikorps* soldiers, while Toller and Mühsam were captured and imprisoned. Finally, on 7 May, the commander of the government forces General von Oven reported to his superiors that Munich had not only been 'pacified', but also 'cleansed'.[43]

FOUNDING THE REPUBLIC

Despite the wave of violence that was sweeping the country, elections to the National Assembly were held on 19 January 1919. Demographic changes and the extension of the franchise through the National Voting Act of 30 November 1918 had increased the number of people eligible to vote to 37.4 million, of whom over half were voting for the first time. Women now made up 54 per cent of the electorate and there were 2.8 million more women than men eligible to vote. Eighty-two per cent of all women aged over 21 voted and 300 stood as candidates, of which 39 were elected.[44] Although this new female electorate tended to vote for parties of the political right, the elections produced a resounding victory for the MSPD and their moderate allies in the Centre and liberal parties and gave a popular mandate (and legitimacy) to Ebert's provisional government.

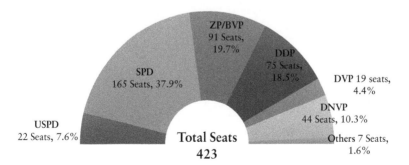

Figure 1.1 National Assembly Election Results, 19 January 1919.

Friedrich Ebert, the first President of the Weimar Republic, photographed in 1922 (Bundesarchiv, Bild 146-2004-0097/CC-BY-SA 3.0).

The Assembly convened on 6 February, not in Berlin but in the sleepy Thuringian town of Weimar. The decision to convene the first elected body of the new republic in a city forever associated with Germany's most famous author, Johann Wolfgang von Goethe, was designed to distance the new regime from Prussian militarism and evoke the spirit of German Romanticism. However, there were also very practical reasons for not attempting the serious business of drafting a constitution in the Reich capital: 'Red Berlin' was still considered much too dangerous, and Weimar was much smaller and easier to defend than the Prussian capital.

Ebert was elected president by the Assembly on 11 February and Scheidemann became Chancellor of a coalition made up of the moderate left-leaning parties. The first major tasks facing the National Assembly were to transform the temporary armistice of November 1918 into a permanent peace treaty and to formulate a constitutional framework for the new republic. The debate over the Treaty of Versailles exposed the divisions in German society over the peace terms and led to the collapse of the republic's first government after only 130 days (see Chapter 2). Meanwhile, between February and July a 25-man committee of experts led by the eminent jurist Hugo Preuß and including such luminaries as the sociologist Max Weber and the historian Friedrich Meinecke worked on a constitution for the republic. Following a series of parliamentary debates on key issues, the constitution was approved by a vote of 262 to 75 on 31 July and it was signed into law on 11 August 1919.

THE WEIMAR CONSTITUTION

The constitution of the new republic was intended to embody advanced principles of democracy while providing a degree of continuity with the past. At the same time, the experience of the November Revolution left many fearful of mob rule and convinced that a strong guiding hand was needed, especially in times of national crisis. Thus the framers of the Weimar constitution sought to devise a document that would reconcile 'a truculent bourgeoisie and an insurgent working class, both of which had been alienated from the state by the war and its aftermath'.[45] The result was a state based on the notion of compromise that sought to incorporate the popular demand for democracy and freedom, while at the same time protecting the vested interests of important groups within Germany society.

The Weimar Constitution opened with a clear statement that the legitimacy and sovereignty of the republic came from the German people. The tradition of federalism was continued, and the federal states (*Länder*) were represented at the national level in the upper house of parliament (the Reichsrat), whose members were selected by the elected assemblies in each state. The lower house of parliament, the Reichstag, was a directly elected chamber whose members were elected every four years by all Germans over the age of 20 through a system of proportional representation. The electoral system was designed to provide a parliament in which the views of the electorate were represented as fully as possible. The country was divided into 35 electoral districts (*Wahlkreis*) for each of which the parties put forward a list of candidates. Electors voted for a party, not a specific candidate, and one seat was awarded per 60,000 votes cast in each district. This system was one of the most democratic in history and did consistently and accurately represent the political will of the German people. It also, as the framers of the constitution intended, made it difficult for any single party to gain an absolute majority, thus forcing various political factions to come together and compromise to form a functioning government. However, it also enabled small single-interest or extremist parties, some of which were fundamentally opposed to the republican system of government, to gain representation in parliament which in turn made the business of forming a stable governing coalition harder. The result was that governments tended to be short-lived and often struggled to muster a majority to pass their legislation (there were 20 different governments in the 15-year lifespan of the republic, 10 of them between January 1919 and May 1924, only three of which could command a majority in the Reichstag).

The head of government, the Chancellor, was not elected but was appointed by the president. Nevertheless, the Chancellor and his cabinet were subject to approval by the Reichstag and were required to resign if they lost a confidence vote. Legislation could be proposed by any member of the Reichstag and was passed by a simple majority vote in the lower house. These bills were then passed for approval to the upper house. The Reichsrat had the power to veto legislation, though the lower house could overrule the veto if a two-thirds majority of deputies voted in favour of doing so. Thus, while theoretically the *Länder* had little power over national legislation, the fragmented nature of Weimar party politics meant that in effect bills vetoed by the upper house frequently died. In unusual circumstances (if the proposed legislation was particularly controversial or would have a serious impact on foreign affairs) the president could decree that a proposed bill should be presented to the public in a referendum before it could be passed into law. Constitutional amendments could be proposed by any member of the lower house in the same way as other legislation but required a clear two-thirds majority in the Reichstag to be enacted.

As a counterbalance to the strong legislature, the Weimar Constitution also provided for an equally powerful directly elected executive. This has often been presented as one of 'Weimar's birth defects', but at the time it was seen as a means of ensuring that the people would choose their leaders and preventing politics from being dominated by the bureaucratic 'party dictatorships' that would emerge if parliament were given too much power.[46] The president of the republic was directly elected by universal suffrage for a seven-year term (the exception was the first president, Friedrich Ebert, who was elected by the National Assembly rather than by a popular poll due to the precarious political situation and died before his seven-year term had expired). As supreme commander of the armed forces the president had the final say on military matters, held the power to convene and dissolve parliament, and appointed the Reich government. Furthermore, Article 48 of the constitution allowed the president to suspend civil rights and rule by decree in the event of 'public order and security' being 'seriously disturbed or endangered', and to order the use of force to compel state governments to fulfil their obligations under the constitution or Federal law.[47] Any German citizen aged 35 or above was eligible to stand for election as president as long as they were not a member of the Reichstag at the time. In the event of parliament losing confidence in the president, the Reichstag could force a referendum on his 'recall' before the expiration of his term in office. To do this a vote of no confidence had to be passed by a two-thirds majority in the lower house (Article 43).

As well as setting out the institutional structure by which the republic was governed, the Weimar constitution also enumerated the rights of German citizens and attempted to meet the demands of the people for legislation to offset some of the social and economic disparities in German society. The constitution established a Supreme Court on the American model which was supposed to be above politics and to which citizens could appeal in the event of disputes with the state. It also guaranteed certain fundamental civil rights – equality before the law (Article 109), the right to free speech and assembly (Articles 114, 118 and 123), equality for women (Article 109), economic justice (Article 151) and the right to strike (Article 159). It also established a welfare state (Article 161) that took the system of unemployment benefit, sickness insurance and old-age pensions first introduced by Bismarck in the 1880s even further and for the first time enshrined in law the principle that it was the role of the state to assist the less fortunate in society (a principle that would be built upon by the republic's post-war successor). Primary education was made compulsory and the Reich government, state assemblies and local communities had joint responsibility for ensuring its provision.

The Weimar constitution achieved much that was ahead of its time, but it failed to heal the deep divisions within German society: industry, land and public services were left unreformed and in private hands, while the armed forces, civil service and universities continued to be dominated by the conservative upper and upper–middle classes whose commitment to the new republic was lukewarm at best. This can be blamed on the fact that the constitution had, by necessity, to be a compromise between differing political forces that sought to provide stability and security for the German people as a whole. Those on the left could not push for more radical social and economic reforms without risking prolonging the violence and uncertainty that had gripped Germany since November 1918. Nevertheless, the republic's founders were to some extent guilty of wishful thinking: 'the SPD leadership hoped that structural change would follow in the wake of legitimate constitutional reform',[48] but in the event little fundamental change was accomplished without state intervention to assist in breaking down vested interests in big business, the landed estates, the army, and the judiciary. The exception that proved the rule was Prussia, which became an unlikely bastion of republicanism for much of the Weimar period. While at a national level many Imperial officials remained in post, the same could not be said in Prussia. Under the Social Democrat Minister President Otto Braun and Interior Minister Carl Severing, 'regional and local government ... saw many monarchist officials replaced by republicans ... the police force reformed, illicit military and paramilitary activities suppressed, and all manner of right-wing extremists pursued with increasing conviction'.[49]

Furthermore, the new republic suffered from a certain degree of constitutional uncertainty – did ultimate power lie with the representative assembly of the people or the popularly elected head of state? The liberal intellectuals who had formulated the constitution had attempted to create a political system that reconciled their ideal of a democratic *Volksstaat* (citizen state) with the conservative desire for a state where power was concentrated in the hands of a strong executive. The result was a system with a 'strong' presidency that was, in theory at least, tempered by parliamentary checks and balances. This tension between these 'two radically different visions' has been seen as 'the underlying fault line of the Weimar Republic'.[50] Although initially there was thought to be no contradiction here, with hindsight it is easy to see in the system of proportional representation used to elect the Reichstag or the emergency powers given to the President under Article 48 the roots of Weimar's later political fragmentation and slide into dictatorship. Yet whatever its limitations the electoral system was adopted for the laudable reason that its creators wanted to make parliamentary elections as democratic as possible. Unfortunately, they did not recognize that the divided nature of German society meant that this would result in such a fragmented parliamentary landscape in which compromise and consensus became increasingly difficult to achieve. Similarly, it is easy to detect echoes of the Imperial authoritarianism of the past or the totalitarian tyranny of the future in Article 48, but it is important to note that it was not the provision of emergency powers themselves that led to dictatorship. Most political systems, including that of the United States, allow governments to adopt sometimes sweeping powers in times of emergency, so the idea is not unique to Weimar. Furthermore, Article 48 was frequently used constructively to defend the republic, particularly during the early 'years of crisis' between 1919 and 1923. When used as intended as a short-term measure to defend the republic and the German people at a time of public disorder, as was the case under President Ebert, emergency powers were not a problem. However, when the president was a figure who was at best ambivalent towards the very idea of republicanism and democracy, as was the case after 1925, Article 48 became instead a means to circumvent the Reichstag and revive the authoritarian political culture of the old Imperial elite. We therefore should not blame the collapse of the republic on the supposed 'flaws' of its political system, but rather look to the groups and individuals who manipulated that system to undermine democracy.

The Weimar Republic, like the German Empire that preceded it, was born in war. But whereas the German nation state of 1871 was forged in the elation of rapid victory, the republic emerged from the dejection of defeat. Four years of bloody mass industrial warfare had reshaped German politics and the economy, while draining the resources, manpower and morale of the German people so that by 1918 the Imperial system looked increasingly unsustainable. News of defeat and fears that the people's aspirations for peace and reform would not be realized sparked a wave of popular protests that rapidly gathered pace to become a full-blown revolution that toppled the monarchy, though what it was to be replaced with was less clear. The stage was set for a bloody confrontation between different visions of Germany's future in which the moderate socialists made a fateful decision to rely on military force to head off the challenge from their opponents on the extreme left. As we shall see, this was to be a decision that they would come to regret as it became clear that they had unleashed forces that they were unable to control.

The German revolution of 1918–19 has traditionally been denigrated by historians 'who fixated on its shortcomings and missed opportunities'. But as some of the more recent accounts have demonstrated, it also delivered 'an armistice, a republic, parliamentary democracy, and the first-ever socialist government of an advanced industrial economy'.[51] These were considerable achievements and none of them were guaranteed. Nevertheless, it failed to reconcile different groups within German society and left a legacy of bitterness that was to dog the republic throughout the next 15 years. Weimar's tragedy was that not only was the republic created in the most difficult of circumstances, but also that it was never given the time and stability to process the trauma and heal the wounds of the war and revolution that gave it birth.

2

CRISES AND CONSOLIDATION, 1919–23

Although Chancellor Otto Bauer hailed the adoption of the new constitution on 11 August 1919 as the beginning of a new era, this momentous change was greeted with little enthusiasm by the public. One British observer noted that 'The ceremony was witnessed by a large crowd, but there were no cheers.'[1] This might be taken as evidence for the accusation often levelled at the Weimar Republic that it was unable to generate much, if any, popular support. But it also reflects the tense and uncertain atmosphere in which the republic was founded and the preoccupation of its leaders with the practical business of governing a country facing serious domestic and international challenges. Germany's transition from authoritarian monarchy to 'the most radical democracy in Europe'[2] was not a smooth one, and the path did not grow any easier. In the first three years of the new decade, the Weimar state was forced to sign an unpopular peace treaty; had to negotiate the difficult process of transitioning back to a peacetime society; faced violent challenges from both right and left; and had to cope with the virtual collapse of the economy. It is little wonder that this period has traditionally been seen as Weimar's 'years of crisis'. Yet this was also a period of consolidation when new institutions were established, and democratic norms laid down. Under the presidency of Friedrich Ebert, the state weathered the storm and laid foundations that were to be the basis of the brief period of stability that the republic was to enjoy after 1924.

MAKING PEACE

One of the chief demands of the strikers and revolutionaries of 1918 had been an end to the war and with it all the hardship and privation that Germany had suffered over the previous four years. The armistice of 11 November 1918 was only a temporary cessation of hostilities, not a permanent end to the conflict. Until a peace treaty was signed Germany technically remained at war and the threat of invasion by the Western Allies was still a very real possibility. Most importantly, the Allied blockade remained in place and shortages of essential goods like fuel and food continued, leading to 'perhaps a quarter of a million civilian deaths' between the armistice and the lifting of the blockade in July 1919.[3] At the same time, hundreds of thousands of German troops remained in the occupied territories in Eastern Europe and in some cases were drawn into conflicts between the Bolsheviks, counter-revolutionary 'White' Russian forces and local nationalists seeking independence from Russia. These troops needed to be brought home, the violence ended, and Germany's borders needed to secured if the government was to concentrate on the business of restoring political and economic order at home.

The German delegation to the Paris Peace Conference in Versailles, 1919 (Bundesarchiv, Bild 183-R01213/CC-BY-SA 3.0).

Peace was therefore a priority for Germany's new republican rulers, but the type of peace they got, and the manner in which it was delivered, came as a shock. One of the chief reasons why the military leadership had been willing to hand power over to civilian authorities in the autumn of 1918 was the belief that a broad-based civilian administration would be better suited to negotiate a peace treaty with the Allies. And once the revolution and elections to the National Assembly had delivered a civilian government with a democratic mandate, the Germans believed that they would be invited to discuss terms based on President Wilson's Fourteen Points.[4] But in the event, there was no negotiation. In a departure from previous diplomatic practice, the Germans were not invited to the Paris Peace Conference until the Allies had already decided on the terms of the treaty. Instead, the German delegation was presented with the draft terms of a peace treaty on 7 May 1919 and given a mere two weeks to consider them and submit written comments. This was in part an attempt to cover up the very real differences between the victors, but it also reflected the popular feeling in the Allied nations that the Germans were to blame for the war and had to be punished. Everything was done to humiliate the Germans, to remind them that they were not equals, but defeated enemies.[5]

By the terms of the treaty Germany lost the territories of Alsace and Lorraine which had been taken from France after the Franco–Prussian War of 1870–1 (Article 51); East Prussia was detached from the rest of Germany and a 'corridor' of territory transferred to Poland (Articles 27–8 and 87–8); the mostly German-speaking territories of Eupen-Malmedy were transferred to Belgium (Article 34); while North Schleswig, the most economically important part of Upper Silesia, and Memel (Niemen) were all later lost after plebiscites (held in 1920, 1921 and 1923, respectively) returned majorities in favour of union with Denmark, Poland and Lithuania. Germany was forced to surrender its overseas colonies to the Allies (Article 119), while the Saar basin was placed under the administration of the League of Nations for 15 years and France given exclusive rights over the exploitation of its coal mines (Article 45). An *Anschluss* ('joining') between Germany and the new Austrian Republic was forbidden (Article 80), even though opinion in Austria favoured such a union (and Article 2 of the new Austrian constitution declared Austria to be part of Germany). The German Army was ordered to demobilize and from the end of March 1920 it was forbidden to exceed seven infantry and three cavalry divisions (a total of 100,000 men, of which no more than 4,000 could be officers) in strength (Articles 159–63). The General Staff (regarded by the Allies as the wellspring of German militarism since the days of Bismarck) was ordered to disband and severe limitations were placed on the armaments that Germany was permitted to develop and store. The Navy was to be reduced to little more than a coastguard of 15,000 men and 36 ships and forbidden the use of dreadnoughts and submarines (Article 181), while other modern military material such as aircraft (Article 198) and tanks were prohibited. On top of this, the Germans were to compensate the Allies for their losses during the war through the payment of reparations in cash and in kind (Articles 233–5). Finally, in order to ensure that the terms of the treaty were met, a strip of territory to the west of the Rhine was to be occupied by the Allies for a total of 15 years, the whole of the Rhineland was declared a demilitarized zone, and Germany was not permitted to build any fortifications or station any military material or personnel in the region (Articles 428 and 42–3).

When the peace terms became known, there was an immediate outcry. The theologian and founder of the German Democratic Party (*Deutsche Demokratische Partei* [DDP]), Ernst Troeltsch, called them 'an imperialist monstrosity … reminiscent of the way Rome once proceeded against Carthage',[6] while the *Berliner Mittagszeitung* denounced Article 231 as 'the greatest crime against humanity ever committed'.[7] Scheidemann's government resigned rather than sign the treaty, the Chancellor asking rhetorically 'Which hand would not wither that binds itself and us in these chains?'[8] Attempts to negotiate concessions – offering reparations of 20 billion gold marks by 1926 and the further 80 billion to be paid later, calling for immediate membership of the League of Nations and the establishment of a commission to investigate the question of war guilt – proved futile and the Germans were given the stark choice of signing the treaty as it was presented or facing an Allied invasion. Advised by General Groener that military resistance was not an option, Otto Bauer's new administration had no choice but to sign the document, which they did – under protest – on 28 June.

Any hope that the conclusion of peace would mark an end to a painful episode and allow the government to move on to other matters were almost immediately dashed. Germans of all political persuasions saw the terms of the treaty as unreasonable and unacceptable. Indeed, the Treaty of Versailles was about the only issue in German politics on which there was almost universal agreement during the Weimar period. Almost immediately voices were raised calling for the revision or circumvention of its terms, and throughout the Weimar period opponents of the republic used it as a stick to beat individual politicians and the democratic system in general. Those who had signed the peace treaty were reviled as 'traitors' and for many democracy itself was tainted by association with the hated treaty.

Part of the problem was that many Germans, particularly those on the political right, had trouble accepting that Germany had lost the war at all. No less a figure than Field Marshal Hindenburg declared publicly that the collapse of the army on the Western Front had come not as a result of defeat, but rather as a consequence of the 'intentional mutilation of the fleet and the army' by left-wing forces at home,[9] a view only underlined by the unfortunate wording of Friedrich Ebert's speech to returning troops on 10 December 1918 in which he told them that 'no enemy has vanquished you'.[10] Such statements led to the widespread belief that the German Army had not been beaten by the Allies but had been 'stabbed in the back' by the forces of sedition and revolution, thus giving birth to the *Dolchstosslegende* (stab-in-the-back myth). In the minds of those who refused to accept that Germany had been defeated, the humiliating Treaty of Versailles therefore became inextricably linked with the November Revolution and the republic that was born out of it.

On top of this there was outrage in Germany that the final peace terms seemed so different from President Wilson's Fourteen Points. There was a widespread view among politicians and public alike that a negotiated peace would be based on these principles and when they were presented with what they saw as the *diktat* of Versailles, the Germans felt that they had been 'grossly deceived'.[11] They argued that the peace treaty as it was presented made a mockery of Wilson's desire for 'covenants of peace, openly arrived at', and the confiscation of their overseas territories did not seem to be a 'free, open-minded and impartial adjustment of ... colonial claims'.[12] Furthermore, the prohibition of an *Anschluss* with Austria and the existence of sizable ethnic German populations in Czechoslovakia, Poland and Romania seemed to expose the fact that 'national self-determination' applied only where it suited the Allies.

When it came to the actual clauses of the treaty, these too were regarded as unnecessarily vindictive and disproportionate. The loss of territory was a definite blow and while some were prepared to swallow the bitter pill that was the loss of overseas colonies and Alsace–Lorraine (which had been German for only half a century), there were few who could accept the creation of the 'Polish Corridor'. The loss of West Prussia and Posen 'outraged German opinion more than any other territorial change'[13] as it transferred what were seen as inherent parts of the German (or perhaps more accurately Prussian) nation to people who many Germans saw as 'alien' and 'backward' and left East Prussia cut off from the rest of the Reich.[14]

Equally, the demand for reparations was considered to be a deliberate attempt to kick Germany while it was down and prevent it from recovering its former economic strength. There was a degree of truth to this, as the French were acutely aware of the threat that a German economic revival would pose to their own trade and had insisted on an astronomical reparations bill not only to cover the costs of reconstruction but also to try to stifle economic competition.[15] The problem was not so much the demand for reparations, as the scale of the indemnity imposed on Germany. It had always been expected that whoever lost the war would have to make some sort of reparations payment. This was normal practice: France had paid an indemnity of 700 million francs after the Napoleonic wars and more recently Germany itself had demanded reparations payments of five billion francs from France by the Treaty of Frankfurt (1871) and three billion gold roubles from Russia in the Treaty of Brest-Litovsk (1918). What most Germans objected to was what they regarded as the unrealistic scale of the reparations demanded by the Allies. In 1919 Germany was presented with demand for a one-off payment of 20 billion gold marks, a down payment on the final figure to be decided upon by a Committee and presented to the German government in May 1921. In effect Germany was compelled to sign a blank cheque when they signed the Treaty of Versailles. This was bad enough, but when the Reparations Commission presented Germany with a provisional figure of 226,000 billion gold marks to be paid over 42 years, the Germans were appalled. They suggested their own figure a month later: a modest one-off payment of 30 billion gold marks. This was unacceptable to Britain and France, and French troops occupied Düsseldorf and Darmstadt. At the end of April 1921 the Reparations Commission fixed a global total of 152 billion gold marks, and at the beginning of May Britain and France issued an ultimatum to Berlin giving the Germans a month to agree to the bill or the Ruhr would be occupied. The Germans had no choice but to agree. The first instalment of reparations was paid punctually in August, but with inflation rampant it became increasingly clear that Germany would not be able to raise enough hard cash to cover the next payment.

However, perhaps what hurt the most was the enforced admission for responsibility for the war. 'War guilt' was a new concept in international relations. Prior to the First World War it had generally been the case that the causes of a conflict were kept out of the process of peace making, with the result that as a rule it was the loser who paid. This principle was applied in 1919, but the victors sought to put a gloss of legal legitimacy on the business of hard-headed politics by forcing Germany to sign a document in which they admitted sole responsibility for the death and destruction caused by four years of conflict. The British Prime Minister David Lloyd George admitted as much when he declared at the London Conference in 1921 that 'German responsibility for the war ... is the basis upon which the structure of the treaty has been erected, and if that acknowledgment is repudiated or abandoned, the treaty is destroyed'.[16] Article 231 was the lynchpin of the treaty, the clause by which all the other clauses – and especially the Allied claim for reparations of sufficient magnitude that they would cover the costs of war pensions – were justified.

As such it was at this clause that Germany aimed its most vociferous denunciations. In response to accusations of war guilt the German Foreign Office, the *Auswärtiges Amt*, rushed to publish 'carefully chosen, edited and – if necessary – falsified' official documents to prove that Germany had not been responsible for the war.[17] Forty volumes of these were published between 1922 and 1927. Such was the desire to refute the accusation of war guilt that a special section of the Foreign Ministry, the *Kriegsschulderferat* (War Guilt Department), was established to encourage and subsidize the publication of attacks on the Versailles settlement. They worked closely with business, teachers and other groups to produce and distribute anti-treaty propaganda in Germany and abroad, with the aim of getting the terms of the treaty revised. This was the Holy Grail of German foreign policy throughout the Weimar period and beyond, but although (as we shall see) successive governments were to make some progress in chipping away at the reparations clauses and getting the Allies to agree to an early end to the occupation of the Rhineland, a comprehensive renegotiation remained elusive.

THE ECONOMIC SITUATION

The other pressing task facing the new Republic was the return to a peacetime economy. There was a widespread consensus that a rapid economic revival was vital to both the restoration of order at home and Germany's international rehabilitation. All were agreed that this could only be achieved through a smooth and speedy dismantling of wartime economic measures and the reintegration of returning soldiers into the workforce. For this, cooperation between workers and employers was essential, and this was what lay behind the Stinnes–Legien Agreement of 15 November 1918.[18] However, although the new republican authorities, in cooperation with the unions and employers, were remarkably successful in quickly switching Germany's economy back to a peacetime setting, successive administrations made fateful decisions regarding economic policy that were to prove disastrous in the medium term. To make matters worse, the promise of a new harmonious era of labour relations heralded in the Weimar Constitution was not to be realized and the fragile alliance formed between big business and organized labour in November 1918 soon broke down.

The industrialist and future Foreign Minister Walther Rathenau declared in a speech on 28 September 1921 that 'economics is destiny'.[19] This was true for the Weimar Republic in so far as it inherited a bitter economic legacy that was to some extent to shape its politics and society throughout its lifetime. The First World War left the German economy 'deformed and exhausted'.[20] Industry had been geared to war production at the expense of consumer goods, which when combined with the Allied blockade had led to severe shortages, while agricultural production had been disrupted by the conscription of the labour force and wartime requisitions of livestock and machinery. Industrial production had fallen to 57 per cent of its 1913 level by 1918, machinery had not been maintained and raw materials – half of which had been imported before 1914 – were in short supply. By 1917 military spending was taking up over half of gross national product (GNP), compared to only 3 per cent in 1913, while at the same time national income was falling. Germany also faced a looming fiscal crisis created by the decision to pay for the war by piling up debt that would then be paid off with reparations once Germany had won. In an attempt to bridge the gap between income and expenditure, the government sold their debts to the Reichsbank in return for cash (the monetization of public debt), precipitating a dramatic rise in the amount of paper money in circulation.

Until 1914 Germany had limited the amount of paper currency by maintaining a gold standard in which one paper mark was worth a single gold mark and could (in theory at least) be exchanged for gold on demand. The Reichsbank was obliged by the Bank Law of 1875 to hold enough gold to cover one-third of the issue of paper notes. But as the war progressed Germany, like the other combatant nations, increasingly sought to circumvent such restrictions, leading to a massive increase in the amount of paper money in circulation. At the same time, Germany was exporting gold bullion – twice as much as Britain – to finance the import of much needed food and raw materials. As a result, the national debt ballooned to 150 billion marks (compared to an annual national debt of about five billion before the war) with the German government owing 1.6 billion marks to the Netherlands alone. Unlike the currencies of the Allied nations, the value of the mark fell precipitously, and Germany emerged from the conflict with a currency worth roughly half its 1914 value. Inflation was then only made worse by the removal of wartime price controls that led to a surge in prices for staple goods between 1918 and 1920.

The Weimar Coalition had two options if they wanted to get inflation under control: increase taxation or cut government spending. In the precarious political situation after the war neither option was attractive (some might say practicable) as they would both serve to alienate the population and lead to further hardships and social unrest. This was especially the case given the raised expectations for a more equitable system of industrial relations and social life raised by the November Revolution. On top of this, the new republic faced a huge bill not only for pensions owed to more than 800,000 wounded veterans, 530,000 war widows and 1.2 million orphans, but also to cover the costs of the ambitious new welfare state promised in the Weimar constitution. Stuck in this bind, the government chose neither option and instead allowed the national debt to grow in the hope that this deficit financing would create jobs and stimulate demand. Public spending in 1919 was double what it had been before the war, but taxation only covered about half of this expenditure (up from 20 per cent during the war), falling to a mere 10 per cent by 1923. However, an essential part of this policy was allowing inflation to continue as 'lubricant' for 'the wheels of the economy'.[21]

If Germany's new leaders failed to get a grip on inflation, they were more successful in getting people back to work. This was seen as 'the key problem of the post-war transition'[22] and the one on which wider problems of returning to normal peacetime society hinged. It was not just that the 6 million men returning from the Front needed to be absorbed into the labour force, the whole German economy and labour-market needed to be restructured and wartime controls needed to be removed. The mobilization of industry behind the war effort had seen the massive expansion of certain sectors while others (such as construction) had withered to almost nothing through lack of demand in wartime. This had led to considerable internal migration as people moved from cities and regions where civilian industries (such as textiles) were located to those focused on heavy industry, leaving rural areas short of manpower. During the war, wages and working hours had been set by the state (in consultation with the trade unions and employers) and people had been told where and when they should work. The end of the conflict required the dismantling of this apparatus and a return to a normal labour market in which workers and employers determined their own destinies. And after the terms of the peace treaty were published it became clear that jobs would need to be found for those men who could no longer be employed in the reduced armed forces and those returning from Germany's former colonies and territory ceded to its neighbours.

The laborious task of releasing men from their wartime military service was largely taken out of the hands of the authorities when the army effectively disintegrated following the armistice. But this meant that the government had only a hazy idea of where these men were, and this limited the extent to which they could coordinate the reorientation of the labour-force. To try to get back the initiative, the Council of People's Representatives set up the Reich Office for Economic Demobilization (*Reichsamt für die Wirtschaftliche Demobilmachung* or *Demoblimachungsamt*) on 12 December 1918 'to take charge immediately of the entire operation of the economic demobilization'.[23] Through the winter and into the spring of 1919 a series of decrees set demobilization policy and constructed the machinery 'to keep the economy going, to place workers, in so far as they can no longer be employed in the armaments factories, as well as discharged soldiers, back in work and in their old regions'.[24] Loans and subsidies were made available to keep businesses afloat (and therefore continue to provide jobs) and to finance public work projects such as road works and tree planting to provide gainful employment for returning soldiers. Local authorities were required to provide support for those without jobs, and in the spring of 1919 a nationwide system of employment agencies was established. This was the basis for the Reich Labour Exchange which was set up in May 1920 to provide job counselling, training programmes and unemployment relief at a federal level.

The problem of employment was partly solved by a huge expansion of the public sector, particularly in the postal service and railways, but also in the federal and regional administrations. But employers and trade unions also played a role. The Stinnes–Legien Agreement had included a clause stating that 'all workers have the right to take up again the job they had before the war started',[25] and this was a principle that was kept to, though only at the expense of some workers. On 8 November 1918, the War Ministry had issued guidelines that established the principle that the pre-war gender order in the workplace should be restored. Although they acknowledged that some women would have to work, they should only do so in areas where there were labour shortages, in those 'corresponding to their nature' and where they would not compete with men for jobs. In response, German businesses began laying off women in large numbers to make way for returning soldiers: Bosch sacked 3,500 female employees in November 1918 and by the end of the year Krupp had dismissed just over 90 per cent of its female workforce. Women's access to unemployment benefit was restricted by the Unemployment Assistance Ordinance of 13 November 1918 that made only those who had to work 'through economic necessity' (which excluded married women whose husbands were in work, for example) eligible to claim, while benefits were withdrawn from those who refused to take jobs in areas sanctioned by the (male) authorities, such as domestic service. These attempts to purge the workforce of women were at once ideological and practical: there was a widespread view amongst (male) intellectuals, workers and policymakers that the war had upset the 'natural' order in which women belonged at home; while at the same time the only way that jobs could be found for the 6 million returning soldiers was to remove women from the labour market.[26]

These principles were reaffirmed by the National Assembly through the Decree on Job Vacancies during the period of Economic Mobilization of 28 March 1919, and although some employers would have liked to retain female employees (who could be paid lower wages and were generally thought to be less insubordinate), they came under huge pressure from trade unions to sack them. Nevertheless, women workers did not go down without a fight: women's organizations protested the dismissal of female employees and on 1 August 1919 a cross-party group of female delegates to the National Assembly lodged an official complaint and called for women to have more say on their economic future. And once the men returning from the Front had been absorbed into the labour force, the brief boom in production caused by the inflation led to increased demand for female workers, allowing some who had been laid off in 1919 to return to work, as well as providing opportunities for even more women to enter the labour force.[27]

In defiance of the expectations of the government itself, the process of economic demobilization went surprisingly smoothly – one Demobilization

Commissar went so far as to say that 'the entire dismantling of the war industry and the allocation of peacetime work was by and large carried out almost without a hitch'[28] – and the Demobilization Office (which had become a Ministry in March) was abolished in April 1919 (though Demobilization Committees and Commissars continued to operate at a local level until as late as 1924). Although there was a brief spike in unemployment in January–February 1919 (1.45 million people were registered as unemployed in January), this was caused by a temporary shortage in raw materials and once this was solved, pent-up demand for consumer goods and a resumption of foreign trade led to a brief economic boom and demand for labour. As few as 12,000 people were claiming unemployment benefit by 1922, though the labour market was far from stable, and many people did not stay in the same job for very long.

Underpinning these moves was a more fundamental and ambitious determination to make the German economy and society fairer and to provide support for the less fortunate. The Majority Social Democrats have often been accused of 'betraying' the November Revolution because of their reluctance to implement a fundamental reorganization of socio-economic life along socialist lines. But their resistance to radical economic change in the short term did not mean that they believed any less in the goal of establishing a socialist society, merely that to do so in the winter of 1918–19 would mean further disruption, hardship and violence for the German people. Instead, they saw the establishment of democracy and the revival of the economy as necessary preconditions to 'socialization' (*Sozialisierung*, public ownership of industry). As Ebert put it:

> We must work and create value ... Socialism is ... only possible if production is carried out at a sufficiently high level of efficiency ... In a time of need like the present, there should be no more room for private monopolies and profits gained without effort. We want to remove the profit element in a planned way where economic development has made an industry ripe for socialisation.[29]

Indeed, the programme of the Scheidemann government contained some quite radical proposals, including the nationalization of those 'branches of the economy ... suitable for overall control by society', allowing workers a say in setting wages and working conditions, and the introduction of a progressive system of direct taxation.[30]

In the event the drive for 'socialization' was defeated by a combination of economic realities, fears that nationalized industries would become subject to reparations and opposition from employers and the general public, who, after the war, wanted to 'free up' the economy, 'get the state off their backs' and return to 'normal'.[31] This was to prove fateful for the republic because when the promises of a better, fairer life were not realized 'the natural authority of republican democracy foundered on blighted expectations'.[32] Nevertheless, this disillusionment lay in the future. Between 1919 and 1922 the Weimar Coalition was able to lay the groundwork for an impressive and progressive system of social welfare. Health insurance was extended to more people than ever before, a network of welfare bureaus was established to provide assistance to disabled veterans, widows and orphans, a new child protection system was introduced, and laws were enacted to prevent landlords charging unaffordable rents and to extend the rights of those in rented accommodation (the majority of the population).[33]

THE KAPP–LÜTTWITZ PUTSCH

By the spring of 1920 it seemed as though the political situation was stabilizing, while an end to the Allied blockade meant that the economic situation was also improving. With rising employment and more food in the shops, labour disputes and demonstrations became less common and the government began to feel secure for the first time since November 1918. With the formation of a regular army, the Reichswehr, on 1 October 1919 the government felt that the continuing existence of the paramilitary *Freikorps* was not only unnecessary but potentially dangerous to their position, and they attempted to disband the volunteer corps. The result was a violent backlash that plunged Germany into a renewed cycle of political violence.

Many volunteers had joined up because their prospects in civilian life were limited, and now once again demobilization brought the prospect of unemployment and social isolation. At the same time, the decision to demobilize the *Freikorps* brought to a head pre-existing tensions between certain sections of the old officer corps and the government. While the politicians and diplomats believed that military power had been decisively vanquished and that the key to a revision of the Treaty of Versailles was economic revival and negotiation with the Western Powers, a hard core within the officer corps interpreted the signature of the treaty as an attack on the army which 'demonstrated that the republic was anti-military'.[34] This suspicion seemed to be confirmed by

The Kapp Putsch: Under the black, white and red flag and with swastikas on their steel helmets, members of the Naval Brigade Ehrhardt distribute leaflets announcing the coup, 13 March 1920 (Bundesarchiv, Bild 183-R16976/CC-BY-SA 3.0).

the attempt to demobilize the volunteer forces that had done so much to defend the new regime from the threat posed by the extreme left, and led some dissatisfied officers to make common cause with a small number of right-wing conspirators who were already plotting to overthrow the republic.

On 10 March 1920, the commander-in-chief of military forces in Berlin, General Walther von Lüttwitz, confronted the President and demanded a halt to demobilization, the resignation of the government and his own appointment as supreme commander of the Reichswehr. When Ebert refused, Lüttwitz ordered former Navy Captain Hermann Ehrhardt and his *Freikorps* to seize control of Berlin on 13 March. The government appealed to the military for support but were told in no uncertain terms by the generals that 'Reichswehr troops never shoot on other Reichswehr troops'.[35] With no soldiers to defend them the president and cabinet fled to Stuttgart, pausing only to urge the working classes to 'Go on strike, put down your work, stop the military dictatorship' and 'fight with every means for the preservation of the republic'.[36] An East Prussian civil servant, Wolfgang Kapp, was declared Chancellor and Lüttwitz was appointed commander-in-chief of the army. However, the coup lacked significant support even amongst conservatives and senior army officers. The working classes heeded the government call for a general strike, the Reichsbank refused to issue money without the proper authorization and civil servants refused to carry out the orders of the putschists. After just four days the coup collapsed, and the conspirators fled in panic.

The most immediate consequence of the Putsch was the revival of the threat from the left. Passive resistance to the attempted coup spilled over into a left-wing insurrection in the Ruhr as militant workers responded to the call for a general strike to defend the republic with their own political demands. Unlike the previous uprisings in Berlin in January and March 1919, the *Märzaufstand* (March Uprising) of March–April 1920 was well-organized and carried out by around 50,000 well-armed and disciplined members of the 'Red Army of the Ruhr' who rapidly succeeded in defeating detachments of police, volunteers and units of the Reichswehr to take control of Germany's largest industrial region. However, the victory of the Communists was short lived. After a 12-day truce between the insurgents and government forces collapsed, General von Watter led a combined force of regular army units and paramilitaries into the Ruhr on 2 April. This 'surge attack' was as violent and bloody as the suppression of the Munich Soviet the previous year, with one estimate suggesting that 1,000 'Reds' were killed in the first two days of the operation.

In the Reichstag elections of June 1920, the SPD and DDP's share of the vote roughly halved, while the Independent Socialists and Nationalists saw their support blossom. In large part this was in reaction against the Treaty of Versailles as the public punished the Weimar Coalition (and the DDP in particular) for having agreed to its terms. But these elections also had a wider significance: they effectively marked the end of the revolutionary period (and with it the opportunity to enact radical progressive social and economic policies), gave the first sign of the decline of the liberal democratic parties, and were perhaps the first instance of what Richard Bessel has termed 'a defining characteristic of Weimar politics': the tendency of the electorate to punish those 'parties that had accepted governmental responsibility, and thus responsibility for necessarily unpopular decisions', in the polls.[37]

These events did nothing to improve Germany's relations with the Allies. The refusal to hand over war criminals had already produced a stand-off in February 1920. Ultimately a compromise was agreed in which Germany promised to establish a specially constituted Reich court in Leipzig to investigate accusations of war crimes. However, the Kapp Putsch caused alarm in London and Paris as it seemed for a moment as though a right-wing nationalist government determined to repudiate the treaty might come to power. Matters were made worse when the fighting in the Ruhr spilled over into the demilitarized zone in the Rhineland. Fearing that the Germans were using internal political turmoil as a

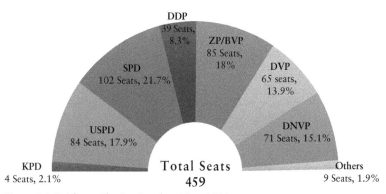

Figure 2.1 Reichstag Election Results, 6 June 1920.

means of avoiding their obligations under the treaty, the French occupied Frankfurt in April 1920 to send a clear signal that breaches of the treaty would not be tolerated under any circumstances.

REVISIONISM

French fears that the Germans might repudiate the treaty were not without some basis. Almost from the moment the treaty was ratified, Germany had tried to avoid fulfilling its obligations. Many of these early attempts were focused on the military clauses and aimed at finding inventive ways to circumvent the restrictions placed on the size and strength of the German Army. Throughout the Weimar period, the Reichswehr played a game of cat and mouse with the Inter-Allied Commission of Control, attempting to avoid the prohibition of the General Staff by dividing its functions between various ministries, and training men in secret under the pretence that they were police offers, not soldiers, or that they were members of private sporting or shooting clubs. But the hard line taken by the Allies and the occupation of Frankfurt in 1920 convinced the military and foreign office that they needed to find more inventive ways to escape the treaty. Two strands of thinking emerged regarding the best way of gaining a revision of the peace settlement: re-build military strength and secure alliances in preparation for a revision of the peace settlement by force, or seek to secure German interests and achieve a return to Great Power status through negotiation and conciliation with the Western Powers.

From the beginning there had been those who argued that the best way to escape from the economic and diplomatic straight jacket imposed on them by the Treaty of Versailles was to make common cause with Europe's other pariah state, the Soviet Union. Ironically enough, considering that Soviet Russia was the world's first Communist state, this was a view most often endorsed by right-wingers. Prussian aristocrats such as Baron Adolf Georg Otto ('Ago') von Maltzan, the head of the Russian department of the Foreign Office, and the head of the Reichswehr Hans von Seeckt, as well as some prominent businessmen, argued that Germany should seek to cultivate closer economic and military relations with Russia at the earliest opportunity. Yet this was not as strange as the obvious ideological differences between the Bolsheviks and the German political and military elite may make it seem. Common antagonism towards Poland provided a bond between Berlin and Moscow, and there was a widespread feeling in the Foreign Office that the Bolshevik regime would not last and would sooner or later be replaced by something more in keeping with Western political and economic norms. The policy of pursuing closer ties with the Soviet Union was therefore regarded as paving the way for relations with a post-Soviet regime, while in some quarters it was seen as simply a revival of the traditional eastward alignment that had dominated Prussian foreign policy in the nineteenth century. Even those who argued that the best chance for revision lay in negotiation rather than confrontation with the Allies saw no harm in seeking to normalize relations in the east, if only as a means of aiding economic recovery and forestalling Russian claims for reparations (an option left theoretically open to them by Article 116 of the Treaty of Versailles). But Russia also offered opportunities for economic and military renewal and development. Continuing discriminatory tariffs on German goods in the West meant that Germany sought new markets for its exports (always a key part of its economy), while the Soviet state was in dire need of capital investment from abroad. Moreover, there were those in the Reichswehr who saw on the Russian steppes the hope of circumventing Allied prohibitions on developing modern weapons and training a new army away from the prying eyes of the Allied Control Commission, something that the Russians were only too keen to acquiesce to in the hope of sharing in the military technology that was developed.

The issue of the repatriation of the 1.2 million Russian prisoners of war still in Germany (and 100,000 Germans in Russia) was used as a means to resume contact. An agreement to this effect was signed on 19 April 1920, to be followed a year later by a Russo–German Trade Treaty and the opening of official diplomatic missions incorporating trade legations in autumn 1921. At the same time, 'preliminary contacts with a view to military collaboration' had been authorized as early as January 1920, and in September 1921 secret meetings between senior German and Russian officers were held in the Berlin apartment of Kurt von Schleicher, while a front company was set up to channel 75 million marks into the establishment of aircraft, munitions and poison gas factories on Russian soil.[38]

At the same time, the occupation of Frankfurt in April 1920 had convinced the civilian government that they had little choice but to bow to Allied demands for reparations and to hope that through attempted compliance they could prove that these demands were unrealistic and thereby achieve peaceful revision of the treaty. This came to be called *Erfüllungspolitik* – the policy of fulfilment – a dual policy of economic development at home and reconciliation and appeasement abroad. It was most closely associated with Chancellor Josef Wirth and his Foreign Minister, the businessman Walther Rathenau. Along with Mattias Erzberger, Wirth had been regarded as one of the foremost 'progressives' within the Centre Party and had served as finance minister under Hermann Müller and Konstantin Fehrenbach, during which time he had supported a progressive tax regime as a means of stabilizing Germany's precarious financial position. Appointed as Chancellor at the age of forty-two (making him the youngest Chancellor in German history) when Fehrenbach's administration collapsed after the German People's Party (*Deutsche Volkspartei* [DVP]) withdrew in May 1921, Wirth believed that nothing could be gained from continuing attempts to circumvent the reparations clauses of the Treaty of Versailles and that the only way to convince the Allies of Germany's inability to pay was to make every effort to do so.

But Wirth and Rathenau's commitment to a policy of reconciliation with the Western Powers did not mean that they were willing to abandon the Russian connection and on 16 April 1922 they managed to pull off a diplomatic coup with the signing of the Rapallo Treaty. This was not an alliance as such, but rather a treaty of friendship that established full diplomatic relations between the two states, saw them agree to renounce all claims for war damage and reparations and grant one another most-favoured-nation status. It was followed on 11 August by a secret Military Convention between the Reichswehr and the Red Army that extended existing military cooperation and led to the development of a tank base at Kazan and an aviation school at Lipetsk. The Allies were horrified by this 'unholy alliance' and saw it as part of a German-led conspiracy to overturn the Treaty of Versailles. It also caused consternation at home. President Ebert strongly opposed the agreement, believing (with some justification) that it antagonized the Western Powers without delivering much of benefit to Germany, while the Social Democrats feared that better relations with Russia would increase the influence of the KPD. Even so, Rapallo 'did not mark ... a fundamental turn to the east',[39] but was seen rather as a complement to the policy of conciliation in the west. By bringing an end to post-war isolation the agreement with Russia secured Germany's eastern flank and opened the way for economic reconstruction through trade links in the east. It also provided a means of avoiding the old nightmare of encirclement, while for some 'hardliners' it opened the possibility of joint military action against Poland which would ultimately lead to the collapse of the Versailles settlement.

THE THREAT FROM THE RIGHT

The indiscriminate violence against the left by right-wing paramilitary forces in 1919–20 has traditionally been seen by historians of evidence of both the 'betrayal' of the revolution by the Social Democratic leadership and of widespread hostility towards the new republic on the right. Yet more recently some scholars have successfully challenged the view of a vast stratum of resentful upper- and middle-class Germans opposed to the new regime.[40] While many in the officer corps, the civil service and the judiciary had no love for the new republic, the majority of them were willing to work towards their aim of restoring Germany to its former glory within the legal framework provided by the Weimar constitution. Conan Fischer draws comparisons with the French Third Republic, where conservative and monarchist forces were relatively reconciled to the new moderate republicanism and a 'functional loyalty', if not love, for the republic developed over time. He argues that similar examples of 'functional loyalty' can be seen in Weimar Germany, such as the civil service's resistance to the Kapp Putsch.[41] Similarly, the ultimate aim of certain sections of the officer corps might have been the restoration of the monarchy or the overturning of the Versailles settlement, but they recognized that, for the time being at least, a broad-based liberal parliamentary republic was the only means of preventing Germany sliding into anarchy and civil war and the best way for the country to regain its strength after the trauma of revolution and defeat.

Nevertheless, the threat from more radical elements within right-wing opposition to the republic had not disappeared with the failure of the Kapp Putsch. Indeed, the ridiculously lenient sentences handed down to the ringleaders of the coup (of the 775 army officers who participated in the putsch, only six were dismissed and von Lüttwitz was allowed to retire on a full pension) meant that many of the core conspirators remained at large. These were able to join the welter of right-wing secret societies, paramilitary organizations and *völkisch* groups that proliferated in the early days of the republic. One contemporary commentator identified at least 59 such groups committed to the overthrow of democracy, but this should not lead us to conclude that the republican system faced concerted and coherent opposition from the right. Right-wing opposition was often isolated, without common goals or strong leadership.

The breeding-ground for far-right organizations determined to overthrow democracy was Bavaria. Before the First World War, Catholic Bavaria had been the home of the most trenchant critics of Prussian militarism and its capital Munich was a haven of left-leaning writers and artistic experimentation. But after the destruction of the *Räterrepublik* and the White Terror that followed, Bavaria became the heartland of the German right, the centre of a Central European network of counter-revolutionaries. Under the rule of a conservative clique made up of Gustav, Ritter von Kahr, the Reichswehr commander General Otto von Lossow and the chief of police Hans von Seisser, the authorities turned a blind eye to the activities of right-wing groups banned by the federal government in Berlin, while official funds were syphoned off to help the anti-republican cause. Among the political refugees who found succour in the south was Hermann Ehrhardt, who, shielded by sympathetic landowners and the local chief of police, established the Organization Consul in Bavaria in 1921. There followed a 14-month campaign of politically-motivated murders which had two aims: to mete out 'justice' to the 'traitors' who had betrayed Germany in November 1918 in the manner of the medieval *Femegerichts* (tribunals that had administered swift and brutal justice in times when no official judicial system existed), and to provoke a left-wing uprising which could then be crushed by the resurgent right and lead to the establishment of a military dictatorship. It is estimated that these 'Feme' killings accounted for around 350 political murders between August 1921 and June 1922. Most victims were civil servants who were prepared to work within the republican system, informers and former members of the Organization Consul, but Ehrhardt also set his sights on prominent republican politicians.

By far the highest profile of these killings were those that began and ended the campaign: the assassinations of the government ministers Matthias Erzberger and Walther Rathenau. Hated by the right for his part in the 1917 peace resolution and the armistice negotiations as much for his public declaration of Germany's need to fulfil its obligations under the Treaty of Versailles, Erzberger had already survived one assassination attempt, but his opponents finally caught up with him during a holiday at the spa resort of Bad Griesbach. On 26 August 1921 he was attacked by a nationalist death squad while out for a walk with one of his Centre Party colleagues. Erzberger was shot 12 times and died of his wounds, while the assassins, Heinrich Tillessen and Heinrich Schultz, returned to Munich from where they were spirited away to Hungary whose right-wing government refused to extradite them.[42]

The murder of Erzberger was followed by an attempt on the life of the former Chancellor Philipp Scheidemann. But the attack which caused the most public outrage and forced the authorities to take drastic action against the 'Feme' was that on the serving Foreign Minister Walter Rathenau. Already a hate figure for the right due to his Jewish ancestry and his advanced political views (which involved the formation of a European free-trade area), Rathenau further earned their ire as foreign minister by pursuing *Erfüllungspolitik* (the policy of fulfilment) with the Allies and signing the Rapallo Treaty with the Soviet Union. On the morning of Saturday 24 June 1922 Rathenau left his home in the Berlin suburb of Grunewald to make his way to his office in the Wilhelmstrasse. A little after eleven o'clock his car was overtaken by another containing a group of right-wing assassins who sprayed Rathenau's vehicle with small arms fire before throwing a grenade through the window. The Foreign Minister suffered wounds to his head and chest and by the time a doctor could be summoned he was dead.

Far from leading to a left-wing insurrection or a growth of nationalist feeling, the effect of the assassination was to precipitate a great outpouring of popular disgust at the murderers and support for the republic. Indeed, such was the public anger at the crime, that the Organization Consul decided that it was politic to suspend its campaign of political violence and lie low for a while. But Rathenau's murder had more profound consequences than merely bringing to a halt the campaign of nationalist violence. It enabled the supporters of parliamentary democracy to seize the moral high-ground from the anti-republican right – who had hitherto portrayed themselves as the true patriots and defenders of the 'German spirit' while lambasting their republican opponents as traitors, the 'November Criminals' who had stabbed the army in the back in 1918 – and associate them with murderous extremism. In a dramatic moment in the Reichstag the day after Rathenau's murder the Chancellor Josef Wirth denounced the political right for inculcating an 'atmosphere of murder' in the country and for failing to condemn the assassination, ending by declaring 'there is no doubt: the enemy stands on the right!'[43] At the same time, Rathenau was quickly transfigured into a republican martyr, a man who had selflessly given his life in the service of the republican state and the German people. In more practical terms the murder of Rathenau finally galvanized the Reichstag to take measures against the threat from the right and led to the passage of the Law for the Protection of the Republic on 18 July 1922. This not only prohibited extremist organizations and established special courts to deal with cases of political violence, but also prohibited the language and imagery of extremism.[44]

FROM INFLATION TO HYPERINFLATION

Meanwhile, the inflationary spiral that had begun during the war continued. In the short term, this did not seem to be such a bad thing. Indeed, to some extent the inflation helped to stimulate Germany's post-war economy. The decreasing value of the mark allowed canny businessmen to borrow to purchase raw materials, manufactured goods, or industrial plant, and then pay back the loan when it was worth a fraction of what it had been a few months before. This ensured that until the middle of 1922 the rate of economic growth was high, and unemployment virtually disappeared. Low taxation also helped to stimulate demand and Germany managed the move to a peacetime economy more smoothly than some other European nations who were suffering less from inflation.[45] Indeed, Carl-Ludwig Holtfrerich has gone so far as to argue that deficit financing was an inspired and successful policy that enabled the Weimar Republic to compete effectively with other European economies that went into recession in 1920–1 and had much higher rates of unemployment (17 per cent in Britain in 1921 compared to Germany's 1.8 per cent).[46]

However, the government's policy of deficit financing could not be sustained indefinitely. Even during the period of apparent growth and prosperity there were clear indicators that all was not well. Price controls on agricultural goods alienated farmers, while rent controls created a housing shortage in the big cities. More worrying still for ordinary Germans was that the purchasing power of the mark fell even as prices continued to rise. Between 1914 and 1920 the cost of living rose 12 times (compared to three times in the USA, four in Britain and seven in France). A family of four could be fed on 60 marks a week in April 1919, but this went up to 144 marks in December 1920 and had risen to 249 marks a year later. Staple items such as tea and eggs were roughly 30–40 times more expensive than they had been before the war. By 1922 consumers were really beginning to feel the pinch. In July alone food prices rose by 50 per cent and a bank clerk's annual salary would provide only enough to feed his family for a single month.

This only served to heighten social and political tensions, providing 'a constant stimulus to labour militancy and anger at the marketplace'.[47] As the purchasing power of the mark continued to fall there were outbreaks of strikes, protests and riots in German cities. State employees on fixed incomes were particularly badly hit as their wages did not keep pace with price rises, and in February 1922 there occurred the 'first (and last) major civil servant strike in German history'.[48] There was very little understanding amongst the public as to what was happening, which only increased people's sense of helplessness and fuelled social tension. Many looked around for someone to blame and came up with a variety of scapegoats – foreigners, the trade unions, big business, war profiteers and in particular, Jews. In Bavaria banknotes became known as *Judenfetzen* (Jewish confetti),[49] and as the slide into hyperinflation gathered pace there was an upsurge of anti-Semitic attacks on Jewish shops and businesses. To some extent the government encouraged this tendency by denying that the amount of money in circulation was anything to do with the problem and continuing to peddle the line that inflation and rising prices were a consequence of the unreasonable demands placed on the German economy by reparations.

THE RUHR CRISIS AND THE COLLAPSE OF THE MARK

Having already failed to make the second scheduled reparations payment in December 1921, the Germans announced in July 1922 that they would again not be able to pay the next instalment. At the same time, under pressure from the United States to repay their wartime debts, the British urged France to repay the money loaned to it during the war. Like Germany, France had emerged from the war heavily in debt and beset by inflation. Increasingly anxious about their own economic situation, the French became fixated on the reparations issue, looking to injections of German cash to both help solve their own fiscal problems and provide economic security by hamstringing German heavy industry and its latent military potential. With Britain demanding repayment, the French government cast around desperately for a way to compel Germany to make good on its commitments. Having already occupied Düsseldorf and Darmstadt in January 1921 when Germany rejected provisional proposals for the final reparations figure, that the French believed Germany was capable of paying when placed under pressure. In November 1922 it was decided to revive a scheme first drafted during the Kapp Putsch to invade and occupy the industrially important Ruhr district if Germany could not be convinced to pay. When renewed negotiations over reparations stalled the following January secret orders were sent to French forces in the Rhineland telling them to prepare for the invasion of the Ruhr.

In the early hours of 11 January 1923 French and Belgian troops seized Essen and Gladbeck, and within four days the whole of the Ruhr had been occupied. In response the German Chancellor Wilhelm Cuno appealed to the population of the region to meet the invaders with 'passive resistance', asking them to down tools and not cooperate with the occupation forces. Germans of all parties and classes rallied to the call, and for a time the nation was united in an upsurge of 'republican-style patriotism'.[50] The only problem was that the government were unwilling to raise taxes to cover the costs of passive resistance. As the months passed and a negotiated settlement to the crisis proved elusive, the government, unable to obtain supplies of coal confiscated by the French, were forced to fritter away their last remaining gold reserves on importing food and fuel.

With expenditure seven times greater than income by April 1923, the government stepped up the printing of paper currency. During February 1923, the number of notes in circulation rose by 450 billion a week and in early March the 'floating debt' rose by 800 billion in one day. At the height of the inflation 30 paper mills, 150 printing firms and 2,000 printing presses worked around the clock to produce a never-ending stream of paper money. In a speech on 17 August 1923 Rudolf Havenstein proudly declared that under his auspices the Reichsbank was issuing 20 billion marks of new money each day, of which 5 billion was in large denominations. The consequence was a reckless descent into hyperinflation.

Until the spring of 1923 the fall of the mark had been dramatic, but steady, and therefore to some extent manageable, but as hyperinflation gathered pace over the summer the value of the mark fell and prices rose not on a monthly or even a daily, but on an hourly, basis. Between May and June 1923, the price of an egg rose from 800 to 2,400 marks and a litre of milk from 1,800 to 3,800. In the Ruhr wages doubled, but prices trebled. The 1,000-mark note (the highest denomination note in circulation since 1876) was withdrawn because it cost more to produce than it was worth, and new 10-, 20- and 50-million-mark notes were issued. The rate of currency depreciation became so great that a 5,000 mark cup of coffee was worth 8,000 marks by the time it had been drunk and 'the only thing to do with cash ... was to turn it into something else as quickly as possible'.[51] Barter took over as the main form of commerce: a cinema seat cost a lump of coal, a bottle of paraffin could buy a shirt and one man paid the rent on his mistress's flat with a pound of butter a month. Many regions, municipalities and even workplaces introduced their own emergency currencies, known as *Notgeld*. These were temporary alternatives to state issued paper money and were often marked with an expiry date, though they soon became collectors'

Table 2.1: Exchange Rates During the Great Inflation

Date	German Marks to the Pound Sterling	German Marks to the US Dollar
January 1920	233	64.8
July 1920	152	39.5
January 1921	243	64.9
July 1921	278	76.7
January 1922	811	191.8
July 1922	2,200	493.2
January 1923	83,190	17,972
July 1923	1,594,760	353,412
August 1923	21,040,000	4,620,455
September 1923	449,375,000	98,860,000
October 1923	112,503,000,000	25,260,208,000
November 1923	9,604,000,000,000	4,200,000,000,000

Sources: Edgar Vincent, Viscount D'Abernon, *An Ambassador of Peace*, vol. 2 (London: Hodder & Stoughton, 1929), 298–300; Paul Bookbinder, *Weimar Germany* (Manchester: Manchester University Press, 1996), 255.

items with a value beyond that of initial exchange. This was because *Notgeld* tended to be highly decorative, often featuring local landmarks, references to local history or folktales, or humorous stories or cartoons. Some forms of *Notgeld* were made of more durable materials such as cloth, leather, aluminium foil or even porcelain, illustrating 'the creative ways in which people coped with the inflation's challenges'.[52]

The result of hyperinflation was human misery on a massive scale. Particularly badly hit were those who relied on fixed incomes such as state employees (civil servants, teachers, railwaymen and postal workers), students, those on benefits and pensioners. These groups were disproportionately exposed because increases in their incomes failed to keep pace with the rate of inflation. Although those in work were generally more insulated from the worst effects of the inflation, during the chaos of 1923 working-class living standards declined because the trade unions were no longer able to negotiate wage increases that kept pace with price rises. At the same time, the economic upheaval caused by the hyperinflation and the Ruhr Crisis provided employers with an excuse to unilaterally revise important aspects of the Stinnes–Legien Agreement, such as the eight-hour working day.[53]

The banker Max Warburg saw Germany as 'a country divided into three classes of society: one that suffers and goes under in decency; another that profiteers cynically and spends recklessly; and another that writhes in desperation, and wishes to destroy in blind fury whatever is left of a government and a society that permits such conditions'.[54] Although this perhaps reflects the perception rather than the reality, it is true that the effects of the inflation were not felt evenly across German society. People in the countryside were better off than those in towns and cities because they had ready access to essential goods (foodstuffs and timber for fuel) and were therefore less reliant on money to secure the necessities of life. At the same time some farmers and landowners were able to 'use hyperinflation to wipe out debts or purchase new machinery and household items on cheap credit (or in exchange for food)'.[55] Similarly, the old idea of 'the destruction of the middle class' needs to be unpicked somewhat. As Geoff Layton has suggested, 'the key to understanding who gained and who lost from the inflation lies in the nature of an individual's income and degree of indebtedness'.[56] Those in debt had the potential to pay off their loans or mortgages with depreciated marks, while those with good business sense could make use of cheap credit and inflated profits to acquire land, businesses, art collections and real estate from the desperate and naïve. Many of Germany's leading industrialists took the opportunity to engage in a rash of mergers and takeovers, creating in the process a series of large industrial *Konzerne* (corporations). Professionals such as doctors and lawyers suffered from a decline of business but were better suited to weather the storm than some because they had skills that remained in demand and could adjust the amount they charged for services in pace with inflation. Likewise, while some small businessmen went under (especially when currency stabilization led to a rash of bankruptcies in 1924), shopkeepers often managed to survive either by resorting to a sort of barter system or by taking advantage of the thriving black market. Furthermore, the inflation era and subsequent currency stabilization led to a 'levelling tendency' not only in the salaries of civil servants (provoking the resentment of senior officials who felt that their economic and social status was being undermined) but also between young and old, male and female and skilled and unskilled workers.[57]

But material hardship was only one side of the story. As important, maybe more so, was the cultural and psychological legacy of the inflation era on the German population. Hyperinflation created 'a lunatic world in which all the familiar landmarks assumed crazy new forms and all the old signposts became meaningless',[58] making it difficult for people – and older people especially – to navigate an environment where familiar concepts of value and worth were challenged or overturned. Whether or not they actually 'lost out' there was a general perception amongst some sections of the middle classes and many on the political right that the inflation and the measures introduced to restore economic stability from late 1923 onwards represented a further round in the fundamental assault on traditional German values that had begun with the November Revolution. This was especially the case as material pressures caused many previously law-abiding citizens to dramatically revise their moral outlooks. As more and more people were forced to bend or break the law simply to survive, a new moral landscape developed in which the boundaries between legitimate and illegal business transactions became blurred. While the working classes engaged in prostitution and petty crime as a way to make ends meet, those with the means and the know-how to do so engaged in more lucrative white-collar crime. Tax evasion became widespread, as did fraud, embezzlement, and currency speculation. Law and order virtually broke down and the German prison population rose by on average 100,000 a day. This was part of a general post-war rise in criminality, but the statistics show a marked increase in trials and convictions during 1923. The 'pervasive, soul-destroying influence of the constant erosion of capital or earnings and uncertainty about the future'[59] led to a decline in ethical standards and an atmosphere where the old virtues of thrift, hard-work and honesty became, if not vices, then mere foolish sentimentality.

THE GREAT INFLATION IN CONTEXT

The period of hyperinflation has cast a long shadow over the German collective imagination and has often been said to influence German economic attitudes to this day.[60] Yet Germany was not unique amongst European nations in facing acute economic difficulties in the aftermath of the First World War. The other defeated Central Powers encountered similar economic, social and political difficulties to those faced by Germany, but it is often forgotten that many of the victorious powers also emerged from the war with severe economic problems. Like Germany, France had gambled on securing reparations as a means of financing the war and a continued reluctance to raise taxation ensured that government spending exceeded income by as much as 12 million francs a year, while the value of the French currency depreciated from 90 francs to the pound in December 1924 to 240 to the pound by July 1926. Italy, too, had resorted to borrowing and printing money as a method of financing its war effort, leading to ruinous inflation that saw the purchasing power of the lira fall by 25 per cent between 1915 and 1918. Together with rising unemployment (2 million out of work in 1919) and labour militancy these were important contributing factors in bringing Mussolini's Fascists to power in October 1922. Even Britain, which had generally managed its war finances well, experienced a short period of inflation after the war.

Germany's hyperinflation was much more severe than anything experienced in Western Europe, but it was comparable with the economic upheavals felt by Austria and Hungary. The collapse of the multi-ethnic Habsburg Empire left Austria an impoverished rump state cut off by new national boundaries from its chief sources of fuel (coal from Czechoslovakia) and food (grain from Hungary), while Hungary lost a third of its pre-war territory and with it supplies of natural resources badly needed to keep its industry going. Industrial production stood at 30 per cent of pre-war levels in 1920, while agricultural yields were half what they had been in 1913. A third of the Hungarian population were out of work and living standards were 40 per cent lower than they had been before the war. This, together with a record of war finance similar to that of Germany led to severe food shortages and rampant inflation. In Austria, the krone depreciated even more rapidly than the German mark, leading to panic-buying, food hoarding and political unrest. By August 1922, the pound sterling was worth 350,000 Austrian kronen (compared to roughly 22 kronen to the pound in 1914) and only intervention from the League of Nations was able to stave off the collapse of the economy and with it the Austrian Republic. It was a similar story in Hungary, where by 1919 the currency was worth only 10 per cent of its pre-war value, falling to 0.3 per cent by 1923. As with Austria, only an international bail-out combined with stringent austerity measures enabled the government to stabilize the currency and bring a measure of economic normality back to Central Europe.

Germany was thus not alone in experiencing a dramatic hyperinflation followed by a traumatic period of stabilization that bequeathed a legacy of long-term structural weakness to the economy. Germany's hyperinflation neither caused widespread cases of starvation as it did in Austria, nor led to a fascist takeover of power as in Italy. Why then has it become a byword for economic instability? Firstly, it was perhaps because those hardest hit by the inflation and stabilization were the best educated and most articulate sections of society who found the experience particularly traumatic because they had previously enjoyed nearly 50 years of prosperity and growth. Secondly, the collapse of the economy struck a further blow to national pride already dented by the humiliation of unexpected defeat. Coming on top of war, revolution and virtual civil war, hyperinflation reinforced the feeling that old certainties and values had been destroyed and replaced by chaos and disorder.

STABILIZING THE CURRENCY, SAVING THE REPUBLIC

By the summer of 1923 Germany was facing not only economic, but also political collapse. Passive resistance had failed and with the French refusing to make concessions, the domestic and international picture looked bleak. With a wave of strikes sweeping the country and the threat of further political unrest, the Cuno government lost a confidence vote on 12 August 1923. The following day, a grand coalition that aimed to include 'all elements loyal to the constitutional idea and the state'[61] was formed under the Chairman of the DVP, Gustav Stresemann. Often lauded as the most adept politician of the Weimar era, Stresemann was to prove during his short spell as head of government and in his subsequent role as foreign minister (a post that he held in every administration until his untimely death at the age of only 51 in October 1929) that he had the political and moral courage to take the difficult and unpopular decisions that were necessary for the preservation of the republic.

On 26 September passive resistance was called off and Stresemann announced that reparations payments would be resumed. A month later the government asked the Reparations Commission to look again at Germany's economic situation, a move that would result in a new repayments schedule, the Dawes Plan. Simultaneously, the government acted to stabilize the currency. On 13 October, the Reichstag passed an Enabling Act (*Ermächtigeungsgesetz*), temporarily providing the government with power to pass legislation without reference to parliament. On 15 October, a new central bank, the *Deutsche Rentenbank* (National Mortgage Bank), was established with its reserves backed not with gold, but with material assets such as real estate. A month later a new temporary currency, the *Rentenmark*, was introduced. One *Rentenmark* was equal to 1 trillion paper marks and the international exchange rate was set at 4.2 *Rentenmarks* to the US dollar.

However, the effects of these measures on the economy were not immediate, and in the autumn of 1923 the government faced renewed threats from both left and right. Communists, Nationalists, and separatists (who wanted to break away from the Reich) all saw the collapse of the economy as an opportunity, and all made plans to challenge the government in Berlin. In Saxony and Thuringia the Communists entered into coalition with the SPD in October and began recruiting 'Proletarian Hundreds' (around 50,000 left-wing paramilitaries). That same month there was an attempted coup in Hamburg that ended in bloody clashes between local Communists and the police. Waves of looting and unrest spread throughout the country, the worst of which were perhaps the riots of 5–6 November in Berlin's Scheunenviertel district, when in the words of the writer Alfred Döblin, 'social tensions [were] unloaded on the Jews'[62] as an anti-Semitic mob stormed through the area which was home of a large Jewish population, looting shops and businesses and beating and robbing innocent bystanders.

Finally, on 9 November 1923, a previously obscure right-wing group, the National Socialist German Workers Party (*Nationalsozialistische Deutsche Arbeiterpartei*, NSDAP or Nazis for short), inspired by Mussolini's seizure of power in Italy the previous year attempted to seize power in Munich as a prelude to a 'March on Berlin'. On the evening of 8 November 1923, the Nazis succeeded in taking Bavaria's leaders, State Commissioner von Kahr, General von Lossow and police chief von Seisser, hostage at Munich's Bürgerbraukeller. But the attempted coup soon descended into farce when the hostages were released and promptly went back on their pledges of support for the Nazis' 'national revolution'. Despite this the march on the Bavarian War Ministry took place as planned on the morning of 9 November. However, when the Nazi Storm Troopers reached the Odeonplatz they found their way blocked by armed police, who ordered them to halt before firing a single volley at the marchers. Faced with real bullets, the Nazis broke and fled. Hitler, along with other leading figures like General Ludendorff, was arrested, while the remainder of the Nazi leadership fled abroad.

In this atmosphere of political challenge, the government in Berlin acted decisively – and fatefully – to protect the republic. President Ebert declared a state of emergency on 26 September and handed extensive powers to the military. When the Saxon government refused to disarm left-wing paramilitaries, the Reichswehr occupied the state, and its government was deposed. Similar measures were carried out in Thuringia in early November and both *Länder* were briefly administered by 'commissioners' (*Reichskimmissare*) appointed by the federal government in Berlin. Although the central government fell short of such an intervention in Bavaria following Hitler's attempted coup, the head of the Army, General Hans von Seeckt, was granted power 'to take all necessary measures for the safety to the Reich',[63] including a clamp down on the press and the suspension of civil liberties.

All of these measures were undertaken with the best of intentions, but they came at a heavy price. Most immediately, the action against the left-wing governments in Saxony and Thuringia led to the collapse of Stresemann's coalition when the SPD walked out in protest. Thereafter the Social Democrats retreated into opposition, content to allow the 'bourgeois' parties to steer the course of the republic until 1928. More broadly, though, the way in which the republic was preserved during the 'stabilization crisis' set a dangerous precedent for the future. For around six months in 1923–24 normal politics was suspended and the legislation necessary to stabilize the currency and oppose extremism was enacted through emergency decrees issued under the Enabling Acts of 13 October and 8 December and Article 48 of the constitution. Worse still, the fallout from all of this reinforced the feeling that the government acted more harshly against leftist challenges than those from the political right. Not only had the nationalist government in Bavaria not suffered the same fate as the left-wing coalitions in Saxony and Thuringia, but the conspirators behind the Beer Hall Putsch were given ludicrously light sentences when they were brought to trial in 1924. Hitler himself was sentenced to a mere five years in prison, even though his treasonable actions were punishable by the death penalty. More broadly, of the 400 murders with an obvious political motive that were committed in Germany between 1918 and 1922, 354 were carried out by right-wing killers and 22 by left-wingers. Of the perpetrators of these 22 killings, 17 received harsh sentences, including ten sentenced to death. Of the 354 right-wing murderers, 326 went completely unpunished. The average jail sentence for a left-wing political prisoner was 15 years. For a right-winger it was four months.[64]

3

RELATIVE STABILITY, 1924–29

After 1924 it seemed as though the Weimar Republic had finally put the economic and political turbulence of its early years behind it. Inflation was brought under control and with the help of foreign investment the economy entered a period of relative growth. Political violence receded into the background and with the Social Democrats in opposition, the republic was governed by a series of centrist coalitions that were able to reach agreement on most issues based on a broadly similar ideological outlook. Germany's relations with its European neighbours began to normalize and steps were taken to reach negotiated agreements that would bring an end to the tensions caused by the Treaty of Versailles. Although there remained deep inequalities in German society, for the first time in a long time, many Germans were able to feel a sense of security and certainty and to look to the future with optimism.

But behind the facade of '*die goldenen zwanziger Jahre*' (the Golden Twenties, as historians have often called the Weimar Republic's middle period), there were worrying signs of structural problems. Germany's economic recovery was dependent on investment from abroad and successive governments continued to be reluctant to burden the population with the levels of taxation necessary to deliver on the promises of 'welfare democracy'. The apparent consensus at the heart of Weimar politics hid the fact that there remained forces that were irreconcilably opposed to democracy, while social and economic pressures resulted in a slow shift in the attitude of the electorate. And although great progress was made in restoring Germany's international position, that progress did not go far enough or fast enough to satisfy public opinion (especially on the nationalist right) and key issues remained unresolved.

During the late 1920s democracy became normalized and the republic managed to establish itself, but it was still a comparatively new state and it remained susceptible to outside influences and economic and political shocks. For all of the republic's achievements it still remained fragile, and it is Germany's tragedy that democracy was not given longer to bed in before being rocked by a renewed economic and political crisis after 1929.

PARLIAMENTARY POLITICS

Following the upheavals of 1922–3 there was widespread agreement that politics needed to be steadied and rationalized 'as a necessary counterpart to currency revaluation'.[1] The experience of the 'years of crisis' brought a realization (at least amongst the political class) that they had to work together to make the political system work, even if they did not always agree on what the best interests of the country were. On 28 February 1924 the head of the army, General Hans von Seeckt, voluntarily relinquished the executive powers granted to him following the Beer Hall Putsch, allowing a return to normal constitutional government that continued until at least 1930. In the meantime, the government had attempted to get finances under control using the powers granted by the Enabling Act of 8 December 1923 to introduce

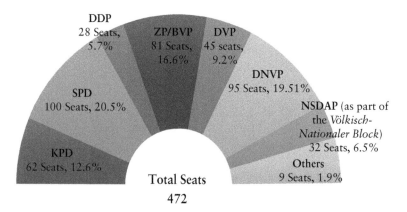

Figure 3.1 Reichstag Election Results, 4 May 1924.

a raft of austerity measures. Between October 1923 and April 1924 400,000 public sector workers, most of them women, were dismissed. For those who kept their jobs, wages were reduced by as much as 60 per cent of pre-war levels and taxes were increased. When the Reichstag reconvened on 15 February 1924 the SPD, KPD and German National People's Party (*Deutschnationale Volkspartei* [DNVP]) combined to try to block these measures, with the result that snap elections were called for the 4 May.

The DNVP was the clear winner of the May 1924 elections, benefitting from discontent amongst the middle classes who had lost out because of the inflation and revaluation of the currency, while the parties who had governed during the crisis were punished by the electorate. But at this point the Nationalists were unwilling to abandon their opposition to the Dawes Plan (see below) and accept the responsibility of government. Wilhelm Marx (who had been Chancellor since Stresemann's fall in November 1923) therefore formed a minority government made up of the Centre, the DDP, DVP and various Independents. With only 138 seats out of 472 in the Reichstag, the government was forced to rely on either the Social Democrats or the DNVP to get legislation passed. Although with the help of the SPD and some sections of the DNVP (who put economic self-interest before Nationalist ideology) Marx managed to get the Dawes Plan through the Reichstag, the situation was unsustainable and new elections were called for the 7 December 1924.

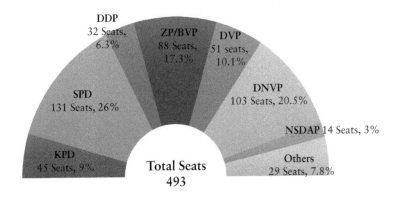

Figure 3.2 Reichstag Election Results, 7 December 1924.

The results of these elections saw a swing away from the extremes and indicated a 'de-radicalization of the electorate'[2] as the economic and political situation began to stabilize. The SPD, DDP and DVP all made up some of their losses from the previous poll, indicating that the success of the KPD and far-right in the May elections had largely been a howl of protest in response to parlous economic conditions of the winter of 1923–4. With the DVP announcing that they would not join a government that included the Social Democrats (and Stresemann keen to draw the Nationalists into a situation where they had to take responsibility for tough decisions and thereby link them to the republican system), a centre-right *Bürgerblock-Regierung* (Bourgeois administration) made up of the Centre Party, Bavarian Peoples' Party, the DVP and, for the first time, the DNVP was formed. The problem was that although the partners in this centre-right coalition saw eye-to-eye on many aspects of domestic and social policy, there was little common ground when it came to Germany's foreign policy. This was highlighted by the disagreement within the government over Stresemann's negotiations regarding a settlement with the Western Powers that resulted in the Locarno Treaties (see below). For sections of the DNVP anything short of a complete renunciation of the Versailles Treaty was unacceptable and in October 1925 they withdrew from the government.

Hans Luther continued as Chancellor with a minority government until May 1926, having failed to lure the SPD out of opposition and into a 'grand coalition' due to ideological differences between the Socialists and the DVP. Luther's government collapsed when a disagreement broke out over which flag (the black-red-gold colours of the Weimar Republic, or the old black-white-red of the monarchy) could be flown in German embassies and consulates, and he was replaced as Chancellor by Wilhelm Marx who, after a few months of minority government, revived the *Bürgerblock* in January 1927.

The DNVP acted remarkably responsibly and showed themselves willing to compromise on domestic politics, making significant concessions to their coalition partners, particularly on the extension of the Law for the Protection of the Republic. In July 1927 the Law on Labour Exchanges and Unemployment Insurance (which extended the existing system of unemployment insurance and set up a nationwide system of state employment agencies to help people find work) passed with cross party support, with only the Communists and Nazis voting against. The DNVP and Centre Party also shared common ground on the issue of religious education, but when the 1927 Schools Bill was put

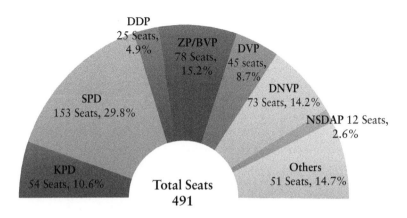

Figure 3.3 Reichstag Election Results, 20 May 1928.

forward it was met with a storm of protest from the liberals (including the DVP) and the left. With the Centre Party unwilling to compromise, the government collapsed, and new elections were held on 20 May 1928.

The 1928 Reichstag elections saw a swing to the left, the collapse of support for the liberal parties, and the emergence of a number of small splinter parties. This had two results: the formation of a grand coalition under the Social Democrat Hermann Müller on 28 June 1928, and a degree of panic within the 'bourgeois' parties concerning their eroding support and the 'threat' from the left. In October and December 1928 respectively both the DNVP and the Centre elected new party chairmen – Alfred Hugenberg and Ludwig Kaas – who were to drag their parties to the right, with fateful consequences for the republic as a whole.

THE WEIMAR PARTY SYSTEM

As the overview of domestic politics in the 'Golden Twenties' given above shows, the governing coalitions of the Weimar Republic frequently broke up and reformed themselves as the electoral arithmetic demanded. This was because the political culture of the Weimar Republic, like German society as a whole, was deeply fragmented and dominated by several subcultures based on ideology, class and confession. All of Weimar's political parties fitted into one or other of these 'camps' with little or no crossing of boundaries. The language of social unity and an idealized national community (*Volksgemeinschaft*) was often deployed, but each party remained wedded to their particular vision of state and society and drew their support mainly from established social milieus, making little effort to expand their appeal beyond their core constituencies.

Despite the fact that most German political parties re-organized themselves in the winter of 1918–19 there was considerable continuity in the party system between Imperial and republican Germany. Of the nine main political parties operating under the Weimar Republic, five were identical to or had evolved out of the main political factions of the Imperial Reichstag (see Appendix 1). Many of the individuals who came to dominate Weimar politics had entered the Reichstag before the war and enjoyed political careers spanning the Wilhelmine and republican periods (Ebert had entered the Reichstag in 1912 after over a decade in local politics in Bremen; Scheidemann had been active in politics since 1883 and was elected to the Reichstag in 1903, the same year as Matthias Erzberger; and Gustav Stresemann was elected as a representative of the National Liberal Party in 1907). This provided a high degree of consistency between the political classes of the Empire and the republic.

Nevertheless, the experience of war and revolution had a transformative effect on German politics and society, breaking traditional political loyalties and forging new ones. As we have seen, war and revolution had led to a split in the labour movement that transformed the SPD from the sole political representative of the German working class into just one of three (two from 1922) political parties espousing Social Democratic and Marxist ideals. Similarly, although the re-ordering of the political establishment in 1918 initially seemed to offer an opportunity for the two wings of nineteenth-century German liberalism to overcome their differences and forge a united liberal party, differing visions of the state and the annexationist position of the leader of the National Liberals, Gustav Stresemann, ultimately meant that the 'bourgeois centre' entered the Weimar period even more fractured than it had been under the Empire. And while the various parties of the right had more success in overcoming their differences and forming a single political grouping, the revolution and collapse of the old order only served intensify the process of radicalization that had already begun during the war.

From the very beginning, Weimar's political parties were viewed with some suspicion by their contemporaries – even those who were staunch democrats, such as the sociologist Max Weber and the Austrian jurist Hans Kelsen, were likely to see them as at best a necessary evil and at worst enemies of true democracy. Commentators complained that Weimar's party system promoted mediocrity and rule by self-serving party hacks, and figures from such diverse political backgrounds as the anarchist Gustav Landauer, the liberal presidential candidate Willy Helpach and the Social Democrat Heinrich Diest all advocated alternative forms of popular political participation that they thought would more directly embody the will of the people. This reflects not so much a lack of faith in democracy itself, as older interpretations have suggested, but rather a plurality of views concerning the nature of democracy that do not necessarily neatly align to our contemporary view of what liberal democracy looks like.

The SPD entered the Weimar period as the strongest of Germany's political parties with a clear ideological vision and an established organizational base. By the early twentieth century, the SPD was the largest political party in the world with over a million members and despite the emergence of two rival Marxist parties after 1917 it carried over much of this support into the Weimar period as the result of a working class long socialized and 'indoctrinated' to see the Social Democrats as their natural political champions. The SPD were consistently the single largest party in the Reichstag between 1912 and 1932 and their experience of wartime cooperation with the state and 'bourgeois' parties stood them in good stead after 1918 as champions of the new republican order. Nevertheless, throughout the Weimar period the party remained ostensibly committed to a Marxist interpretation of history that saw liberal democracy as merely a step on the road towards a utopian socialist future. Although by 1929 only 60 per cent of its members were industrial workers (the remainder were white-collar employees, housewives [17 per cent] and left-wing intellectuals), the SPD continued to see itself as 'the party of working people in town and country' whose aim was 'the progressive reshaping of the whole capitalist economy ... to free working people from the bonds of capital's domination'.[3] For this reason it withdrew into opposition in 1923 and remained there until 1928. This meant that the largest party in the Reichstag was more often than not outside the governing coalition (even if it did extend its informal support or tolerance to the government of the day), thus weakening the government and denying the SPD the chance to gain credit among voters for the relative stability and prosperity of Weimar's middle years.

Elsewhere on the left, the more radical Independent Socialists (USPD) lost their direction and cohesion after the war and foundation of the republic. United only in their opposition to the war, once peace came, they lost much of their *raison d'être*. The formation of the German Communist Party (KPD) highlighted the ideological divisions within the USPD and in October 1920 the party split, with the majority joining the Communists, while the rump of the party limped on for another two years before merging with the SPD.

Much more ideologically and organizationally robust was the Communist Party. From its inception the KPD remained fundamentally opposed to parliamentary democracy and wedded to the goals of bringing about revolution and the establishment of the communist utopia. Not only the bourgeois parties but also the 'reformists' and 'opportunists' in the moderate left were branded as class enemies and anyone who deviated from the party line (as dictated from Moscow) was ruthlessly purged from the party. Nevertheless, in the first years of the republic there was considerable division within the KPD over what tactics would best achieve their ends. The influence of those within the party who favoured violent revolution was still strong, as demonstrated by the 'March Action' of 1921 and the uprisings in Thuringia, Saxony and the Ruhr in 1923, but the KPD was increasingly under pressure from its Soviet masters to forego direct action and engage in a united front of German labour while at the same time pressing for greater socialization. This became the official party line with the appointment of Ernst Thälmann as leader of the KPD in 1925, an event which brought the German Communist Party firmly under the control of Moscow. From then on the party pursued a policy of the 'concentration of forces', which implied 'awaiting a future struggle ... whilst proclaiming itself not reconciled to the republic, continuing to contest elections with some success and playing an opposition role in the Reichstag, as well as working inside the trade unions.'[4] Nevertheless, this failed to gain them a mass following, especially as the violent tactics of the early 1920s had alienated the majority of the working classes. The KPD's core constituency remained the unskilled working class and the ranks of the unemployed and they struggled to peel the majority of working-class voters away from the more moderate, reformist SPD. This, together with the inflexibility imposed from Moscow, severely hampered the KPD's ability to either capitalize on the opportunities presented by the Great Depression or to mobilize resistance to the Nazi threat after 1929.

If the political left remained divided between two parties that espoused radically different methods of achieving the same ends (the liberation of the working class and the creation of a socialist society), the centre ground was even more fragmented. An attempt in 1918 to merge the two main liberal parties of the Imperial era came to nothing and German liberalism remained divided on roughly the same lines as it had been during the *Kaiserreich*. On the one hand the German Democratic Party (DDP) espoused a belief in progressive social policy and support for the republic combined with a desire for a more centralized state and a commitment to revise the Treaty of Versailles. On the other hand, the German People's Party (DVP) was more ambivalent towards the republic, initially favouring a constitutional monarchy instead, and championed unrestricted private enterprise. Both these parties competed for middle-class votes with the right-wing DNVP and the Catholic Centre Party, whose internal ideological divisions were more than made up for by its shared confessional identity which also gave it broader electoral support. This made the Centre Party perhaps the nearest thing to a genuine *Volkspartei* ('people's party'), whose appeal crossed social boundaries, in the Weimar era: its supporters included industrial workers, farm labourers, teachers, industrialists and aristocrats and although it was strongest in the Catholic south and west of Germany, it had pockets of support throughout the country. It also tended to be more flexible than either the SPD or the liberal parties, which meant that it became the mainstay of governments throughout the period: it participated in every national governing coalition between 1919 and 1932 and supplied more Chancellors than any other party. However, as the economic and political situation worsened in the late 1920s the Centre Party shifted to the right, while the DDP and DVP found it increasingly difficult to survive as their traditional supporters abandoned them in favour of parties who offered more radical solutions to Germany's problems. The death of Gustav Stresemann in 1929 left the DVP leaderless and bereft of its greatest electoral asset, while the defection of key supporters to the host of middle-class splinter parties that emerged in the late 1920s (the Business Party, the *Deutsche Bauernpartei*, etc.) forced the DDP to rebrand itself as the more nationalist State Party (*Deutsche Staatpartei*) in 1930 in an attempt to stave off electoral eclipse.

In contrast, the political right seemed much more cohesive and clearer in its goals. For most of the Weimar period right-wing opposition to the republic was focused on the German National People's Party (DNVP), an amalgamation of the old Conservative and Free Conservative parties, the Pan-German League, the Christian Social Party and the racist *Deutsche völkische Partei*. Yet although the right managed to carry out the kind of merger that eluded the liberals, the DNVP remained deeply divided in terms of both ideology and support, encompassing every shade of right-wing anti-republican opinion from monarchist landowners and army officers to anti-socialist businessmen, lower middle-class nationalists, conservative Christians and racist extremists. Indeed, the old Conservatives under Count von Westarp only joined the DNVP reluctantly and maintained their own separate organization throughout the Weimar period (breaking away completely in 1930 to form the Conservative People's Party [KVP]), while the various nationalist clubs and societies who made up most party activists resisted any attempt to impose central control on them. It has been suggested that what held the DNVP together was its commitment to a restoration of the monarchy,[5] but it is perhaps more accurate to see the unifying principle behind the party as a shared hostility towards the republican system. Although the party's programme explicitly called for the 'renewal of the German empire as established under the Hohenzollerns',[6] there were also many within the DNVP who were as ambivalent towards monarchism as they were towards the republic.

As the second largest party in the Reichstag after 1924 the DNVP was divided between those who were prepared to constitute a loyal opposition within the republican system and those who remained implacably opposed to democracy. Although it joined the government twice (in 1925 and 1927), the DNVP was engaged in an intra-party struggle between these factions throughout the middle years of the republic which was only resolved with the election of the dictatorial press magnate Alfred Hugenberg as party chairman in 1928.[7] Under Hugenberg the party shifted towards the right and made the disastrous decision to bring the Nazis into a 'National Opposition' against the Young Plan, a move which ultimately only served to improve the fortunes of the NSDAP who increasingly picked up support from those who had once given their loyalty to the Nationalists.

Even further to the right than the DNVP and even more implacably opposed to the republic were the host of nationalist and anti-Semitic (*völkische*) groups that emerged in the wake of the war and revolution. Many had their origins in pre-war nationalist pressure groups such as the Pan-German League or the wartime Fatherland Party, but others emerged in the wake of the revolution to espouse a radical new vision of state and society that blended extreme nationalism or Prussian conservatism with a vague socialism based on the comradeship of the trenches. There were at least 15 of these groups in Munich alone in 1919 and throughout the 1920s these societies waged 'a broad cultural war' against 'the socialist and republican left' through mass demonstrations and political agitation.[8] Out of this welter of anti-republican extremist societies emerged a group that by 1933 could genuinely claim to be a mass movement and had displaced the SPD as Germany's largest political party.

Founded in Munich in 1919 the *Deutsche Arbeiterpartei* (German Workers Party [DAP]) sought to bring nationalism and anti-Semitism to the working masses by combining them with an ill-defined socialism. It was soon joined by Adolf Hitler, an embittered Austrian who had fought in a Bavarian regiment during the war and subsequently been ordered by military intelligence to keep an eye on the activities of groups such as the DAP. Under Hitler's influence the party added the words 'National Socialist' to its name and adopted a 25-Point Programme that called for the radical revision of the Treaty of Versailles, the establishment of a strong central authority under a single leader, and the implementation of radical socialist, corporatist and racialist policies.[9] By 1921 Hitler had displaced Anton Drexler as leader and the party had acquired its own newspaper, the *Völkischer Beobachter*, and developed a paramilitary wing mostly made up of former *Freikorps* men dubbed the *Sturmabteilung* (Storm Detachment [SA]). Nevertheless, for much of the Weimar period the NSDAP remained a marginal and regional force within Weimar politics. Despite a strong following in Bavaria by 1924 the Nazis could only contest national elections as part of the *Völkischer-Block*, a short-lived electoral alliance between the Nazis, the German Racial Freedom Party (*Deutschvölkische Freiheitspartei* [DVFP]) and the National Socialist Freedom Movement (NSFB). Even after Hitler's release from prison in December 1924 and the re-founding of the party in 1925 with a commitment to achieve power through legal means, National Socialist electoral performance continued to be poor. They attracted little support during Weimar's middle period and won only 12 seats in the Reichstag elections of 1928. What dramatically altered their fortunes was the onset of the Great Depression. This new economic crisis allowed the Nazis to present themselves as a radical alternative to the more established parties who seemed unable to bring rising unemployment under control and they picked up support from both unemployed workers and middle-class voters who feared loss of status and a Communist takeover. By 1932 the NSDAP had displaced the SPD as the largest single party in the Reichstag and was being considered as a possible coalition partner by the right-wing Chancellor Franz von Papen.

THE DAWES PLAN

Despite the tendency towards factionalism in the Weimar party system and the frequent changes in coalition government during Weimar's middle years, there was a high degree of continuity in German foreign policy. Not only did it continue to be dominated by the issue of reparations, but it was also dominated by one man: Gustav Stresemann, who held the foreign affairs portfolio in every cabinet from 1923 until his death in 1929. Although he had once been an ardent nationalist, the war had convinced Stresemann that the key to German prosperity was not economic rivalry and territorial expansion, but the common interests of the European states in the face of the economic challenge from the Anglo-Saxon world (and particularly the United States). It was an argument based on economic self-interest, but it also assumed that such self-interest could lead to greater cooperation and understanding between nations. The Ruhr Crisis further convinced him that interdependence had another strand: that German security depended on French security, for as long as the French felt threatened by the prospect of a resurgent Germany, they would do all they could to keep their neighbour down.

However, before serious steps could be made towards *rapprochement* with France, the Ruhr Crisis needed to be ended and that meant some sort of solution to the reparations issue. On 30 November 1923 the Reparations Commission established two committees of experts to review Germany's liabilities under the London Schedule of Payments of 1921. The committee under the American financier Charles G. Dawes reported back in April 1924, proposing an economic and political compromise that would ease the financial strain placed on the Weimar Republic while going some way to satisfy French demands for a secure and durable payment schedule. The so-called Dawes Plan, which was approved in August 1924, provided Germany with an 800-million-mark loan designed to kick-start its economic recovery and a moratorium on reparations payments until 1925. After this the republic was liable for an annual annuity of 1 billion marks, rising to 2.5 billion by 1928–9. No schedule of payments or even total figure was specified, and as a guarantee of future payments the Allies insisted that Germany hand over control of the railways and accept the appointment of an Allied currency commissioner.

Almost immediately the plan provided some relief to Germans suffering under the inflation and stabilization measures. Interest rates fell to 30 per cent, halving unemployment, while a series of international loans (Germany received £200 million in loans from the United States alone between 1924 and 1926, and by 1929 had been in receipt of a total of around £1 billon) and investments helped to bring the official unemployment figure down to 436,000. As the German economy began to recover, the Dawes Plan seemed to have, for the time being at least, resolved the conundrum of reparations, vindicating those like Stresemann and Wirth who had long argued Germany's priority should be to become once more a 'credible ally' (*bündnisfähig*) for the West. Yet Germany still faced international hurdles in its path. The reparations issue might have been settled on a reasonably acceptable basis for all but the most hard-line nationalists, but the other clauses of the Treaty of Versailles remained unaltered, and Germany was still far from being reintegrated fully into the community of nations.

THE 1925 PRESIDENTIAL ELECTION

On 28 February 1925 President Friedrich Ebert died of peritonitis, aged only 54, having delayed seeking medical attention so that he could give evidence in the libel trial of a journalist who had accused him of being a traitor.[10] His sudden death highlighted the continuing divisions in German politics as the parties all scrambled to field their own candidates for the presidency. No fewer than seven candidates were put forward in the first round of voting so unsurprisingly none of them managed to secure the necessary outright majority. For the second round the 'people's bloc' made up of the Centre, SPD and DDP all agreed to support the former Chancellor Wilhelm Marx who seemed certain to win. Following the failure of the Kapp and Beer Hall Putsches, 'the right had committed itself to the quasi-legal course of altering the political system from within rather than by means of a violent overthrow' (hence the DNVP's participation in government in 1925 and 1927) and seizing the presidency was seen as 'key to the eventual foundation of a more authoritarian system of government'.[11] Alarmed by the prospect of another seven years of republican rule the political right rallied behind a latecomer to the contest, the 77-year-old wartime hero Field Marshal Paul von Hindenburg. Presented by his right-wing supporters as the apolitical 'saviour' of the nation, Hindenburg's carefully constructed mythic status as the 'victor of Tannenburg' enabled him to secure a narrow victory over Marx and his other opponent, the Communist Thälmann.[12]

Table 3.1: Results of the Presidential Elections, 1925

	First Round (29 March 1925)	Second Round (26 April 1925)
Turnout	68.9%	77.6%
Braun (SPD)	7,802,497 29%	–
Held (BVP)	1,007,450 3.7%	–
Hellpach (DDP)	1,569,398 5.8%	–
Hindenburg (Independent)	–	14,655,641 48.3%
Jarres (DVP, DNVP)	10,416,658 38.8%	–
Ludendorff (DVFP)	285,793 1.1%	–
Marx (Centre)	3,887,734 14.5%	13,751,605 45.3%
Thälmann (KPD)	1,871,815 7%	1,931,151 6.4%

Note: Figures for each candidate indicate number of votes polled and percentage of total votes cast.

Source: Anna von der Goltz, *Hindenburg: Power, Myth and the Rise of the Nazis* (Oxford: Oxford University Press, 2009), 96.

Although the hopes of his supporters and fears of his detractors that the new president would bring about an immediate shift to the right were not realized, Hindenburg's election did mark a turning point in Weimar politics and would prove to have fateful consequences for the republic. Although he had no great love for democracy, the Field Marshal had sworn an oath to discharge his office in accordance with the law. He therefore always kept within the letter of the constitution and greatly endeared himself to republicans by backing Stresemann's foreign policy and retaining Ebert's State Secretary Otto Meissner as presidential chief-of-staff. Nevertheless, there were clear indications of the new president's attitude towards the republic: he remained an honorary member of the anti-democratic veterans association, the *Stahlhelm*, publicly endorsed the 'stab-in-the-back' myth and continued to 'lend his weight to

President Paul von Hindenburg leaving Berlin Cathedral, April 1928 (Bundesarchiv, Bild 102-05749/CC-BY-SA 3.0).

numerous right-wing causes, especially those of symbolic importance'.[13] Under Hindenburg there was a gradual shift away from the primacy of parliament towards a more presidential style of government which was facilitated by the difficulties in securing workable parliamentary majorities. This enabled the president 'to bring his personal and political preferences to bear on the formation of governments' which effectively meant that 'if at all possible the DNVP should be included in government' and the SPD kept out of office as a matter of principle.[14] Almost from the very beginning Hindenburg made no secret of his desire for a more right-wing configuration of politics, while at the same time jealously guarding the powers and privileges granted to him by the constitution.

FOREIGN POLICY UNDER STRESEMANN

There were high hopes that the adoption of the Dawes Plan would herald the beginning of a new era in Germany's relations with the Western Powers, but almost immediately a new crisis threatened to erupt. In December 1924, following a report by the Military Control Commission demonstrating extensive violations of the disarmament clauses of the treaty, the Allies decided that the area of the occupied Rhineland around Cologne would not be evacuated in January 1925 as scheduled. This rang alarm bells in the German Foreign Office, who feared that this was the first step towards a new Anglo-French agreement that would leave Germany permanently isolated and stiffen French intransigence just when the prospect of increased mutual understanding seemed in the offing. At the same time, Stresemann was acutely aware of the effect that the failure to evacuate the Cologne zone would have on his right-wing critics at home.

Thus, in an effort to 'balance French claims for security with German demands for Treaty revision',[15] Stresemann launched what he later called 'a peace offensive on a grand scale'[16] by reviving the idea of a tripartite 'Rhineland Pact' that had first been proposed by the Cuno administration in 1922. Early in 1925 the German Foreign Office offered to renounce their claim to Alsace and Lorraine in return for a revised schedule for the withdrawal of Allied troops from the Rhineland. The French were hesitant at first – particularly after Hindenburg's election as President, which stimulated French suspicions that the Weimar Republic was little more than a front for the aggressive, nationalist Germany of old – but with the encouragement of Britain and the USA the proposal was treated seriously. The main sticking point was the lack of any guarantee of Germany's eastern frontiers (the most Stresemann was prepared to offer was mutual arbitration treaties with Poland and Czechoslovakia), which the French feared would leave their eastern allies dangerously exposed. After protracted negotiations and exchanges of notes (during which time Stresemann faced down pressure both from the Soviets – who threatened to reveal the extent of their military links with the Reichswehr – and the DNVP) it was agreed to hold a foreign minister's conference at Locarno in Switzerland to discuss the proposal. The conference opened on 5 October 1925 and agreement was reached 11 days later. The resulting Locarno Treaties were signed in London on 1 December. These were designed to allay the security fears of all the participating nations and put an end to territorial disputes. The Treaty of Mutual Guarantee saw the five European powers (Germany, France, Britain, Belgium and Italy) guarantee Germany's existing frontiers with France and Belgium while agreeing to uphold the demilitarization of the Rhineland. Germany undertook not to wage war against France and/or Belgium and all three powers agreed to offer any disputes to the League

The Deliberations in Locarno, 1925: German Foreign Minister Gustav Stresemann, British Foreign Secretary Austen Chamberlain and French Foreign Minister Aristide Briand, October 1925 (Bundesarchiv, Bild 183-R03618/CC-BY-SA 3.0).

of Nations for arbitration. Britain and Italy acted as guarantors of the treaties and pledged to assist the victims of aggression, while all the signatories pledged to renounce military action except in self-defence.

Locarno marked a turning point in Weimar Germany's relations with the outside world. Though it faced concerted opposition from the extreme right the ratification of the agreement ushered in a period of détente in Europe that, in spite of the strains later placed upon it, lasted until at least 1929. Locarno dramatically improved Germany's international standing and made it much harder for the Allies to justify the continuation of the occupation of the Rhineland, while at the same time improving the republic's financial position as it opened the way for more foreign investment and trade treaties with the United States, Britain, France, Italy and Poland. Thereafter Germany was treated more like an equal than a former enemy, and the way was smoothed for Germany to be readmitted into the community of nations through membership of the League.

This possibility had first been raised in September 1924 by the newly elected British Prime Minister Ramsey MacDonald, but it soon ran into problems. Although the initiative was welcomed by Stresemann as a step towards Germany's rehabilitation as a Great Power, it also presented a problem as it was unclear how compatible this would be with Weimar's commitments to the Soviet Union. A staunch anti-Communist who was sceptical as to the value of military cooperation with the Red Army (as Chancellor he had tried to bring an end to this, only for the Reichswehr to carry on regardless[17]), Stresemann never saw close relations with Russia as being as important as an accommodation with the Western Powers, but he did see their value as a means of balancing Germany's commitments. This was partly because he viewed close relations with the Soviet Union as a means of maintaining pressure on Poland, but also because he was aware of the entrenched domestic opposition from Hindenburg, Seeckt and the nationalist right to abandoning Germany's 'eastern option' in favour of closer ties with the West.[18] He therefore argued for German entry to the League only on terms that would not drive a wedge between Germany and Russia. This proved unacceptable to the Allies and the matter was dropped. Negotiations were resumed in the wake of Locarno, only to stall again in March 1926 when Germany insisted on a permanent seat on the League Council while vehemently opposing France's suggestion that this should be balanced by the extension of the same privilege to Poland. Nevertheless, over the summer Germany's path to membership of the League was smoothed and on

10 September it was formally admitted (although the Germans had to consent to Poland becoming a non-permanent member of the Council).

Meanwhile, protracted negotiations with the Soviet Union had been taking place. Alarmed at Stresemann's policy of détente with the West, in December 1924 the Soviets proposed an extension to the political and military agreement made at Rapallo. Feeling that reconciliation with the Western Powers promised more immediate and important gains, the Germans prevaricated, but on 24 April 1926 Germany concluded a commercial treaty with Russia. This was largely designed to counter domestic criticism that the policy of rapprochement with the West was one-sided and gave away too much. But it also had great symbolic importance as a show of Germany's independence and right to act in ways that it thought appropriate to its political and economic interests, geographical position and status as a Great Power.[19]

After securing the Weimar Republic's entry into the League, Stresemann had high hopes of a wide-ranging agreement with France designed to allay French security concerns once and for all while finally ridding Germany of foreign occupation. However, such a final settlement remained elusive. Hopes of a general Franco–German agreement foundered when faced with French reluctance to commit and the realization that no progress could be made on reparations until after the United States' presidential election of 1928. Nevertheless, with the establishment of better relations after Locarno, British and German politicians increasingly regarded the occupation of the Rhineland as an anachronism, and in January 1926 the British withdrew their troops from Cologne, leaving only a token force at Wiesbaden. Further negotiations followed and in August 1927 Stresemann managed to secure a reduction of the occupying force in the Rhineland and the signature of a comprehensive trade treaty with France.

Shortly afterwards the French made an attempt to elicit a 'solemn declaration' of friendship from the Americans. Determined not to be drawn into the European security system the US Secretary of State, Frank Kellogg, countered in December 1927 with a proposal for a multilateral peace pact. The International Treaty for the Renunciation of War as an Instrument of National Policy, or Kellogg–Briand Pact as it became known, 'directed that its signatories renounce war, but provided no means of enforcement' while 'in its final form, the draft was diluted to exclude wars of self-defence and for the fulfilment of existing treaty obligations'.[20] Nevertheless, it caught the public mood and seemed to offer an opportunity to breathe new life into the flagging Locarno spirit. Furthermore, it was consistent with Germany's policy of seeking to persuade the Allies that they had turned over a new leaf and thereby pave the way to a revision of Versailles and the restoration of equality with other nations. This being the case, Stresemann seized eagerly on the opportunity and Germany was the first nation to accept Kellogg's proposals.

Nevertheless, a final settlement on the Rhineland and reparations remained an important goal that could not be overlooked. By the beginning of 1929 the government was acutely aware that Germany would not be able to meet its obligations under the Dawes Plan and that unless some agreement was reached foreign investors would lose confidence in the German economy. American bankers were to some extent open to proposals to revise the Dawes Plan as it was clear that Germany lacked sufficient funds to both pay the full annual instalments of reparations stipulated by the 1924 agreement and to meet interest payments on loans from the United States. On their side the French were also willing to agree to a revision if it also took into account war debts. To this end, the League of Nations established a commission to review the question under the chairmanship of the American banker Owen D. Young. The resultant 'Young Plan' provided a total figure of 112 billion marks to be paid over 59 years and abolished Allied controls on German banking and railways. Although the plan faced opposition from both the French and the far-right in Germany, Stresemann was aware that the French needed an agreement on reparations and war debts as badly as the Germans, and managed to force their acquiescence to the evacuation of French occupying forces by 30 June 1930 by threatening not to sign the Young Plan.

THE ECONOMY

Following the introduction of the Dawes Plan, Germany was able to return to some measure of economic normality after the trauma of war, defeat, revolution and hyperinflation. On 30 August 1924 Germany reverted to the gold standard and the *Rentenmark* was replaced by the *Reichsmark*. Stimulated by American capital, the German economy experienced a boom. Yet the consequences of the revolution and the inflation cast a long shadow and left the economy particularly exposed to any new economic crisis that might come along. This being the case, the question remains as to whether, economically at least, the lustre of Germany's 'Golden Twenties' was little more than fool's gold.

Part of the problem was deep-seated 'structural' weaknesses in the Weimar economy that were partly a legacy of the revolution and ideological attempts to impose greater regulation and social mobility on Germany, and partly a consequence of the dramatic expansion and intrusion of the state into economic life that had taken place during the Great War. 'Modernization' and 'rationalization' – defined by the National Board for Economic Viability as 'the application of all means offered by technology and systematic organization to the rising of economic viability, and therewith to increasing the production of goods, reducing their cost and improving them'[21] – were the buzzwords of the day and the state worked hard to promote these principles in the face of opposition from the unions who feared that the result of the implementation of 'modern' business models borrowed from America would be job losses. The *Reichswirtschaftsrat* (Reich Economic Council), established in August 1919 as the pinnacle of a three-tier pyramid structure (comprised of Factory and Regional Councils) and designed to safeguard the interests of workers at the same time as increasing production through the promotion of rationalization and modernization, was symptomatic of the widespread tendency towards 'organizationalism' in the Weimar economy. It was made up of 326 members representing both employers and workers and was supposed to foster dialogue that would be beneficial to both. However, it ultimately proved ineffectual in bridging the gap between labour and capital and although it continued to exist until 1934 it played a negligible role in economic life after 1923 as the post-war agreement between employers and unions increasingly broke down.

Accompanying, and related to, this trend was the increased power of economic interest groups who had been brought in to assist with labour shortages and economic mobilization during the war and remained in a privileged position after it had ended. Business resumed the pre-war habit of forming cartels (there were 2,500 in 1925, rising to over 3,000 in 1930) to set prices and standardize products. In the wake of the inflation there was a widespread belief that 'the big firm is the model of the future'[22] and several businesses merged in the mid-1920s (for example, I.G. Farben in 1925 and Vereinigte Stahlwerke and Daimler-Benz in 1926). These *Konzerne* joined the numerous new economic institutions and pressure groups that had been established after 1918, such as the *Reichsverband der deutschen Industrie* (National Association of German Industry), who together with traditional institutions such as the Reichsbank jostled for influence over economic policy. This welter of complex competing, and interconnected interest groups and institutions ultimately led to confusion and lack of coherence and hampered the government in responding effectively to the challenges posed by the Great Depression.[23]

For ordinary people the effects of economic stability were often hard to discern. After 1924 real wages rose gradually, but so did housing costs and prices for staple goods. Likewise, employment figures were erratic in the period of 'stability' and 'recovery'. Seven per cent of Germans were out of work in 1925, a figure that rose to 18 per cent in 1926. It fell again to between 8 and 9 per cent in 1927, only to begin to climb again in 1928, a trend which continued until 1933. In contrast to the dynamic, research-driven economy of Imperial Germany, Weimar's industrial output looks practically moribund: technological advances were limited and restricted to a few well-established industries (chemicals, mining, automobiles), while productivity and growth remained sluggish over the whole period, to the extent that one study has concluded that there was no growth in total factor productivity between 1913 and 1929.[24] Furthermore, Germany's reliance on exports meant that it was badly hit by the post-war contraction in world trade which saw a 31 per cent fall between 1913 and 1929, with German exports at 87 per cent of their pre-war value in 1925. By 1929 exports to Britain and the United States were 60 per cent lower than they had been in 1913 and German exports were contributing only 14.9 per cent of the total GNP between 1925 and 1929, compared to 17.5 per cent before the war. All this meant that Germany's economic 'recovery' after the inflation was limited, a fact that was not lost on contemporaries who spoke of a 'weak' or 'sick' economy.

Table 3.2: Average Annual Growth Rates of Industrial Output (per cent)

	1913–38	1913–25	1925–29	1929–32
Metal Production	0.8	−2.9	5.1	−28.1
Metal Working	4.2	2.3	6.7	−20.9
Mining	0.8	0.6	5.9	−31.3
Chemicals	5.0	2.4	8.8	−9.4
Textiles	0.1	−1.7	−0.4	−6.8
Gas, Water, Electricity	5.8	5.8	7.7	−7.8
Construction	0.2	–	–	−29.9

Source: Harold James, *The German Slump* (Oxford: Clarendon Press, 1986), 115.

At the same time, in some important respects the inflation sowed the seeds of Germany's unique vulnerability to global economic instability. After the stabilization of the currency in 1924 Germany became enmeshed in a global 'cycle of debt' and thus especially vulnerable in the event of a worldwide economic downturn. German reparation payments to Britain and France were used by those countries to help pay off their own war debts to the United States, who in turn provided most of the foreign capital that was intended to kick-start Germany's economic recovery. Moreover, the government and the banks had not learnt the lessons of the early 1920s and continued to borrow at high interest while refusing to raise taxes. This enabled them to invest heavily in public works and pay reparations, but at the same time left the state finances dangerously exposed to fluctuations in world markets.

When the American economy went into a dramatic free fall in the wake of the Wall Street Crash not only did the foreign investment upon which the German economy had come to rely dry up, but Germany also found itself under increased pressure from both American investors who demanded repayment of earlier loans and from Britain and France who required reparations to help meet their own obligations to the United States. Under such pressures, German businesses went under, forcing millions into unemployment. Equally, already deeply in debt, the German government could see no way out of their economic predicament other than to reduce services, welfare costs and public sector wages and increase taxes. These austerity measures were not only hugely unpopular, but they also decreased demand (which only made matters worse) and had a dramatic impact on the financial and banking system.

A REPUBLIC WITHOUT REPUBLICANS?

If the comparative stability in the German economy between 1924 and 1929 was to some extent a facade which covered more worrying structural and long-term problems, the situation was something of the opposite when it came to politics. As we have seen, the governing coalition broke up and re-formed no fewer than six times between November 1923 and the collapse of Müller's grand coalition in March 1930. This gives the impression of a weak and unstable political system, but the high turnover of governments masks that fact that there was considerable continuity in terms of the individuals making up successive cabinets: over the 15-year lifespan of the republic there were 19 different cabinets, but the 223 ministerial posts were filled by just 79 politicians, 19 per cent of whom held office five times or more. Otto Gessler (DDP) became defence minister on the removal of Noske in March 1920 and remained in post until June 1928, serving in 13 different cabinets regardless of the party affiliation of the Chancellor. Heinrich Brauns (Centre) had a similar ministerial career, and Gustav Stresemann (DVP) served twice as Chancellor in 1923 before becoming a successful foreign minister until his death in 1929. There was also consistency in the Presidium of the Reichstag (the officials who oversaw parliamentary debates and procedures): Paul Löbe (SPD) was president of the Reichstag (equivalent of the Speaker of the British House of Commons or US House of Representatives) between June 1920 and May 1924 and again from January 1925 to 1932. It was a similar situation in the *Länder*: apart from two brief gaps between April and November 1921 and February and April 1925, Otto Braun was Minister President of Prussia from 1920 to until the illegal deposition of his government in 1932, Carl Severing was Prussian minister of the interior between 1920 and 1926 and again from 1930 to 1932, while in Bavaria, Heinrich Held (BVP) was Minister President from July 1924 until he

Constitution Day celebrations in Berlin, 11 August 1929. The *Reichsbanner Schwarz-Rot-Gold* marches past the Brandenburg Gate and the memorial to those who died in World War I (Bundesarchiv, Bild 102-08216/CC-BY-SA 3.0).

was ousted by the Nazis in March 1933. This suggests that there was perhaps more continuity and stability within the democratic system than has often been appreciated.

Similarly, we need to revise the notion that the foundations of German democracy were weak. Although the power and influence of the Reichstag and the political parties had been limited during the Imperial era, Germans had nearly 50 years' experience of universal male suffrage and participatory politics. During this time, Germany had developed 'genuinely competitive and representative political parties'[25] and a political class who continued to dominate German politics into the Weimar period. Until the onset of the Great Depression, the Reichstag and other institutions of the democratic state mostly functioned well. What is more, if we take membership of political organizations and electoral turnout as measures of democratic health, then Weimar Germany looks much more robust than many modern liberal democracies. Weimar's citizens joined political parties and associated social, youth and paramilitary organizations in large numbers and were involved in various forms of political activism. Electoral turnout under the Empire had been high, and it continued to be so under the republic, with 60 to 80 per cent of the population voting in both regional and national polls. This suggests that rather than being a politically immature nation with weak democratic institutions and traditions, Weimar Germany had in fact a thriving political culture in which contested elections and intensive electioneering were the norm. Rather than being estranged from or indifferent towards the republic, most of the German population 'positively participated in the republic and to a greater or lesser degree ... reaped the benefits of the welfare state'.[26]

Similarly, we must question the persistent assertion that the majority of those who participated in the democratic process and a sizable number of those who openly declared their support for the republic were fair-weather friends, so-called 'rational republicans' (*Vernunftrepublikaner*) who supported the democratic state for want of anything better. That there was no public appetite for either a restoration of the monarchy or a more radical left-wing state was amply demonstrated by the overwhelming support for the moderates during the November Revolution and subsequent elections to the National Assembly. This was underlined repeatedly during the 'years of crisis' by the lack of popular support for violent attacks on the republic and its politicians from both the left and the right. The assassinations of Matthias Erzberger and Walter Rathenau provoked a tide of outrage and revulsion and led to mass demonstrations in support of the republic. As the aristocratic diarist Count Harry Kessler noted on observing a pro-government demonstration in Berlin's Lustgardten the day after Rathenau's murder, 'the bitterness against Rathenau's assassins is profound and genuine. So is adherence to the republic, a far more deeply rooted emotion than pre-war monarchical "patriotism" was'.[27] And it was not just the faceless masses who demonstrated a more genuine commitment to democracy than has sometimes been suggested. Even amongst the ranks of the army, civil service, judiciary and big business, who have traditionally been seen as at best ambivalent towards the republic, there were some important and influential individuals – such as the state secretary for the foreign office Count von Maltzan and the industrialists Peter Klöckner and Paul Silverberg – who argued that the republican settlement was the best deal for Germany. Finally, the fact that even in 1932 the pro-republican *Reichsbanner Schwarz-Rot-Gold* was the largest of Germany's paramilitary associations with over a million members and that 'roughly one third of electors voted for parties that either explicitly or generally favoured the constitution, and a further fifth supported parties that, while not explicitly pro-democracy, nevertheless were not openly fighting the republic' suggests that 'To assert that the Weimar Republic was a "republic without republicans" is simply wrong.'[28]

At the same time, the oft repeated assertion that Weimar failed to develop unifying myths and symbols with which the population could identify needs to be reassessed. While it is true that for many on the right the republic was seen as fundamentally 'un-German', a foreign imposition, inspired by internationalist political creeds such as socialism and completely alien to Germany with its long tradition of monarchy,[29] its supporters were able to counter such assertions with their own appeals to German history and tradition. In an interesting inversion of the *Sonderweg*, some republican commentators saw Bismarck's Empire as 'a withered side branch on the tree of our people'; while as the heir to the liberal nationalism of 1848 the Weimar Republic was 'a fundamentally legitimate and appropriately national form of state'.[30] Furthermore, the authorities consistently sought to link the republic with 'events of national, historical and cultural importance' as part of a 'deliberate strategy to embed the young democracy into a tradition of German culture and history'.[31]

Despite the long insistence that the Weimar Republic lacked a political symbolism of its own which left it at a disadvantage vis-à-vis its conservative nationalist and Communist opponents, the republic was in fact better at developing such symbols than the Imperial regime it had replaced. The black-red-white colours of the Hohenzollern monarchy had only been formally adopted as the flag of the German Empire in 1896, there were no nationwide national holidays, and the empire never managed to agree on a national anthem. In contrast the republican authorities acted quickly to address the issue of shared national symbols for the new state, establishing the office of federal art expert (*Reichskunstwart*) at the Ministry of the Interior in October 1919 with the express task of replacing the old symbols of the monarchical state (everything from the national flag and coats of arms to coinage and postage stamps to national monuments and the staging of state occasions) with those more appropriate for the democratic republic. Like the framing of the constitution, this was a difficult balancing act between continuity and innovation: on the one hand the new democratic republic wanted to distance itself from the trappings of the authoritarian Empire, while on the other it recognized that tradition and precedent play an important role in legitimizing such symbols. To this end, the German eagle, which became the state symbol of the republic, was reminiscent of the heraldic symbol of the Prussian monarchy; the black-red-gold flag of the liberal revolutionaries of 1848, which had connotations of both democracy and nationalism, was adopted as the national colours; and the *Deutschlandlied* (with words written in 1841 set to a tune written in 1797) was officially recognized as the national anthem in 1922. These decisions were not uncontroversial and were the subject (like almost everything else) of bitter arguments between the left and the right, but the very fact that the republic treated the issue of finding national symbols that expressed the ethos of the state and with which its citizens could identify so seriously demonstrates that they were not as blind to the necessity for 'symbols and fantasy' in politics as some contemporaries and historians have suggested.[32]

Meanwhile, under the auspices of Edwin Redslob the *Reichskunstwart* worked hard to develop a framework of national symbolism and political theatre that would foster a sense of community and togetherness, both seen as hallmarks of the republican state.[33] Through a number of set pieces of national theatre heavy with republican symbolism such as the state funerals of Walther Rathenau (1922), President Ebert (1925) and Gustav Stresemann (1929), the inauguration of President Hindenburg (1925) and the annual Constitution Day celebrations, the authorities sought to provide focal points for a new form of republican patriotism based on notions of 'personal sacrifice for the sake of democratic principles and ideals rather than on race'.[34] Despite the fact that this was never officially adopted as a public holiday – the Reichsrat approved the measure, but it was never passed by the Reichstag – Constitution Day (11 August) became increasingly significant as an opportunity to celebrate republican aims and ideals. From modest beginnings in 1921, this evolved into a genuinely popular expression of republican patriotism that involved widespread social events as well as official ceremonies. One of the highlights of the celebrations in Berlin was a torchlit parade through the city centre made up of the *Reichsbanner*, the trade unions, the German Association of Civil Servants, the Jewish War Veteran Organization, local choirs and other civic groups numbering 12,000 in 1927, rising to 30,000 a year later.[35] For the celebration of the tenth anniversary of the adoption of the constitution in 1929, hundreds of thousands of people turned out to mark the occasion in Berlin alone while the provinces reported similar crowds.[36] So established had the occasion become that even though the celebrations had to be scaled down due to public spending cuts during the Depression, Constitution Day remained a fixture of the public calendar until the Nazis abolished it.

TOWARDS A NEW CRISIS

Although democracy and the republican system were by no means as weak and devoid of friends and champions as some older accounts would have us believe, by the time Hermann Müller's grand coalition came to power in the summer of 1928 there were already ominous signs that the fragile consensus and stability achieved after 1924 was beginning to break down. Both the Communists on the left and *völkische* nationalist groups on the right had continued to snipe at the republic from the sidelines and their newspapers and party propaganda stoked division and discontent in the hope that they would gain political capital from the destabilization of the republic. At the same time, the inability of Weimar's sluggish economy to deliver on promises of prosperity and social improvement left many voters dissatisfied and aggrieved, fuelling the rise of a host of single-issue 'bourgeois' splinter parties such as the Business Party (*Wirtschaftpartei*) and German Peasant's Party (*Deutsche Bauernpartei*) in the mid- to late-1920s. This put pressure on parties of the moderate centre and centre-right and the scrabble to appeal to alienated middle-class voters led the Centre, DDP, DVP and DNVP to run to the right.

There were also indications that the violence and uncertainty of the 'years of crisis' had also not been completely laid to rest. Agricultural crisis led to a series of mass protests in Schleswig-Holstein in January 1928 organized by the Rural People's Movement (*Landvolkbewegung*). These were followed by tax strikes, but under the charismatic leadership of Claus Heim and Wilhelm Hamkens the movement soon graduated from protests and withholding taxes to bombings and arson attacks against tax offices and public buildings in the summer of 1929.[37] At around the same time, Berlin was rocked by three days of rioting sparked by the heavy-handed police response to a KPD-organized May Day rally. 'Bloody May' (*Blutmai*) left 33 dead, 200 injured and 1,200 people in police custody (though only 44, were ultimately convicted and imprisoned for their role in the riots). For the Communists this confirmed their view of the Social Democrats (who held power in Prussia) as 'Social Fascists' who were worse than the class enemies on the right because they cloaked their reactionary tendencies with the language of social revolution. It also undermined public trust in the Berlin police force whose bloody suppression of the riots was reminiscent of the events of 1919.[38]

However, we should not overstate the significance of these trends and see them as evidence that the collapse of the Weimar Republic was inevitable or even likely. The drift of voters towards the right and the parties' adjusting their platforms and policies to follow them was a normal response to economic, social and political conditions within a liberal democracy (and arguably one that we have seen in Europe and the United States in the first decades of the twenty-first century). Even after the onset of a new economic crisis after October 1929 (see Chapter 6), the majority of Germans did not abandon democracy per se, and at least until the electoral breakthrough of the Nazi Party in September 1930, the choice before the electorate was between social democracy on the one hand and 'stability based on conservative and traditionalist authority' on the other.[39] Both options fitted in with the political consensus that had been developed during Weimar's 'Golden Twenties', and while some influential figures and extremist groups might have dreamed of a fundamental reordering of the German political system, there is little evidence to suggest that this was what the majority of Germans desired, even as late as 1932.

4

EVERYDAY LIFE IN WEIMAR GERMANY

Between 1924 and 1929 Weimar Germany returned to some semblance of economic and political normality. Yet the deep divisions that had existed within German society during the Imperial era persisted, and in some cases became more pronounced as a result of the demographic changes caused by the Great War. These focused new attention on potential areas of social discord that had existed before 1914, such as anti-Semitism, female emancipation and generational conflict, but which gained new significance in the 1920s. Interwar Germany was, then, a divided society and there was no single, universal experience of everyday life in the Weimar Republic. The lived experience of individuals and the ways in which they understood their society and their place within it was determined by a variety of factors which included class, gender, geography (where in Germany they lived and whether they lived in a city or the countryside, a leafy suburb or an inner-city slum), sexuality or any number of other characteristics. Nevertheless, it is possible to discern certain general trends that give us a sense of social relations during the Weimar Republic and what life was like for those who lived through the period.

SOCIAL CLASS IN WEIMAR GERMANY

Although Article 109 of the constitution abolished aristocratic ranks and titles and declared all Germans to be equal before the law, the Weimar Republic remained a stratified, hierarchical society in which social class (largely determined by wealth rather than birth alone) mattered.

To the frustration of many on the left, the November Revolution did not produce any immediate or significant redistribution of wealth or property. Weimar's 'welfare democracy' provided a safety net for those at the bottom of the social pyramid and living standards did in general slowly improve, but although class barriers were more permeable than under the monarchy, social mobility was limited.

There was also a considerable degree of stratification within broad class boundaries. There is a tendency amongst historians to talk about social classes as though they were homogenous groups, but as Stephan Malinowski has pointed out in the case of the German nobility, the reality was very different.[1] The German nobility was made up of Prussian *Junkers* (the term usually applied to the landed nobility of Prussia, particularly those who owned large estates east of the River Elbe[2]), the landowners of southern and western Germany and various impoverished branches of noble families with a claim to a famous name or aristocratic title but no money or property to speak of; the middle classes encompassed everything from the 'salaried masses' of clerical workers, to shopkeepers and small businesspeople, educated professionals (doctors, lawyers, teachers, etc.), and bankers and industrialists; while the working classes included skilled workers, manual labourers and the unemployed. There were therefore large disparities in standards of living, access to opportunity and everyday experience within each class. Even so, the three traditional social classes remain a convenient way to organize a discussion of the social hierarchy of Weimar Germany.

THE OLD ELITES: ARISTOCRACY AND OFFICER CORPS

The German revolution of 1918–19 was not accompanied by the kind of social upheaval and bloodletting as other, similar events such as the French Revolution of 1789 or the Russian Revolution of 1917. There were no tumbrils or guillotines, no expropriation of land, and the revolutionaries showed an 'astounding willingness to compromise and come to agreements with the old order'.[3] Nevertheless, for the around 80,000 individuals (roughly 0.14 per cent of the total population) who made up the nobility, news of the military collapse and formation of the republic was greeted with a mixture of shock and horror. They saw in the transition from monarchy to republic the collapse of everything they believed in and had been brought up to trust and admire. This engendered a profound sense of dislocation and anxiety which was only intensified by what many saw as the sudden loss of their economic and social power in the urban, industrial, and (supposedly) egalitarian republic. While some sections of the nobility were able to maintain a certain degree of their former status, many amongst the minor nobility felt particularly disenfranchised and embittered by the transition to the republic. It was these individuals in particular who increasingly gravitated to more extreme forms of right-wing politics.

For all the anxiety that they felt, certain sections of the old elites continued to be able to exert a degree of influence on the republic and even dominated some of its institutions. The Prussian system of large estates owned by aristocrats remained in place and was even subsidized by the public purse. Forty-one per cent of land in Germany's largest state belonged to these estates, many of which had been held by the same family for centuries. Traditional loyalties remained strong in the countryside and noble families continued to exercise influence locally and to play a role in provincial administration, in spite of the efforts of the Social Democratic government.[4] Similarly, the nobility continued to dominate the upper ranks of the Reichswehr. In reducing the manpower of the German Army in accordance with the terms of the Treaty of Versailles, preference was given to retaining regular officers who were mostly from aristocratic backgrounds. Of the 38 general officers in 1925, 21 were nobles, while 40 of the Reichswehr's 90 colonels were also from aristocratic backgrounds. In 1931, 19 of the 41 generals were noblemen as were 38 of the 104 colonels. In the army as a whole the nobility was disproportionately represented, making up 21.7 per cent of its strength in 1920, falling to 20.5 per cent in 1926 but rising again to 23.8 per cent in 1932.[5]

Hindenburg's *Junker* background and closeness to the army meant that the political influence of the nobility increased after he became president in 1925. The elderly field marshal owned lands in East Prussia and therefore had a personal interest in agricultural prices and supported state subsidies and tax breaks for East Prussian landowners, while opposing proposals in 1931 to break up unprofitable large estates and parcel out the land to unemployed workers. That Chancellor Brüning would even consider such proposals went a long way to discrediting him in the eyes of the President. Towards the end of his life, Hindenburg spent as much time as possible on his country estates and in the company of his aristocratic neighbours, giving them privileged access to the Head of State. He made no secret of the fact that he considered noblemen to be the 'natural' rulers of the country and this was reflected in the

Papen and Schleicher governments. Of the 11 members of Franz von Papen's short-lived 'Cabinet of Barons' (June–November 1932), seven had the aristocratic 'von' in their names, one was a Graf (count) and four *Freiherren* ('Free Lords', roughly equivalent to an English baron).

THE MIDDLE CLASSES

More than any other section of Weimar's social strata, the middle classes have been the focus of historical research. This is because they have traditionally been seen as the chief supporters of the Nazis after 1930 and because they were the section of society that provided the country's intellectual and cultural elite. Initially supporting the Weimar coalition in large numbers, the *Mittelstand* gradually turned first to the DNVP, then to special interest and splinter parties such as the *Wirtschaftpartei* (Business Party), and finally to the Nazis in search of protection from the perceived threat of the loss of their political, economic and cultural status. This fear of 'proletarianization' – a loss of social position leading to being subsumed into the working classes – haunted the lower middle classes throughout the Weimar period and was only exacerbated by the economic upheavals of hyperinflation and the Great Depression. Many blamed big business and the corporate rich for their perceived woes, but it was the left and the unions that filled them with an atavistic horror and left them feeling that if market forces did not rob them of their wealth and position, radical social legislation and/or violent revolution would.

The Weimar *Mittelstand* complained about their hard-earned taxes being misspent on expensive welfare projects for 'lazy' and feckless workers and 'benefit scroungers', but it was the fall-out from the inflation period that caused perhaps the most resentment, so much so that 'the agitation for redress of the wrongs of the inflation served to undermine the political stability of the Weimar Republic'.[6] The introduction of the *Rentenmark* had serious implications for those who had either borrowed or lent money under the old system. Either these debts would become worthless along with the old currency – effectively wiping out the debt, freeing the debtor from his or her obligations and leaving the lender out of pocket – or some way of transferring debts into the new currency had to be devised. Public pressure led to the introduction of the Revaluation Law of 16 July 1925 which was designed to redistribute wealth from those who had gained from the inflation to those who had lost out, but the complexities of the issues involved – and the vastness of some of the sums – quickly led to a moratorium on revaluation payments. This did not stop people challenging the principle of revaluation in the courts, and between 1925 and 1933 there were around two million such legal cases, resulting in hundreds of thousands of people feeling that they had been inadequately compensated for their losses during the inflation, while (to their eyes) workers had been able to take advantage of the economic chaos to negotiate higher wages.

However, like all other social groups the middle classes were far from being homogeneous. Historians have often divided them into 'upper' (academics, doctors, lawyers, etc.) and 'lower' (shopkeepers, tradesmen, etc.), but they might also be differentiated as 'old' and 'new'. While the 'upper' middle classes to some extent were better able to maintain their place in society, this did not insulate them from the sense of anxiety that infected their less fortunate fellow citizens. In particular they were deeply concerned about the perceived loss of respect for and the value of education and *Bildung* (literally 'formation', but the term more accurately reflects the idea of self-improvement through education and cultural consumption), while the hardships wrought by the inflation and depression created fears of 'an academic proletariat' and drove the professional classes into the arms of the DNVP and the Nazis.[7] The so-called 'old' lower middle classes were those whose livelihoods and values 'were rooted in an idealized vision of a pre-industrial past' like craftsmen, artisans and shopkeepers.[8] This gave them a strong sense of social identity but in the post-war era they faced ever more competition from mass-production and large-scale retailers (trends that had existed before the war but intensified after 1918) which only heightened their rejection and fear of industrial modernity. The 'new' lower middle classes were made up of those in the service industry (such as shop workers) and other white-collar workers such as clerks and junior civil servants, what the cultural critic Siegfried Kracauer termed 'the Salaried Masses' (*Die Angestellen*).[9] Between 1907 and 1925 the number of such employees rose from 1.3 million to 5.3 million, but this expansion brought with it a lack of job security. At the same time, women coming into the labour market were blamed for driving down wages (female white-collar workers earned on average 33 per cent less than their male colleagues) and increased competition for jobs, causing more anxiety and tension.

THE WORKING CLASSES

According to the census of 1925, about 32 million people, half of the German population, could be counted as being working class. Roughly two thirds of these worked in industry, while the rest were agricultural workers or were employed in the service sector. These figures mask considerable diversity in the lived experiences of working-class Germans, not least because those employed in industry worked in everything from small firms with five or fewer employees to big businesses employing thousands of people in sectors such as mining, steel production or the electro-chemical industry. Conditions varied greatly, but in most sectors work was hard, involving at least a degree of manual labour, and usually dirty and dangerous. In 1925, 1.3 million people worked as domestic servants, 99 per cent of whom were women, most of them aged between 18 and 30. Approximately 406,000 Germans, again mostly women but some of them children, worked from home finishing mass-produced goods or in small-scale manufacturing such as toy-making. These were often the lowest paid and most isolated members of Germany's working class, and they enjoyed little job security or legal protections.[10]

In contrast to what many middle-class Germans believed, it was the urban poor who suffered most from Germany's post-war economic upheavals. Despite the efforts of the Social Democrats in government at both national and regional levels, life for working people remained difficult and there were still extremes of wealth and poverty in Weimar Germany. The Stinnes–Legien Agreement that gave full legal recognition to the unions and established an eight-hour working day – both long-standing demands of organized labour – was a step forward, but it did not benefit all workers evenly and remained a source of contention not only between workers and employers, but also between different sections of the working class. In the immediate aftermath of the war and during the inflation period workers' real income tended to be lower than before the war. City-dwellers faced severe shortages of affordable food, fuel and housing, making them particularly susceptible to infectious diseases such as tuberculosis and rickets. Large numbers of people lived on horse or even dog meat. Even as late as 1929 one official study suggested that consumption of meat, bread, dairy products, fruit and vegetables was much lower than it had been before the war.

Owing to a shortage of affordable housing, overcrowding was the norm in working-class areas of most German towns and cities. Most families lived in small (one to three room) apartments, often with several

Tenant's strike in Berlin, September 1932. View of the courtyard of the house in Köpenickerstrasse 34/35. On the wall the tenants have written 'First the food, then the rent.' Some residents have hung out Communist and some Nazi flags. (Bundesarchiv, Bild 146-1970-050-13/CC-BY-SA 3.0).

people sharing a room or bed. Around half of these lacked their own toilets or bathrooms. Even with government set price controls in place, rent took up on average 10 per cent of an unskilled worker's income, while about 40–50 per cent of a working family's income went on food. This left little for other essentials such as clothing or education, let alone luxury items or entertainment. When it came to leisure, Weimar Germany offered a range of options to working-class people, from engagement with the modern entertainment industry through visits to the cinema, cabarets or amusement parks, to more solitary or traditional pastimes like gardening, hiking, reading or playing a musical instrument. For men, the local pub was a focal point of leisure and social life, while sport played an increasingly important role in the lives of both men and women.

The authorities did make some attempt to alleviate the problems faced by workers, but often in a patchy and unfocused way. The Social Democrats tended to focus their attention on their core constituency of skilled workers, championing their rights and presenting themselves as the party of the working class while to some extent ignoring the unskilled, homeless and otherwise disenfranchised sections of the urban proletariat. Although this drove many young workers into the arms of the Communists, the KPD also 'tended to have a rather scornful view of the urban poor'[11] and young unskilled workers were easily seduced by the Nazis after 1930. At the same time a new breed of middle-class social workers, midwives and welfare reformers attempted to apply new 'scientific' methods to deal with urban poverty, only to face obstruction and small acts of defiance from those who they were trying to help but who resented the intrusive and patronizing attitude of the social services. Similarly, the authorities struggled to control the gangs of young boys (or after 1929 unemployed youths) who roamed working-class districts looking for distraction and who only seemed to confirm fears that the war had caused a complete and irrevocable collapse of parental authority and an unprecedented outbreak of criminality.

Nevertheless, the Social Democratic authorities in Prussia took pains to do all they could to improve the lives of working people, raising social insurance and pensions, and investing in new affordable housing that allowed some of the better-off workers to move out of the old, overcrowded tenements into clean, modern apartment buildings with amenities such as electric lighting and indoor toilets. There were also more opportunities for education and training opened to workers by the extension of adult education. Evening classes specifically designed for working men were offered by philanthropic and educational institutions, but those affiliated with the University of Frankfurt were probably the most successful. Even so, the curriculum was designed to 'raise the consciousness of workers and make them a force for political and social change',[12] rather than to provide re-training or better employment prospects, so the usefulness of such classes is debatable. Article 146 of the constitution called for 'organically developed' public schools in which a good education providing the best life chances would be available to all regardless of wealth and background. Furthermore, it was hoped that these schools would instil the sense of civic responsibility in young Germans, along with the critical faculties necessary for a well-functioning democracy.

However, the ability of the Reich government to achieve these aims was somewhat limited. This was in part due to the provisions of the constitution itself – while central government had responsibility over higher education, the individual states retained control over secondary and primary education. Nevertheless, the SPD authorities in Prussia were assiduous in trying to make the education system more equitable and bring it into line with the principles expressed in the constitution. They raised the age at which pupils were examined to determine which of the three streams of the German school system they would be placed in, changed the rules to allow more movement between streams, and attempted to narrow the gap in opportunities available to boys and girls in an effort to make a university education possible for more people. All these measures were designed to improve the life chances of less wealthy pupils and to encourage more social mobility. However, the reformers faced opposition from the Centre Party who were dismayed at the secularizing trend in Social Democratic educational policy, and from within the educational establishment itself. Many teachers remained opposed to the republic on principle, while old educational methods such as learning by rote remained standard.

FAMILY LIFE, GENDER AND SEXUALITY

For Germans of all social classes the family remained the basic unit of social relations. Under Article 119 of the Weimar Constitution the state and municipalities were committed to the maintenance of 'the purity, health, and social welfare of the family' and marriage was afforded 'the special protection of the constitution' as 'the foundation of family life'.[13] Nevertheless, the German family changed considerably during the 1920s, reflecting wider changes in attitudes towards gender and sexuality that, like almost everything else in Weimar Germany, were highly contested. The Weimar Republic has often been represented in popular culture as a period of exceptionally liberal attitudes towards sex and sexuality. Yet while it is true that in this period Germans experimented with new forms of relationships or lifestyles and that state and national authorities tended to take 'a modern, scientific approach to gender and sex'[14] that stressed education and regulation over prohibition, we should be wary of projecting contemporary notions of progress and liberation onto the past. As Laurie Marhoefer has argued, despite some unease about the changes taking place in German society there was broad support, or at least acceptance, of changes to the gender and sexual order largely because they were 'in keeping with prevailing bourgeois norms of gender and sexuality'.[15]

In Germany, as in other combatant countries, the First World War had a profoundly disruptive effect on family life and gender roles. With so many husbands, fathers, sons and brothers away at the Front, women were forced to break out of the restrictions placed on them by nineteenth-century gender values and take on the roles of provider and disciplinarian in addition to their more traditional nurturing responsibilities. In many families this was a situation that was to continue even after 1918 as many men either did not return at all or proved to be physically or psychologically unfit to resume their 'proper' functions in the family and society because of their war experiences. The absence of men and their inability to fulfil what was considered to be their natural roles fostered a sense that traditional male authority and masculinity itself was under threat and that society was becoming increasingly 'feminized'.

The absence of men, both during and after the war, meant that many women had to abandon hope of ever taking on the traditional roles of wife and mother even if they wanted to, while the gender imbalance in society meant that the rules of the dating game changed. The stigma over sex before marriage had lessened during wartime and the incidence of single parenthood increased, not least because of the number of single-parent families caused by the death of a husband during the war. At the same time economic uncertainty and wider social changes led to a trend towards smaller families. Something like the nuclear family became the norm and by 1933 more than 50 per cent of German families were households made up of between one and four people. Only in the countryside did families tend to be larger, with over a third of households numbering six or more people.[16] Thirty-five per cent of married couples remained childless and Berlin had the highest divorce rate and the lowest birth rate in the world.[17] In Germany as a whole divorce rates tripled from pre-war levels, with the number of divorces per 100,000 people rising from 26.6 in 1913 to 61.6 in 1923 and 65 in 1932.[18] The reasons for this rise are difficult to determine with certainty because each divorce was a result of the breakdown of an individual relationship, but the difficulty that some men had in returning to normal life after the war was one factor, as was 'a general dissatisfaction with traditional marriage as they had witnessed it in their parental homes' among younger women.[19]

Nevertheless, within the family established gender roles remained the norm. Women were still expected to shoulder the burden of domestic chores and childrearing, even if they were also in paid employment. The Imperial Penal Code (*Reichsstrafgesetzbuch*) which gave men sole right of custody of children, the legal power to take decisions related to family life without consulting their partners and control of their wife's assets, remained in force throughout the Weimar period. The state, business and sections of the media all continued to push housewifery as the ideal for German women, who were encouraged to view housework and nurturing their families as a profession (*Beruf*) in itself. This reflected wider anxieties concerning a declining birth rate which was at least in part blamed on the supposed lax sexual morals of young women who were shirking their national duty by pursuing careers rather than having children. 'Female reproduction was still linked to the "people's body" (*Volkskörper*)' and as such women's bodies were seen as the property of all society.[20] The state was prepared to back Article 119 of the constitution with practical action and funds were made available to welfare and public health programmes that stressed 'family values'. Social workers and sex education programmes encouraged (married) couples to have more and better sex, stressing the importance of satisfaction for both partners, but only so that they might have more children.

Even so, despite the efforts of the government and business to re-establish pre-war gender roles, women entered the labour force in unprecedented numbers during the 1920s. After 1925 the trend towards economic rationalization led to more and more women entering the labour market as cheap unskilled workers. The number of female white-collar workers grew by 200 per cent between 1907 and 1925, meaning that two-thirds of those employed in the service sector were women. Of these, 90 per cent were unmarried and two-thirds were under the age of 25. There was a whole generation of young, unmarried women who were to some extent freed from the constraints of home and family by their disposable income. This enabled them 'to enter the spectacle-world of consumption'[21] as businesses woke up to the existence of untapped potential revenue from an increasingly well-educated, independent and solvent section of society. Household goods, fashion items, cosmetics and entertainment were aggressively marketed to female consumers, with advertisers often drawing on the language and iconography of political emancipation.[22]

The way that women looked and behaved was also changing. Gone were the long-hair, corsets, and flowing dresses of the pre-war period, to be replaced by bobbed hair (the so-called *Bubikopf* or page-boy hairstyle), shorter skirts, and 'tubular' styles of dress. It became acceptable for women to smoke in public and a world-weary and 'sophisticated' pose that hinted at sexual experience and availability became standard. The image of the flapper and the vamp, as exemplified by celebrities such as Josephine Baker, Louise Brooks and Marlene Dietrich, became commonplace and was much imitated by fashion-conscious young women who were usually also keen cinemagoers.

As pervasive as the image of this 'new woman' was in literature, advertising and popular culture, it has often been pointed out that it bore little resemblance to the lives of most German women. In the 1925 census 4.2 million women (a third of Germany's female adult population) described themselves as wage earners, half of whom were in poorly paid manual jobs.[23] New white-collar positions in the service industry or secretarial sector offered some degree of social mobility for young working-class women, but most of them found themselves working long hours for little pay in dead-end jobs. Many faced discrimination and sexual harassment both in the workplace and in wider society and there was little job security for female employees. Two thirds of German women were not in work: more young single women received welfare support than men in the years before the Great Depression, in part because employers usually gave preferential treatment to male job applicants. Matters became even worse after 1929 when competition for employment became ever more cut-throat. One of the ways in which the government sought to respond to the growing crisis was by prohibiting married women from working in the civil service, thus giving the move back towards more traditional gender roles official sanction. At the same time, working women were often the focus of anxiety and contempt from the male-dominated labour establishment: unions attacked the 'feminization' of the factory workplace that they saw as part and parcel of the trend towards rationalization, while young women were often dismissed not only by politicians of all parties but also by some older feminists as 'frivolous' and 'flighty', more concerned with fashion and having a good time than with serious social and political issues.[24]

There was little that was unique in the changes and challenges faced by German women in the Weimar period, which reflected wider social and economic changes and a heightened interest and discussion of issues relating to sex and sexuality throughout Europe.[25] But there was a perception both amongst Germans and some foreign observers that war, revolution and democracy had radicalized sex. While this might be going too far, the republic did offer an opportunity to reformers to try to apply the principles of scientific rationalization that were becoming popular in the economy to social and public health issues. The Weimar state wanted to introduce 'a new system of management' for society 'in which welfare paved the way to ethical behaviour' which would in turn lead to better personal and national health.[26] Although abortion remained illegal (under Paragraph 218 of the Penal Code), concerns about the public health implications led to a reduction of the maximum penalty and in 1926 abortion was made legal in instances where the mother's life might be endangered. Similarly, the 1927 Law for Combating Venereal Diseases (*Reichsgesetz zur Bekämpfung der Geschlechtskrankheiten*), which effectively decriminalized prostitution in towns with populations of more than 15,000 people and introduced instead a system of state regulation was passed in the hope of halting the spread of sexually transmitted infections and Germany's demographic decline.[27] At the same time, new discourses about citizenship provided opportunities for members of Germany's LGBTQ+ community to organize and campaign for increased rights.

Under Paragraph 175 of the Reich Penal Code of 1872 (which remained in force throughout the Weimar period and beyond) 'Unnatural sex act[s] committed between persons of male sex' were illegal and 'punishable by imprisonment' and the loss of civil rights.[28] As early as 1897, the sexologist Magnus Hirschfeld (himself a gay man) had helped to establish the *Wissenschaftlich-humanitäres Komitee* (Scientific Humanitarian Committee [WhK]), which was to become one of the main gay rights organizations of the Weimar period. The abolition of censorship during the November Revolution and the establishment of the Weimar Republic seemed to herald a new era of sexual tolerance and equal rights, and across the country gay men formed *Freundschaftvereine* ('friendship associations'). Hirschfeld founded the *Institut für Sexual-Wissenschaft* (Institute for Sexual Science) in Berlin in 1919 with the help of a grant from the Social Democratic government of Prussia. This became the headquarters of the WhK, while the Friendship Associations banded together to form a national German Friendship League (*Deutscher Freundschaftsverband* [DFV]) in 1920. Renamed the League for Human Rights (*Bund für Menschenrecht* [BfM]) in 1923, this organization had 48,000 members by 1929 and was active both in the campaign for repeal of Paragraph 175 and as a publisher of gay literature (including, from 1924, Germany's first magazine aimed at lesbian and bisexual women, *Die Fruendin*). Germany had 26 magazines aimed at a gay or lesbian audience during the 1920s (although most had only limited print runs and even more limited lifespans) and it has been estimated that by 1929 there were between 65 and 80 bars (or *Dielen*) catering for an exclusively homosexual clientele, as well as 50 clubs catering for lesbians, in the Reich capital alone. There was a similar pattern in other large cities like Hamburg, where there were around 30 gay bars, and Cologne, where there were 20. The Berlin police commissioner estimated that there were around 100,000 gay men in the capital in 1922 (not including 25,000 rent boys), a figure that had risen to 350,000 by 1930.[29] This subculture achieved an international reputation that made Berlin a destination for 'sex tourists' who believed that it was a city where they could be themselves and fulfil their erotic desires and saw establishments such as the notorious Eldorado transvestite bar appear in mainstream guidebooks.[30]

The term 'transvestite' (*Transvestit*) had been invented by Magnus Hirschfeld in 1910 and was commonly used in interwar Germany to refer not only to cross-dressing but also to 'a broad spectrum of what would now be referred to as "transgender" experiences and identifications; from self-defined heterosexual male transvestites with wives and children who cross-dressed only at home, to biological females and males living permanently as a member of the "opposite" sex'.[31] The term 'transgender' was coined in 1923 (also by Hirschfeld) but was not in common usage. As with gay men and lesbians, trans people enjoyed a greater degree of freedom and tolerance under the Weimar Republic than previously and began to organize and to push for recognition and acceptance in wider society. Although there was no specific law against cross-dressing, trans Germans could be subject to harassment by the authorities or prosecution under Paragraphs 175 or 183 (which dealt with causing a 'public nuisance'). However, from as early as 1908 German police forces had issued 'transvestite certificates' (*Transvestitenscheine*) which allowed trans people to go about their business free from official sanction and in 1922 guidance was issued to police forces stating that 'apart from male prostitution, transvestism in general has no criminal significance' and that a 'gentle treatment of transvestites' should be the rule.[32] The Weimar period also saw the development of a 'trans media' made up of articles and columns, often in magazines aimed at a lesbian audience, and at least one short-lived transvestite magazine, *Das 3. Geschlecht* (*The Third Sex*). There were also some of the earliest examples of individuals undergoing gender reassignment surgery, the most famous of which is Lili Elbe, a Danish artist who underwent a series of surgeries in Berlin and Dresden in 1930–31, a few months after Dora Richter had become the first person to successfully transition from male to female.[33]

Yet for all the apparent liberalization of sex and sexuality in the Weimar period, there was no real push to completely overturn the existing gender and sexual norms. Gay and trans rights activists in Weimar Germany mostly subscribed to middle-class values and were quick to censure anyone who did not conform to bourgeois standards of 'respectable' dress and behaviour. Within the trans subculture 'Female-to-male and homosexual transvestites were ... sidelined, as were individuals who voiced what would now be termed "transsexual" desires'.[34] At the same time, the reforms demanded by these movements were relatively modest. Magnus Hirschfeld 'was a reformer, not a revolutionary. ... He did not want homosexuals to acknowledge their homosexuality in public ... He did not want people to come out. He was not "out." He also did not want legal protections for same-sex relationships'.[35] The 1929 vote to abolish Paragraph 175 of the German penal code that prohibited sexual acts between men and replace it with a new law imposing an age of consent (21 years and over) and prohibiting male prostitution is often seen as evidence of this growing toleration of what previously had been regarded 'deviant' sexuality, but more recently this interpretation has been called into question. The proposed change in the law was extremely controversial amongst the gay community, many of whom argued that it was a mere 'illusion of liberation', while those who proposed the reform did so from the perspective of merely changing a 'failed' and unenforceable law while still arguing that homosexuality went 'against nature'.[36]

'WEIMAR'S OTHERS'

Class, gender and sexuality were intersectional factors that contributed to shaping an individual's identity and experience in Weimar Germany and determining their status within the social hierarchy. Another such factor was race. Germany has always been a much more ethnically and linguistically diverse country than is often appreciated, with a dynamic population that altered as national and regional boundaries shifted and as economic fortunes changed in the nineteenth century. After 1871 Germany had sizable French-, Danish- and Polish-speaking minorities, while the economic boom of the 1890s and 1900s created an unprecedented demand for labour that could not be met even by Germany's growing, youthful population. Prior to the First World War the employment of foreign workers in Germany became 'a mass movement', with around 1.2 million migrant workers employed by German firms in 1914.[37] The majority of these were unskilled workers from elsewhere in Europe (mainly Poland, Russia and Italy), but there were also temporary visitors or permanent residents from further afield. Robbie Aitken and Eve Rosenhaft estimate that there were 'several thousand' people of African descent living in Germany before 1914.[38]

Following the defeat in the First World War the change of national boundaries imposed by the Treaty of Versailles led to a major transfer of populations as around a tenth of the pre-war population of Imperial Germany became citizens of other countries. Of these, roughly a million ethnic Germans opted to return to the Reich during the course of the 1920s, including 150,000 from the lost provinces of Alsace and Lorraine and 16,000 from Germany's former overseas colonies. But Weimar Germany also continued to be attractive to immigrants, particularly from Eastern Europe. In Prussia alone there were around 30,000 applications for citizenship each year, though this represents only a fraction of the number of people settling in Germany as 'very few new immigrants … applied for citizenship'.[39] This (perceived) influx of refugees and economic migrants caused some anxiety and disagreement amongst the representatives of the federal states who had ultimate responsibility over citizenship applications through the Reichsrat. Jews and 'foreigners from the East of non-German descent' in particular were accused of being a drain on German resources and a destabilizing force in the housing and labour markets. Even the relatively liberal Prussian authorities only approved just over half of all citizenship applications. However, despite concern over and opposition to immigration in Weimar Germany, in practice the German government was 'unwilling or unable to deport immigrants'.[40]

In 1925 there were 564,379 Jews living in Germany, around 0.9 per cent of the total population. Of these, around 108,000, or 19 per cent of the Jewish population, had been born outside Germany's borders, of whom 90 per cent had migrated from Poland and Eastern Europe to escape persecution and economic hardship. Unlike the more established German Jewish community these so-called *Ostjuden* ('Eastern Jews') tended to be poor and to stand out from the rest of German society – speaking Yiddish, sometimes wearing distinctive traditional clothing and adhering to more traditional religious practices – and as such were a particular focus for anti-Semitic attacks. Germany's Jews were mostly an urban population, with over half living in the big cities and as many as a third residing in Berlin. This was at least in part a result of historical restrictions on the sorts of occupations that Jews were allowed to pursue that also led to them being over-represented (for the size of the community) in certain professions. Around 60 per cent of Jews owned small- or medium-sized businesses and 16 per cent of all German lawyers and 11 per cent of doctors were Jewish. Yet Jews were as divided by factors such as class and gender as other Germans and faced the same economic conditions. The very fact that most Jewish families made their living through trade and commerce meant that they were particularly vulnerable to the effects of Weimar's economic upheavals. By 1930 around a quarter of Jews were reliant on welfare provisions such as soup kitchens, homeless shelters and employment bureaus set up by the community.

Jewish community life was organized by the *Gemeinde*, corporations 'empowered to collect tax revenues to pay for the maintenance of their religious institutions and services'. Although these had responsibility for religious matters such as the appointment of rabbis, by the 1920s they had evolved into 'dense networks of social, economic, and welfare institutions' and the places where intra-community conflicts and debates were played out.[41] These debates – between traditionalists and modernizers, for example – to some extent mirrored wider debates within Weimar society more broadly and reflected the general commitment to pluralism within the community. This pluralism also translated into the staunch and long-lasting commitment to the democratic republic exhibited by most Jews.

Regardless of the insistence on their difference by those outside the community, most Jews were intensely patriotic and *'felt German'*.[42] The

P. Busch, Jewish man on the Grenedierstraβ in Berlin's Scheunenviertel district, 1933 (Bundearchiv, Bild 183-1987-0413-506/CC-BY-SA 3.0).

history of nineteenth-century German Jewry had been one of determined assimilation and acculturation in which Jews had made a concerted effort to 'become Germans'. The Jewish community also displayed an 'intense and abiding' loyalty to liberalism,[43] and following the creation of the republic this enabled Jews to see themselves as for the first time 'the most state supporting element' within society.[44] Only with the formation of the republic, it was argued, had Jews become 'truly German', and most Jews 'propagated a liberal-republican vision of society' and a 'constitutional patriotism' in which the link between race and nation was broken and 'whoever feels German' was a German.[45] Yet this did not mean that German Jews did not also have a strong sense of their Jewish identity. Many saw no contradiction in this and were quite comfortable with the idea of seeing themselves (and being seen by others) as a confessional community like Protestants or Catholics, as 'German Citizens of Jewish Faith' as the most prominent Jewish organization, the *Centralverein deutscher Staatsbürger jüdischen Glaubens*, founded in 1893, would have it.

Although in theory Jews enjoyed the same rights and opportunities as other German citizens since 1871, in practice Jews continued to be victims of discrimination and prejudice. From the 1870s onwards a new form of virulent anti-Semitism based on the conception of the Jews as an alien and inferior ethnic group joined the prejudice that Jews had faced on the grounds of cultural or religious difference throughout Europe for centuries. Anti-Semitism increasingly underpinned the world view of the German nationalist right before and during the First World War, but it was the abolition of censorship in 1918 which helped it become a 'mass phenomenon' during the Weimar Republic as public spaces and even private letterboxes were filled with an avalanche of anti-Semitic posters, pamphlets and publications.[46] Anti-Semitism took a variety of forms in the 1920s, from outright violence such as the assassination of prominent Jewish politicians like Walther Rathenau or attacks on '*Ostjuden*' in the Scheunenviertel area of Berlin on 5 November 1923, to more 'low level' instances of discrimination, humiliation and intimidation. Jewish businesses were boycotted, Jewish names and traditions were mocked and Jews continued to be quietly excluded or passed over for promotion in professions like academia and the civil service. Although verbal and physical attacks on Jews most commonly came from people and parties subscribing to a nationalist or far-right world view, stereotyping, prejudice and discrimination could be found across the political spectrum and throughout German society. While not always openly anti-Semitic, politicians and commentators used dog-whistle terms like 'alien elements' or 'cosmopolitanism' to mount veiled attacks on Jews in general and Jewish immigrants in particular. After the death of Gustav Stresemann in 1929 the centre-right DVP 'became openly anti-Semitic' while 'the Catholic milieu was traditionally anti-Jewish' and the Centre Party's public opposition to anti-Semitism was more rooted in a general concern about religious discrimination (which had been directed against Catholics as recently as the 1870s) rather than deep concern for the plight of Jews. On the left, even the KPD sometimes employed lazy Jewish stereotypes in its attacks on big business and 'international finance capital'.[47]

Another group in Weimar society who suffered discrimination owing to their perceived difference were people of colour. There had been a Black presence in Germany since at least the Middle Ages[48] and by the time of the *Kaiserreich*, Germany's somewhat belated emergence as a colonial power had resulted in greater engagement with the African continent and an increased number of people of African origin visiting the country. The Black community in Imperial Germany was spread throughout the country but was largely transitory and mostly made up of young men from Germany's African colonies. Like the other groups discussed in this chapter it was far from homogenous and its members originated from a variety of countries, spoke a range of languages and encompassed people from backgrounds ranging from servants and 'exhibits' in 'human zoos' (such as the one at Hagenbeck's *Tierpark* in Hamburg), to the children of wealthy Cameroonian or Togolese families who travelled to Germany to attend school or university.

The place of people of colour within the German body politic has always been an uncomfortable one. The move towards conceptualizing nationhood and citizenship in racial terms which accompanied German unification in the late nineteenth century and led to an increasingly anti-Semitic form of German nationalism also affected people of colour, who were viewed by the majority white population as 'alien' and 'inferior' and incapable of being 'real' Germans by virtue of their skin colour.[49] Prior to 1914 indigenous people from the colonies were denied German citizenship and instead given the lesser legal status of *Schutzgebietsangehörige* (subjects of protected territories). The transfer of Germany's colonial possessions to French or British rule as part of the post-war peace settlement removed even this dubious legal position, leaving several hundred people effectively stateless and stranded in Germany. Lack of citizenship made everyday life complicated for Black Germans, as did everyday racism. This was particularly the case in the period between 1920 and 1923 when the presence of Senegalese and other African troops in the French occupying forces in the Rhineland led to a press outcry and accusations of the rape and murder of German women by African soldiers.[50]

Lacking full citizenship rights and facing prejudice and discrimination, people of colour in Weimar Germany often found it difficult to find and hold down a job, find a place to live or to get married. In response, and lacking adequate support from the state, Black Germans began to form support networks and self-help organizations of their own. These included the *Afrikanischer Hilfsverein* (African Aid Association), founded in Hamburg in 1918 'to create a centre and with that a support for all Africans living in Germany' to 'replace the tribal society and family of home',[51] and the more overtly political League for the Defence of the Negro Race (*Liga zur Verteidigung der Negerrasse* [LzVN]) which was formed in 1929 and affiliated with the KPD. These organizations tended to be small (the African Aid Association had only 43 members in 1920, the League only around 30 members) and short-lived but they represented the consciousness that Black Germans had of their position as 'others' in German society, a desire to come together as a community, and a determination of fight for recognition and improvements in their rights. At the same time, the explosion of mass popular culture and the popularity of new cultural trends such as jazz provided new employment opportunities for Black people (see Chapter 5). While work in the entertainment industry offered little in the way of job-security, it did provide the potential to make good money and theatres, fair grounds and film sets became spaces where people of colour could come together and support one another.

THE URBAN REPUBLIC

In the wake of the First World War the trend towards urbanization which had begun in the late nineteenth century continued apace. Towns and cities throughout Germany continued to grow as millions of young Germans flocked to them in search of work, and the split between the agrarian east and industrial west became ever wider. The city became the focal point of Weimar political, social, economic and cultural life and municipal authorities became the primary point at which citizen and government interacted in the new democratic state. The large-scale public building and social welfare projects undertaken by the large metropolitan centres became 'barometers of the success or failure of the Weimar experiment and … encouraged a close identification of the republic with municipalities that remain to this day'.[52] But it was 'Red' Berlin that came to be most identified with the Weimar Republic and its culture. Although it is perhaps going too far to say that 'Weimar was Berlin, Berlin Weimar',[53] it is certainly true that during the 1920s the Reich capital for the first time became more than simply *primus inter pares* with the other great German cities, overtaking Munich and Dresden as Germany's pre-eminent political, cultural and social centre.

Berlin was 'a city that's always on the go, always in the middle of becoming something else'.[54] Under the auspices of the Social Democratic city authorities, who felt that modernization and rationalization could bring social harmony, Berlin enjoyed an unprecedented period of expansion: by 1925 it had a population of 4 million people, and this continued to grow by 80–100,000 people a year. This was both a consequence of and a driving force behind Weimar's increasingly rationalized, technologized consumer economy and society, and by 1928 Berlin was the third largest city in the world after London and New York. In order to accommodate this rising population, town planners adopted modern ideas in an attempt to transform the urban environment, rationalizing the city so that 'work, living, leisure, and commerce were … assigned to different zones'.[55] In Berlin and other cities throughout the Reich old slum areas were cleared, to be replaced by new suburban housing estates mostly comprising around 500 to 1,000 dwellings equipped with modern conveniences such as electricity, indoor plumbing and central heating. Fashionable young architects such as Bruno Taut were commissioned to design these new estates, while the city's transport system was overhauled and the latest technology applied to the overhead and underground railway (S-Bahn and U-Bahn) networks in order to bring suburban dwellers to work and shop in the heart of the city.

At the same time, the visual landscape of the city was transformed. Pedestrians vied with greater levels of traffic as a growing population and new technology brought more and more means of transportation into the cities. One 1928 survey recorded that each hour 2,753 vehicles passed through the Potsdamer Platz in central Berlin, where in 1924 the authorities erected a huge and iconic modernist traffic light which was visible a kilometre away.[56] In keeping with the youthful spirit of the age, the city received a facelift: gone were the neo-classical facades and neo-gothic buildings of the nineteenth century, replaced by tall, sleek, functional office blocks and department stores in concrete, glass and steel, exemplified by Erich Mendelsohn's Columbus House. Advertising reached hitherto unseen levels of 'volume and sophistication'[57] during the 1920s and as the decade progressed the hand bills and paper posters that were splashed across walls and billboards were joined by increasing numbers of illuminated neon signs hawking the wares of the new consumer culture.

The city was no less busy by night when it became a veritable smorgasbord of mass entertainment. In 1926 the Funkturm radio tower was erected, putting Berlin at the centre of Germany's modern broadcasting and communications industries; while the Haus Vaterland on the Potsdamer Platz allowed Berliners to frequent a 1,000-seat cinema, the largest cafe in the world and a series of themed bars all under one roof. Germany's largest and most well-known film production company of the Weimar period, *Universum Film A. G.* (Ufa), had an extensive studio complex at Neuebabelsberg in Berlin and this became the centre of the German film industry. The gaudy bars and nightclubs of the Kurfürstendamm in central Berlin achieved an international reputation as the places to go for a good time and even during the worst days of political and economic crisis there were plenty of Germans who were prepared to escape from their problems in the dives and dance halls

Georg Pahl, The modernist traffic tower on Berlin's Potsdamer Platz by night, December 1924 (Bundesarchiv, Bild 102-00892/Georg Pahl/CC-BY-SA 3.0).

of Berlin, while the bitter experience of the inflation discouraged thrift and persuaded many people that it was a much better idea to spend their earnings on a good time while they had the chance.

Yet behind this glitzy exterior, the Weimar cityscape had a darker side. Poverty, deprivation, fear and alienation haunted the less affluent sections of Germany's big cities and Nazi propaganda 'infamously juxtaposed the hard living conditions, anonymity, and moral corruption of the big city with rural and traditional ways of life'.[58] Faced with the daily struggle to survive many working-class Germans were prepared to do anything to make ends meet, especially in the chaotic economic and political conditions of the early and late phases of the republic. The 1920s have been called 'the golden age of Berlin crime',[59] and certainly there was a widespread public perception of lawlessness and disorder during the Weimar period. By 1929 it was estimated that there were around 15,000 missing persons cases reported annually and that the Berlin police were handling over 50,000 complaints a year, ranging from burglaries to murders. Convictions for theft in the capital alone were 81 per cent higher in the three years from 1919 to 1923 than they had been for the three years before the war, while those for receiving stolen goods were 245 per cent higher. Nationwide, annual criminal convictions soared from 538,225 in 1910 to 823,902 in 1923. Yet even when crime rates began to fall after the inflation period until they were lower than pre-war levels there was still a perception of widespread criminality, focusing on the three areas of juvenile delinquency, prostitution and murder.[60]

Between 1913 and 1918 the number of adolescents convicted for criminal offences doubled and youth crime rates continued to rise throughout the early 1920s. It was only after the Juvenile Justice Act of 1923 lowered the age of criminal responsibility and allowed judges greater leeway in sentencing that rates began to drop. This only seemed to confirm claims that Weimar's cosmopolitan consumer culture was riddled with moral turpitude, and it was widely thought that the growth of the number of women and children brought into the workforce during the war, together with the death of so many male authority figures, had fundamentally weakened the traditional patriarchal German social structure, opening the way to widespread criminality and sexual licence.

If youth criminality seemed to confirm conservative accusations of Weimar immorality, the highly visible sex trade only reinforced such claims. Industrialization and urbanization had transformed prostitution from something that professionals did behind closed doors to an occupation undertaken by amateurs who plied their trade in busy urban spaces. For many women, prostitution was 'a way of managing economic crisis', and 'the only certain way of making ends meet' when faced with low wages, unemployment or separation from a male breadwinner.[61] German sex workers in the Weimar era were perhaps surprisingly assertive and independent, facing up to the authorities, forming their own trade union and supported by a wide range of individuals and services in the wider community.

Nevertheless, prostitution was a risky business and those who participated in the trade lived under the threat of potential violence. The fact that the victims of all three of the most celebrated serial killers of the Weimar period included several people (both male and female) who were engaged in the sex trade speaks volumes for the risks that sex workers took daily. Fritz Haarmann, the so-called 'Butcher of Hanover', murdered 24 tramps and male prostitutes between 1919 and 1924; Karl Grossmann is thought to have murdered around 50 women before he was caught in 1921; and, most famously of all, Peter Kürten, the 'Vampire of Düsseldorf', was convicted in April 1931 of nine murders and seven attempted murders, but he confessed to a total of 79 offences, including murder, rape and child molestation, committed over a 17-year period. There were even suggestions of cannibalism in both the Haarmann and Grossmann cases as it was rumoured that the murderers had sold the flesh of their victims during the years of hardship after the war. The public took a salacious fascination in the crimes of all three of these men which were related in lurid detail in the press and only served to reinforce the 'myth of the anonymous killer' which 'was a powerful one for expressing anxieties about urban anonymity and the threat of danger from the margins'.[62]

Yet we should not be misled into thinking that Weimar Germany was in fact the den of iniquity that many of its citizens believed it to be. 'Berlin was by no means the most violent city in Germany'[63] and by international standards German crime rates were not exceptionally high.[64] Weimar Germany had one of the largest and most modern police forces in Europe and the homicide division of the Berlin detective force or *Kriminalpolizei* was used as a model by similar forces in Germany and across the Continent. Under the energetic leadership of Ernst Gennat, the homicide division of the Berlin '*Kripo*' pioneered techniques such as fingerprinting, ballistic tests and psychological profiling, reflecting the Weimar tendency towards rationalism and functionalism evident in other areas of economic and social policy. Nevertheless, Weimar Germany continued to be perceived as being particularly lawless. In part this was a consequence of mass literacy. There were over 4,000 newspapers, magazines and illustrated papers published in Germany by the mid-1920s and Berlin alone had 50 daily newspapers and produced over 30 per cent of all publications by the end of the decade. These communicated stories of violent crime and sexual offences in lurid detail to an avid readership. As Todd Herzog has noted, Weimar Germany was 'fascinated by criminals and their crimes' and 'seemed to take pleasure in the spectacle of crime, in imagining itself as a criminal space'.[65]

Although the First World War in many ways had a profound effect on German politics and society, there was, at least at first glance, no root and branch social transformation during the Weimar period. The old hierarchical class structure remained in place and established elites – the nobility, big business, and the officer corps – retained a certain amount of power and influence. Yet this apparent continuity with Imperial Germany masked more fundamental changes in social relations. The demographic catastrophe of the Great War helped to create circumstances in which pre-war social trends became fixtures of post-war society. The absence of men changed social and sexual attitudes and behaviours in the 1920s and 1930s and opened up educational and employment opportunities for women and the young, at the same time as causing widespread moral panic. The development of a 'new' middle class made up of 'the salaried masses' of young, well-educated men and women fuelled the growth of Weimar consumer culture and urbanization continued apace, further eroding old values and transforming the working lives and leisure activities of the working and middle classes. As the cities expanded beyond recognition they became increasingly identified with the modern, cosmopolitan culture of the republic, exemplified by American imports such as jazz, department stores, mass advertising and the 'new woman'.

Yet there was little about all this that was unique to Weimar. Urbanization and industrialization had already brought about the development of an urban consumer culture by the turn of the twentieth century and the growth of the service sector of white-collar workers had been going on since at least 1900. Generational conflict and female emancipation had also been features of Wilhelmine society (which had its own, earlier, version of the 'new woman' in the 1890s), while anxieties over the effects of industrial modernity on their social position had also haunted shopkeepers and artisans in the Imperial era. At the same time, Weimar Germany was not particularly unique in its collective anxieties and neuroses. Moral panic over juvenile delinquency, female emancipation and the health of the nation have their parallels in later moral panics over the effects of socio-economic change and technology, particularly on the young. Across Europe and the world other nations were facing similar difficulties and expressing their concerns in strikingly similar ways. Industrialized nations throughout the globe struggled to come to terms with the demographic changes wrought by modernity and conflict, while struggles between town and country, labour and capital, raged everywhere. The 'new woman' of the 1920s was an international phenomenon, as was deep concern over the moral and physical well-being of the young in the post-war world.

Nevertheless, this should not distract us from the very real social achievements of the Weimar period. The extension of the welfare state helped to alleviate the suffering of millions, and there was a greater degree of social mobility under the republic (even if it did come at the expense of job security). Despite the limits on female emancipation pointed out by historians such as Kathleen Canning, the Weimar Republic extended equal voting rights to women before Britain, the United States and France, and had more women sitting in parliament than any of the more established democracies by the mid-1920s. The social activism of the Weimar state, together with a debatable degree of sexual tolerance, secured an end to the repressive and intrusive system of state-regulated prostitution and almost succeeded in having the law prohibiting homosexuality struck down (almost 40 years before Sexual Offences Act of 1967 achieved the same result in Britain and Paragraph 175 was repealed in West Germany in 1969). At the same time, the Weimar Republic left a scientific and artistic record second to none, providing new theories in theoretical physics and philosophy that laid the foundations of our present understanding of the world and humankind's place in it as well as deeply influential new styles of music, architecture and visual art. The cinema of the Weimar Republic rivalled that of Hollywood and provided technical and stylistic innovations that helped transform the medium into an art form, while the literature and theatre of Weimar Germany still have an audience today. It is to these cultural developments that we will turn in the next chapter.

5

WEIMAR CULTURE

During the 1920s Germany gained an international reputation for technological innovation (particularly in the entertainment industry) and artistic experimentation. At the same time, the social changes wrought by modernity together with the political and economic upheavals of the early years of the republic combined to create a heightened sense of anxiety which was widely reflected in the culture of the period. Weimar Germany became a 'laboratory of the apocalypse where modern Europeans tested the limits of their social and cultural traditions'[1] and 'the Weimar age … witnessed the emergence of the first truly modern culture'.[2]

Yet what exactly constituted that culture is a more complicated matter than has often been acknowledged. Most accounts focus on particular artistic movements and an established canon of pictures, books and films that are considered to exemplify 'Weimar culture', often stressing stylistic experimentation or 'a restless questioning of what it means to live in modern times'[3] as the key defining features of the intellectual and artistic artefacts of the period. But this tends to ignore the broader sphere of mass entertainment and popular culture, the products of which reached a much wider audience than the work of the avant-garde. Like pretty much everything else during the Weimar period, culture was highly contested and contemporaries were often more ambivalent about the culture of the republic than later historians. Many of the movements and figures associated with the period were well established or began their artistic or literary careers before 1918, and many continued to be active as writers, artists, academics and film-makers (many in exile) after 1933. Gustav Frank has even gone so far as to challenge the very idea of the Weimar period as a distinct cultural moment: 'while novels were written, pictures were painted and films were produced *during* the Weimar Republic, there is no literature *of*, no art *of*, nor even a cinema *of* the Weimar Republic, and this invalidates the concept of "Weimar Republic" as a designation of an epoch of literary or artistic history'.[4] Yet in some ways this very confusion and diversity is what makes the culture of the Weimar period most reflective of the times in which it was produced and worthy of our attention.

WEIMAR GERMANY AS A 'CULTURAL NATION'

The Germans had long prided themselves on being a 'cultural nation' (*Kulturnation*) in which the arts were central to national identity and a source of great national pride. This continued to be the case under the republic, and education and the arts were heavily subsidized by the Weimar state(s). After 1918 'the assumption that the state should use taxpayers' money to subsidize the arts and ensure the broadest possible spread of cultural provision' became a 'crucial feature of German cultural life'.[5] Article 150 of the Weimar Constitution committed the state to the maintenance and preservation of the nation's cultural and natural heritage and prohibited the 'removal of German artistic treasures to foreign countries'. Subsidies and tax breaks were provided to keep cultural institutions afloat through the economic challenges of the inflation period and the Great Depression and in the face of competition from other, less highbrow, forms of entertainment. As much as half of the income of many of Germany's 160 provincial theatres came from the public purse, and municipal and state authorities (who were responsible for funding and promoting arts and culture) on average devoted around 3 per cent of their annual budgets to cultural provision. However, this meant that the political composition of the state government and the dominant values of the region tended to dictate the openness (or lack of it) to modern art. Prussia under the Social Democrats, for example, tended to patronize contemporary artists and writers, while Catholic Bavaria took a more traditional and conservative view of the arts.

Nevertheless, in some instances state institutions and funding did play an important role in fostering new talent and modern styles and ideas. The famous Bauhaus school of art and design was part funded by the Thuringian government until political pressure forced it to move to Dessau in 1925 with the support of the mayor and the city council. Gustav Hartlaub, the director of the Kunsthalle Mannheim between 1923 and

1933, was a champion of modern art and is credited with having coined the term *Neue Sachlichkeit* (New Objectivity) in 1925 to describe a new style of art that he saw as 'the true face of our time'.[6] More broadly, the Social Democratic state authorities in Prussia provided funding and support for Magnus Hirschfeld's *Institut für Sexualwissenschaft* (Institute for Sexual Research) that undertook pioneering scientific research into human sexuality as well as providing medical services, marriage and sex counselling and education and advice to around 20,000 visitors a year.

All of this was underpinned by 'Germany's phenomenal education system' which provided even those who did not go to university with 'a superb grounding in literature, philosophy, history, and classical and modern languages'.[7] The constitution committed the republic to provide free, compulsory and universal education to all German children who were provided with eight years of elementary schooling, followed by the option of staying on until the age of 18. Germany's universities, the traditional training ground of the country's cultural and political elite, also enjoyed considerable financial support from the state, though they tended to be much more resistant to reform and academics have usually been seen as being overwhelmingly hostile to the republic. 'Weimar culture' might have been 'conceived outside the schools and universities and ... never penetrated the academic establishment to any depth',[8] but educational institutions played an important role in fostering that culture. They produced a highly literate and well-educated population who were to be the prime audience for the art, literature and entertainment provided in the Weimar period and they provided the training and economic support that allowed some of the period's great intellectuals to develop and disseminate their ideas. The professoriate in general might have been resistant to new thinking, but individual academics such as the philosopher Martin Heidegger and the physicist Werner Heisenberg were to produce radical, groundbreaking work that transformed our way of looking at the world and our place within it.

Culture was also deployed by the Weimar state for diplomatic and propaganda purposes. 'By 1933 Germans had won more Nobel Prizes than anyone else' (one a year between 1918 and 1932, two in 1918, 1925 and 1927, and three in 1931), 'more than the British and Americans put together'.[9] Nobel laureates like Albert Einstein or Thomas Mann became informal ambassadors for German culture and the modern, democratic image that the state wished to project to the rest of the world. The German Foreign Office provided subsidies and encouragement to academic and literary organizations that were used to help encourage the re-establishment of cultural links with former adversaries and to promote German interests abroad.[10]

POPULAR CULTURE AND MASS ENTERTAINMENT

While state support for the arts and German pride in the nation's cultural heritage meant that Weimar Germany had an incredibly rich and dense network of publicly funded institutions that ostensibly made 'culture' available to 'the masses', it also meant that politicians were to some extent able to dictate the type of culture that was on offer. Funding was channelled towards the educational or 'uplifting', as opposed to entertainment. Theatre was subsidized, but cinema, dancing and variety shows were subject to a 'leisure tax' (*Lustarkeitssteuer*), which both made them more expensive and reflected an assumption that popular entertainment should contribute to the costs of propping up more 'edifying' brands of culture. This reflected the anxiety felt by the educated middle classes (*Bildungsbürgertum*) who increasingly worried that Germany's culture was under threat from a new commercialized mass culture, produced on an industrial scale and drawing on 'alien' influences, particularly from the United States.

By the beginning of the twentieth century industrialization and urbanization had produced a huge mass of people, mainly in towns and cities, who had a degree of disposable income and were hungry for distraction and relaxation in what little free time they possessed. The privations of the First World War and the uncertainties of the immediate post-war era only stimulated demand for diversion and amusement as people sought to escape from their troubles, while the shorter working hours and guaranteed holidays provided by Weimar's welfare settlement meant that Germans had more leisure time (*Freizeit*, a term that entered the German dictionary in 1929) than ever before. They filled this with a range of activities, from cinema- and theatregoing, to watching or playing sport, to dancing and sunbathing, many of which were enabled by the application of new technology. 'The 1920s were undoubtedly an era of remarkable innovation in the popular arts',[11] with the development of new media such as cinema, radio and recorded music and (in some cases) their elevation into an art form. But the period also saw a form of 'media convergence', as 'old' and 'new' media worked together to promote one another, for example through the production of magazines aimed at cinemagoers or radio enthusiasts.[12]

The first film had been shown in Germany in November 1895, but it was only after the end of the First World War that the medium really took off. In 1919 there were 2,836 cinemas (with 980,000 seats) in Germany, rising to 3,700 in 1920 and 5,267 (amounting to nearly 2 million seats)

Yva (Else Ernestine Neuländer-Simon), *Charleston*, multiple exposure photograph, 1926–7.

in 1928, mostly in urban areas. These ranged from opulent 'film palaces' aimed at the respectable middle classes to smaller neighbourhood cinemas catering to a local, working-class audience. The programme and experience differed accordingly, with the films screened reflecting class and regional differences (what played well in Berlin might not go down so well in Munich or Stuttgart) and middle-class audiences watching in silence as at the theatre, while working-class filmgoers would talk to their neighbours, applaud or make their own sound effects. Although the average price of a cinema ticket was around 80 pfennigs which was in theory affordable for the poorest in society, in reality going to the cinema was only an occasional treat for most working-class families. Nevertheless, attendance rates were high, reaching 320 million a year in 1930, which averages out as around seven trips to the cinema a year for every adult in Germany. By the middle of the Weimar period cinema was a mass medium with a broad popular appeal.[13]

In order to keep up with this demand, the German film industry grew exponentially. By the middle of the 1920s there were over 400 German production companies making 180 to 250 films a year. This amounted to three to five new films a week, supplemented by around 300 foreign imports annually after 1924. Most of the home-grown films were cheaply produced comedies, romances or thrillers designed to provide amusement and entertainment for what was assumed to be an undiscerning audience who would watch whatever was shown. But there were also the blockbusters of the day that featured big-name stars, high production values and the latest cinematic techniques and special effects. Although sound film did not really take off until after 1929, as early as 1922 *Universum Film A. G.* (Ufa) premiered its first 'talking picture' in Berlin – five years before what is often considered to be the first 'talkie', *The Jazz Singer*. In 1926 Lotte Reininger's *Die Abenteuer des Prinzen Achmed* (*The Adventures of Prince Achmed*), telling stories from the Arabian Nights through the medium of stop-motion animation, became the world's first animated feature film, a decade before Walt Disney's *Snow White and the Seven Dwarfs*. Fritz Lang developed pioneering special effects in films such as his two-part adaptation of the medieval epic poem *Die Nibelungen* (*The Nibelungs*, 1924) and his science fiction masterpiece *Metropolis* (1927). F. W. Murnau's *Der Letzte Mann* (*The Last Laugh*, 1924) was the first production to use the cinematographer Karl Freund's 'unchained camera technique' in which the cameras moved with the action, while films like Richard Oswald's *Anders als die Andern* (*Different from the Others*, 1919) and Leontine Sagen's *Madchen in Uniform* (*Girls in Uniform*, 1931) were pioneering in their subject matter, being considered early milestones in Queer Cinema.

While cinemagoing was a communal experience, new technology also enabled Germans to access entertainment alone and in the comfort of their own homes. Even more than cinema, radio was seen by many as 'the quintessential "medium of modernity"'.[14] German radio broadcasting was launched in 1923 and in 1925 the Reich Broadcasting Company (*Reichs-Rundfunk-Gesellschaft-mbH* [RRG]) was founded in Berlin. The RRG, like the British Broadcasting Corporation (BBC), was a non-commercial operation run under the auspices of the Postal Ministry and listeners were required to have a licence (costing 2 marks a month) which helped to cover the costs of producing content and broadcasting. Unlike the highly centralized BBC though, the RRG operated on a federal structure with nine broadcasting companies each operating in a different region and a conscious effort was made to ensure that programming reflected regional cultures and identities. This was public-service broadcasting with a mission to educate as well as entertain and the primetime 8–10 pm slot which attracted 80 per cent of listeners was deliberately dominated by orchestral music, opera and educational programmes – material that the broadcasters felt was good for the audience, not necessarily what it wanted to hear. Of the remaining airtime, 15 per cent was taken up by news bulletins, 10 per cent to talks by eminent thinkers, writers or other experts, and 10 per cent to programmes aimed at specific groups like children or women.[15]

As with cinema, radio was a growth industry in the Weimar period. The number of radio sets registered rocketed from 1,580 in 1923 to just over 3 million in 1929.[16] Yet the extent to which radio was a mass medium is debatable. Top-of-the-range radio sets could cost 250–300 marks (the average monthly income of most skilled or white-collar workers), while even a simple set cost 50 marks, more than the average weekly income of a working-class family. In addition, most transmitters were situated in cities which meant that most of the rural population could not easily tune in. In 1927 roughly 40 per cent of city-dwellers had radios, while only 3 per cent of households in rural areas had one.[17] For much of the Weimar period, then, radio was the preserve of a largely middle-class, urban audience. Technological improvements began to make it more affordable after 1929, but it was only when the Nazis began marketing cheap *Volksempfänger* radio sets in the mid-1930s that radio truly became a mass medium that reached most of the population.

The development of radio coincided with the mass consumption of recorded music. Until the late nineteenth century, the only ways to hear music were to attend a communal performance or to sing or play an instrument at home (*Hausmusik*). That changed with the invention of the gramophone in 1887 by German-American inventor Emil Berliner. He founded Germany's first gramophone manufacturing works and record label, *Deutsche Grammaphon-AG*, in Hanover in 1898, but it was not until after the First World War that recorded music really took off. By the end of the 1920s there were 427,200 gramophones in people's homes. Germany was producing around 29 million records a year for domestic consumption and another 14 million for export,[18] with *Deutsche Grammaphon* alone producing almost 10 million records annually (83,000 a day). Recordings of classical music and traditional folk songs, ballads and dance music were popular, but the ability to listen to music at home also stimulated the development of new strands of *Schlagermusik* (popular music).

The 'most entertaining and vital phenomenon' in Weimar pop music was jazz.[19] As Jonathan Wipplinger has demonstrated, 'American jazz was a constant presence' in Weimar Germany.[20] Originating in African American communities in the late nineteenth and early twentieth centuries, jazz blended traditional African rhythms and folk tunes, European classical music, blues and the syncopated rhythms characteristic of ragtime. It was widely seen as modern music for a modern age, 'a piece of the present of all countries ... filled with the youthful energy of America ... the song of a new generation'.[21] The psychologist Alice Rühle-Gerstel called it 'the deepest expression' of the age in which 'what remains of the creative force of this sterile time unfolds'.[22] The satirist Kurt Tucholsky likened the beat of a jazz band to 'the typewriters that the audience left behind two hours ago' and, echoing the nineteenth-century military theorist Carl von Clausewitz, called it 'the continuation of business but using other tools'.[23] Discussions of Weimar's fascination with jazz (like those of Weimar culture more broadly) tend to focus on Berlin, but Germany's introduction to 'real' jazz was through direct contact with American troops and their culture during the occupation of the Rhineland. Following the stabilization of the currency in 1924 jazz became something of a mass phenomenon, with Dr Hoch's Konservatorium in Frankfurt-am-Main offering the first academic courses in jazz anywhere in Europe from 1928. American jazz musicians such as Sam Wooding and his Orchestra (otherwise known as the 'Chocolate Kiddies'), Paul Whiteman, and Mike Danzi (who enjoyed his time in Germany so much that he lived and worked there from 1925 to 1939) were rapturously received when they toured Germany. American performers were soon joined by a host of home-grown imitators such as Eric Borchard and Stefan Weintraub's Syncopators. Borchard was a classically trained clarinettist who had worked with the Dresden Philharmonic but was inspired to turn to jazz after a visit to America in 1918–19. Anglicizing his name to appear more American, his band made 150 recordings between 1920 and 1925 as well as appearing in films such as Fritz Lang's *Dr Mabuse, der Spieler* (*Dr Mabuse, the Gambler*, 1922). The crossover between the modern medium of cinema and the modern music of jazz was also apparent in the case of Stefan Weintraub's Syncopators who performed as the cabaret band and provided the backing music for the 1929 film *Der Blaue Engel* (*The Blue Angel*).[24]

Sport also became a hugely popular form of mass entertainment in the 1920s. There was a longstanding tradition of physical culture in Germany and activities such as hiking, gymnastics and sunbathing had all been popular throughout the nineteenth century. But while more traditional outdoor activities such as these remained popular in the Weimar period, it was sports such as football and boxing that really captured the imaginations of Germans in this period. Sixty-four thousand people watched Hamburger Sportverien beat Union Oberschöneweide to win the German football championship at Berlin's Deutsche Stadion in 1923 and by 1929 over 500,000 matches were watched by an audience numbering in the millions. The Berlin Sportpalast opened in 1910 but really came into its own during the Weimar Republic. An ice rink was installed in 1925 and it became a popular venue for ice hockey, speed skating events and musical revues on ice.

For many in Weimar Germany sport represented not merely distraction and entertainment, but also individualism and emancipation. Watching or playing sports like football, boxing and tennis offered the chance to escape the mundane realities of daily life for a few hours and be caught up in a thrilling communal experience, but for the lucky few the chance to play sport professionally also provided a means of winning fame and fortune. The figure of the athlete, as exemplified by the boxer Max Schmeling or perhaps even more so by women like the tennis players Paula von Reznick and Cilly Aussem, swimmer Gertrude Ederle, the fencer Helene Mayer or the middle-distance runner Lina Radke (all Olympic gold medallists), represented the modern self-made German who through hard work and dedication had brought their bodies to a state of physical perfection and taken control of their own destinies. All this was interpreted as evidence of 'a new vitality, a fresh outlook on life ... people want really to *live* in the sense of enjoying light, the sun, happiness and the health of their bodies. It is not restricted to a small and exclusive circle, but is a mass movement which has stirred all of German youth.'[25]

Like so much else in the Weimar Republic the emergence of mass culture and popular entertainment was controversial and highly contested. Modern media were greeted with 'a mixture of praise and hostility' from cultural critics from both left and right.[26] Commentators variously fretted about the perceived threat that 'industrialized merriment'[27] posed to traditional German values or its supposed homogenizing effect that meant that 'everyone has the *same* responses, from the bank director to the sales clerk, from the diva to the stenographer'.[28] But the boundaries between 'high' art and popular culture were not as clear cut as contemporaries and some later historians would have us believe. Weimar Germany saw the first 'intermingling of high and low culture that would one day become the hallmark of 20th-century pop ... In the big Berlin show palaces like the Wintergarten, Scala, Metropol, or the Grosses Schauspielhaus, the great stars of the day from the more serious realms of classical music, theatre, and opera were persuaded by large fees to appear as part of numbered revues'.[29] The director Erwin Piscator made extensive use of still photography and projected film backdrops in his 'proletarian theatre'; the violinist and band leader Dajos Béla performed with the Berlin Philharmonic as well as his own jazz orchestra and his repertoire included everything from classical pieces to dance tunes and film music; writers and artists like Bertolt Brecht and George Grosz celebrated and were keen to be pictured alongside sporting heroes like Max Schmeling; while artists like Hannah Höch and John Heartfield made use of images clipped from advertisements and popular magazines to create innovative photomontages that challenged the political, racial and gender order of the day.

EXPRESSIONISM AND OBJECTIVITY

Although in retrospect it is easy to identify the miscalculations and fateful compromises made by Weimar's politicians, or the limitations of the republic's ideal of 'welfare democracy', these were not necessarily apparent to people at the time. Throughout the period there were many who were enthused by the opportunities presented by technology and modernity, and who demonstrated 'a fundamentally optimistic belief in the malleability of the future and the possibility of achieving a "better" or a "new time"'.[30] This was accompanied by an 'activist tendency' that saw many intellectuals and politicians argue that the foundations of this brave new world could be laid in the here and now through creative action. This sense of optimism can be seen in the alacrity with which many Germans embraced mass consumer culture, but also in the ways in which the artistic avant-garde sought to push boundaries and break new ground to find new ways of expressing what they saw as the spirit of the times. It was also reflected in the tendency of others to experiment with forms of spirituality and ways of seeing the world outside the mainstream of Western religious or scientific thought.

The two artistic movements most often associated with the Weimar Republic are Expressionism and *Neue Sachlichkeit* (New Objectivity). Expressionism predated the Weimar Republic by over a decade, originating in the work of visual artists including Ernst Ludwig Kirchner and Emil Nolde who formed the Dresden-based group *Die Brücke* (The Bridge) in 1905, and the Munich-based artists Wassily Kandinsky, Franz Marc and Paul Klee who formed *Der Blaue Reiter* (The Blue Rider) in 1911. There were as many as 2,500 self-declared Expressionist writers in Germany by 1924, working in a variety of media from painting and visual art to poetry, music, drama and film. At the core of the movement was, in the words of the painter Conrad Felixmüller, the desire 'to convey not impressions of the external world, but the expression of experienced reality',[31] to *express* the feelings and experiences of the individual rather than to represent what is going on outside the artist. Expressionists sought to show 'the disintegration of the bourgeois world and the chaos of modernity' and their art, drama and literature is 'full of images of anxiety, psychological alienation, [and] spiritual disorientation'.[32] But if Expressionist artists, authors and film-makers often 'concentrated more on shadows than light, on the sinister effects of shade and dark, the qualities of nightmare and alienation',[33] there was also a more hopeful side to Expressionism which manifested itself in 'a search for roots, a desire to return to beginnings', and in dreams of creating a 'new man, of "changing everything"'.[34]

It is often suggested that by 1922 Expressionism had had its day and was giving way to a new naturalism in art, literature and cinema. *Neue Sachlichkeit* has been described as 'a style with no particular artistic programmes or manifestos' but characterized by 'a new rationality of vision, a feeling for what was down-to-earth, feasible, real',[35] with everyday subjects depicted in a more naturalistic or realistic style. Gustav Hartlaub, who coined the term, identified two distinct 'wings' amongst the artists he exhibited under the heading of 'New Objectivity': one was 'so conservative as to be equal to Classicism' while the other was 'incandescently contemporary in its lack of belief in art' and 'attempting to expose chaos, the true feeling of our days' through 'the exposure of the self',[36] which does not sound that different from what the Expressionists were attempting. In truth, the lines between Expressionism and New Objectivity were more blurred than is often appreciated. Many of the artists who would produce work in the new style – Otto Dix, George Grosz, Konrad Felixmüller – had previously produced work in the Expressionist style and many continued to include themes associated with Expressionism in their work.

Expressionism reflected the anxious and anarchic political and economic times of Weimar's 'years of crisis', while New Objectivity mirrored the 'modern urban aesthetic of cool detachment, modern design and rational thought'[37] of the republic's more stable middle period when *Schlichkeit* (objectivity) and 'rationalization' were the buzzwords of the day. Artists, writers and film-makers working in both styles offered savage critiques of the society they saw around them as well as more hopeful, celebratory visions of the present and the future. In this they were not dissimilar to the host of 'alternative' spiritual, occult and *Lebensreform* ('life-reform') groups and practices that enjoyed a degree of popularity during the Weimar years.

Spiritualism, seances, fortune-telling, and a variety of social movements that advocated everything from nudism to vegetarianism and offered critiques of industrial modernity had become popular among middle-class Germans before the First World War.[38] But as Berghard Schmidt has pointed out, 'a critique of modernity need not mean a rejection of modernity'[39] and eastern spirituality, clairvoyants and the supernatural continued to attract large numbers of Germans alongside, and as part of, the spectacle world of mass entertainment of the Weimar period. The Austrian writer Robert Musil observed that in the 1920s 'Germany is awash with sects'.[40] These ranged from the neo-Zoroastrian religion Mazdaznan (of which Johannes Itten, the Expressionist painter and teacher at the Bauhaus was an initiate), and esoteric and occultist movements like Theosophy and its off-shoot Anthroposophy, which claimed to offer a path to enlightenment based on a merging of spirituality with science, to *völkische* neo-pagan movements like Ariosophy and Ludendorff's Deutsche Gotterkenntnis which blended spirituality with extreme nationalism, racism and anti-Semitism.[41] At the same time, Eastern religious traditions attracted adherents due to their comparative unfamiliarity, association with pacifism and distance from traditional European religious practice. A Buddhist commune was established in Utting in Bavaria in 1920 and the country's first Buddhist place of worship was opened in the Berlin suburbs in 1924. German authors (most notably Hermann Hesse, but also Gustav Meyrink, Otfried von Hanstein and others) drew on themes taken from Buddhism and Hinduism in their work. The complete works of the Indian writer and philosopher Rabindranath Tagore sold around 800,000 copies in translation within a year of their publication in 1921 and Franz Osten and Himansu Rai's Indo-German film *Prem Sanyas* (*The Light of Asia*, 1925) told the life story of the Buddha.[42]

Despite laws against telling fortunes for money, there was a revival of interest in astrology and divination in the 1920s. An Academic Society for Astrological Research was founded in 1924 and over 400 books and pamphlets on the subject were published between the wars. The mentalist Erik Jan Hanussen (born Hermann Steinschneider) became a celebrity on the back of his mind-reading and hypnosis act at La Scala in Berlin, and mediums, hypnotists and practitioners of the 'occult sciences' such as August Drost, Erich Möckel, Paul Hildebrecht and Else Günther-Geffers (many of whom were themselves later prosecuted for fraud) were employed by or worked with the police to solve crimes.[43] Themes of madness, alienation, mind-control and supernatural horror were common in both the popular and high culture of the period, with both Expressionist and *Neue Sachlichkeit* artists employing fantastic and symbolic imagery hinting at 'a dark, cold almost nightmarish mystery',[44] while films like *Das Cabinett des Dr. Caligari* (*The Cabinet of Dr Caligari*, 1919), *Der Golem, wie er in die Welt kam* (*The Golem: How he Came into the World*, 1920) and *Nosferatu* (1922) – the first screen adaptation of Bram Stoker's *Dracula* – featured somnambulism, Jewish folklore and vampirism.

This has often been dismissed as representing a retreat from reality and modernity into superstition and irrationality, an expression of the 'eschatological moods' and 'pseudo-religious feelings' that led the German people to embrace Nazism.[45] But such an interpretation is too simplistic. This was, after all, the age of Freud and Einstein, of the radio and cinema, when modern science and technology were putting forward ideas and creating effects that would have seemed to previous generations to be magical. It was not too much of a leap for people to believe that if one could hear the disembodied voices of people thousands of miles away via the radio, then might it not also be possible through some scientific or technological means not yet discovered to hear the voices of the dead or discern the future course of events. Interest in the occult can therefore be seen as a complex response to modernity in which the scientific world view was simultaneously seen as lacking in meaning and the potential means of finding that meaning through experimentation with astrology, seances, mind-reading and other occult phenomena. At the same time, this interest was popularized by and reflected in Weimar culture through horoscopes in newspapers, specialist magazines and journals dedicated to various aspects of spirituality and the occult, in pulp fiction and horror films, but also in the work of Expressionists like Meyrinck, Rainer Maria Rilke, Hanns Heinz Ewers and Wassily Kandinsky, who were steeped in the occult.

THE DIVERSITY OF WEIMAR CULTURE

That Weimar culture was diverse in form and content, encompassing a range of media, ideas and styles, has long been acknowledged. However, traditional narratives of Weimar culture tend to ignore the important contribution made to the arts by women and people of colour and the development of distinct subcultures. Walter Laqueur's seminal book on Weimar culture, for example, provided a survey of the 'classics' of Weimar literature that does not mention a single female writer.[46] While this perhaps reflects the male-dominated and heteronormative nature of the Weimar artistic and literary scene and the attitudes and prejudices of many of its leading figures which 'conspired to marginalise the practice of women artists in the period',[47] it does not reflect the reality of Weimar culture in which women, Jews and people of colour were active and important as both producers and consumers, creators and audience.

The increased visibility of women in the 'public sphere' of the workplace and politics that took place during and after the First World War was accompanied by a corresponding increase in women's involvement in the arts and entertainment. Women 'featured strongly' in Weimar's consumer culture 'as producers, commodified objects, targeted recipients, critical observers and discerning purchasers'.[48] Women were active in every branch of the arts, science and entertainment and produced some of the most exciting and innovative work of the period, making a vital contribution to what we now think of as Weimar culture. In the visual arts Käthe Kollwitz (maybe the most well-known female artist of the era and the first woman to be elected to the Prussian Academy of Arts) produced a series of drawings, posters and sculptures through which she tried to process the trauma of the death of her son Peter in the First World War; Jeanne Mammen worked as a commercial artist, contributing illustrations to fashion magazines, before producing a series of astonishing watercolours depicting Berlin's nightlife and particularly its gay and lesbian bars and cabarets; and Lotte Laserstein was an important exponent of the New Objectivity, producing large paintings in a realist style. Female novelists such as Vicki Baum and Irmgard Keun were hugely popular and gained an international reputation – ten of Baum's novels were adapted into films in the United States, including the Oscar-winning *Grand Hotel* (1932), and she ultimately emigrated to America where she spent ten years as a Hollywood screenwriter. Other women found success in the cinema closer to home: Lotte Reiniger created the first German animated feature film; *Mädchen in Uniform* (*Girls in Uniform*, 1931) had a female director (Leontine Sagan) and writer (Christa Winsloe), as well as an all-female cast; Thea von Harbou wrote most of her director husband Fritz Lang's films of the Weimar period; and Marlene Dietrich shot to fame as the cabaret-singer Lola Lola in *Der Blaue Engle* (*The Blue Angel*, 1929). The physicists Lucy Mensing and Herther Sponer were pioneers in the field of quantum mechanics, while the chemist Ida Noddack won the prestigious Liebig Medal in 1931 and was nominated for the Nobel Prize three times.

Weimar Germany also witnessed the development of a distinctive *Frauenkultur* (women's culture) 'in which female practitioners played active and decisive roles' and 'women's voices were heard, their work sympathetically received, and their identities as trained professionals accepted and even celebrated'.[49] By 1931 there were 175 magazines aimed at a female audience and dealing with issues of interest to women, which ranged from the weekly *Blatt der Hausfrau* (*Housewife's Magazine*) which had been founded in 1866 and by 1931 had a circulation of 1.9 million, to the fortnightly lifestyle magazine *Die Dame* (*The Lady*) which was aimed at a younger, more urban and cosmopolitan audience, celebrated the 'new woman' and had a circulation of over 50,000 by the late 1920s. Books like Crista Brück's *Schicksale hinter Schreibmaschinen* (*Fates behind Typewriters*, 1930) – the first of four novels examining the lives of female office employees – and Irmgard Keun's *Das Kunstseidene Mädchen* (*The Artificial Silk Girl*, 1932) revealed the sexual harassment and exploitation that were routine for young women in the Weimar

Yva (Else Ernestine Neuländer-Simon), *Untitled (lady reading newspaper), c. 1932.*

workplace, while Keun's *Gilgi* (1931) and Vicki Baum's *Stud. Chem. Helene Willfüer* (1928) deal with issues such as abortion and single motherhood. The work of Marta Hegemann, who was active in Cologne's radical art scene, but was largely overshadowed by her artist husband Anton Räderscheidt, dealt with the struggles of being both a working artist and a wife and mother, while in Jeanne Mammen's watercolours we see Berlin's sex workers and cabaret performers from a female – and queer – perspective. In 1929 the Association of Berlin Women Artists (founded 1867) held an exhibition called *Die Frau von heute* (The Woman of Today) consisting of 'ninety portraits of important women from society, politics, science, fashion and sport by sixty-five women artists',[50] providing a platform for female artists whose work was often sidelined or ignored by the male dominated art establishment.

Another group that played an invaluable part in the mainstream of Weimar culture while also seeing a flourishing of a distinct culture of their own was Germany's Jewish community. The Weimar era was one of 'eminent Jewish writers and painters, of outstanding composers and scholars'[51] who made a vital contribution to the cultural life of the nation in the face of increasingly violent anti-Semitic rhetoric from the far-right. Of the 19 German Nobel Prize laureates between 1918 and 1932, 12 were Jewish. No account of Weimar culture would be complete without a mention of German-Jewish composers like Arnold Schönberg and Kurt Weill who had a revolutionary and lasting impact on twentieth-century music; writers like Alfred Döblin, Jakob Wassermann, Lion Feuchtwanger and Arnold Zweig (to name just a few); the greatest journalist and satirist of the period, Kurt Tucholsky; the philosopher Walter Benjamin; the director and producer Max Reinhardt; and film directors Fritz Lang and Ernst Lubitsch; not to mention perhaps the most famous scientist of the twentieth century, Albert Einstein. The great Berlin publishers Mosse and Ullstein Verlag were owned and run by German-Jewish families and played an important role in Weimar's literary and popular culture. Ullstein published the weekly news magazine *Berliner Illustrirte Zeitung* (which had a nationwide readership and the highest circulation in Europe in 1928), the tabloid *B. Z. am Mittag* and the liberal daily *Vossische Zeitung*, widely considered to be Germany's newspaper of record. It also published works by Vicki Baum and Erich Maria Remarque's anti-war novel *Im Westen nichts Neues* (*All Quiet on the Western Front*, 1929).

By the 1920s German Jews had become an integral part of Germany's cultural life, but this left some of the community feeling that something had been lost through assimilation in the nineteenth century. Constantly reminded of their 'otherness' by anti-Semites, a new generation of German Jews 'set out to explore new and creative modes of Jewish culture' and create 'a new tradition, a mostly (though not exclusively) secular Jewish culture' that assimilated German Jews could identify with.[52] This was done through the establishment of adult education centres and study groups, museums and libraries and Jewish schools and youth groups. There were 42 Jewish newspapers focusing on news and matters of interest to the community being published by 1933 and in Berlin five Jewish schools (catering to 2,173 pupils by 1930) were founded during the 1920s.[53] While the development of Jewish schools was to some extent motivated by the prejudice and discrimination that Jewish children could face, the Jewish adult education movement was more focused on providing a place where grown-ups could learn about their heritage and explore their own Jewishness. Institutions like the Frankfurt Lehrhaus, Berlin Jewish Volksnochschule and Akademie für die Wissenschaft des Judentums all provided programmes that involved the study of the Bible and Talmud, but also contemporary Jewish sociology, history, economics and literature. A Berlin Jewish Museum opened just six days before Hitler was appointed Chancellor in January 1933 and along with similar institutions in Kassel, Breslau and Munich, reflected a desire to explore and celebrate their history and culture amongst Germany's Jewish community.

Writing in 1929, the African American newspaper editor Robert S. Abbott observed that 'It is in the arts that Black people who have made their homes in Germany have found the greatest welcome.'[54] The film historian Tobias Nagl has gone so far as to suggest that 'the majority' of people of African descent in Berlin 'worked at least temporarily as "artists" in the entertainment industry' prior to 1945.[55] Robbie Aitken and Eve Rosenhaft have identified forty individuals working in the entertainment industry in the Weimar years, though they note that 'the actual number is likely to have been higher'.[56] The popularity of jazz provided opportunities for Black performers, as did the development of cinema and the popularity of films featuring 'exotic' locations which sought to add 'authenticity' by casting Black or Asian actors in supporting roles or as villains. But although people of colour were highly visible in Weimar culture, their experience of working in the entertainment industry was frequently not empowering: all too often performers were forced to adopt roles that played into the prejudices and stereotypes of a majority white audience and were so ignored by critics that their identities have largely been lost to history. Nevertheless, such was the talent and popularity of some of these performers that the whitewashing of Weimar culture has more recently given way to a rediscovery of the important contribution made by people of colour.

In October 1920 Berlin's *Apollo-Theater* staged a show called *Harlemnächte* (*Harlem Nights*) featuring 20 performers from Germany's former colony Cameroon, 30 Bayadere dancers and starring a 'Sudanese actress' named Myriam Barka and the film star Louis Brody.[57] Brody (born Ludwig M'bebe Mpessa in Duala, Cameroon) had begun his acting career in 1911 and was to appear in more than 30 films including Fritz Lang's *Der müde Tod* (*Destiny*, 1921) and Alfred Hitchcock's directorial debut, the Anglo-German co-production *The Pleasure Garden* (1925). He was a founder member of the *Afrikanischer Hilfsverein* (African Aid Association) and of the League for the Defence of the Negro Race and protested against the racism directed toward Black Germans during the campaign against the use of French African troops in the occupation of the Rhineland. By the 1930s he was the highest paid Black actor in Germany, earning three or four times more than other Black performers. Astonishingly, he continued to live and work in Germany throughout the Third Reich, appearing in 23 films between 1933 and 1945. After the Second World War he worked as a circus performer and played in jazz bands, dying in Berlin of natural causes in 1951.

Brody was a particularly successful and high-profile example of the role that people of colour played in Weimar culture, but his career also reflected the more general experience of Afro-Germans in the entertainment industry. Like many other Black performers he took on 'a wide range of often overlapping roles' – in his case, theatre and film actor, musician, writer, wrestler and circus performer – many of which 'reflected continuing stereotypes ... and tended to reinforce ideas of European superiority'.[58] The same might be said for other performers such as the dancer, actor and political activist Josef Bilé and Adolf Ngange and Jakob Mandenge who performed as The Bonambelas, as well as the Chinese-born actors Henry Sze and Nien-Sön Ling (both of whom appeared alongside Brody in Joe May's *Die Herrin der Welt* (*The Mistress of the World*, 1919–20) which was attacked by Chinese students in Berlin for its racist depiction of their homeland[59]). Film productions with 'exotic' African, Indian or Asian settings provided temporary

Portrait of Cameroonian actor Louis Brody by Yva (Else Ernestine Neuländer-Simon), *c.* 1925.

employment to people of colour as uncredited extras, while popularity of jazz created a demand for Black musicians who were seen as more 'authentic' than white-only jazz bands.

While perhaps not producing a distinct Black German subculture in quite the same way as Germany's Jewish community or the *Frauenkultur* created by and for women, people of colour did come together through involvement in the entertainment industry, and the arts provided opportunities for them to express their own experiences. 'Performing … played an important role in helping to foster a sense of community' amongst Black performers, who came together backstage in theatres and cabarets, on film sets or in circuses, shared experiences and helped each other to find work.[60] It is notable that some of the leading figures in the African Aid Association and the LzVN were performers and in 1930 there were plans to form a Black theatre in Berlin that would stage a show about Black history written by Brody and featuring a majority Black cast.

WEIMAR'S CULTURE WARS

Just as later generations have worried about the harmful effects of new media such as television, home video, video games and the internet, in the Weimar era Germany's cultural elite and guardians of public morality fretted about the potentially corrupting influence that new media like cinema might have on young people and the working classes. The agitation for increased media regulation and the critique of mass culture that underpinned it were just one front in a broad-based culture war that raged throughout the Weimar period. At stake was the soul of the German nation, and all sides competed to put forward their vision of the values and beliefs that they thought should hold sway in society.

Article 118 of the Weimar Constitution stated that 'Every German has the right, within the limits of the general laws, to express his opinion freely by word, in writing, in print, in picture form or in any other way' and that 'censorship is forbidden'; but it also allowed for 'exceptional provisions' to be made regarding the regulation of films. To appease the conservatives, it also provided for the suppression of 'trashy and smutty literature' (*Schund und Schmutzliteratur*) and 'public plays or exhibitions' that might corrupt German youth.[61] This opened the way to state regulation of the media, initially through the *Reichslichtspielgesetz*

(Reich Motion Picture Act) of May 1920 which required films to be passed by local certification boards before they could be shown to the public. Under the law films could be cut or banned altogether if they were considered to include any material that would be corrupting to public morals – depictions of crime, violence, sex, etc. – or to criticize state institutions, moral norms or even Germany itself.[62] In 1926 the Law for the Protection of Youth against Trashy and Filthy Literature (*Schund und Schmutzgesetz*) established review boards in Berlin and Munich similar to those that certified films for general release which had powers to ban books and magazines from public display and prohibit their sale to anyone under 18. By December 1932, 183 books and magazines had been prohibited under the law, mostly serial romance stories, 'pulp' detective fiction and adventure stories.

Both the Motion Picture Law and the 1926 *Schundgesetz* are illustrative of the highly contested nature of culture in the Weimar Republic and of the fears and anxieties that haunted the educated classes in the period. They displayed the middle-class concern that culture (and with it the social status of the *Bildungsbürgertum*) was under threat from corrupting foreign influences (such as American pulp fiction) and the 'dumbing down' of popular culture and represented a means of holding off 'social chaos, [as] epitomised by a [perceived] flood of sleaze'.[63] But they also reflected a wider sense that there was something 'wrong' with modern society and culture and the desperate search for a remedy to this. In the case of the conservatives and the coalition of moral campaigners who were behind the campaign for the *Schundgesetz* this solution was to be found in a return to the (largely imagined) moral and political order that had existed before 1918, but for others on both the left and right, their vision of both society's ills and their proposed solutions were expressed in more radical, though often in less practical and more unfocused, terms.

It is notable that both the Motion Picture Law and the *Schundgesetz* attracted broad support from across the political spectrum. Commentators from both left and right 'weaponized' cultural critique as part of a broader political assault on democracy and the Weimar state. Right-wing writers and intellectuals in particular propagated and popularized 'Many of the ideas essential to National Socialist propaganda'[64] such as the 'stab-in-the-back' myth, anti-Semitic stereotypes, or the idea of an idealized national community. The ill-defined term 'cultural bolshevism' was deployed as a means of disparaging art and literature that showed a 'freedom of expression and form'[65] or was otherwise regarded as being unacceptable on the grounds that it was too liberal, too commercial, too cosmopolitan, not 'German' enough. But modern art, mass consumer culture and modern media were also attacked by many on the left of politics who sought to expose what they saw as the hypocrisy and essential conservatism of the 'bourgeois' republic and its 'sham democracy'. At the same time, mass entertainment was criticized for its tendency to distract the masses from the reality of their economic plight and the necessity of overthrowing the capitalist system.

The cultural life of the Weimar Republic was rich, multifaceted and highly contested. What exactly constitutes 'Weimar culture' is still highly subjective, but broadly speaking it encompassed highly experimental avant-garde art, literature, architecture and design that played with form and employed the most up-to-date ideas and materials, as well as an easily accessible popular culture: mass spectator sport, records of popular dance tunes and traditional ballads, trashy detective novels, and glossy magazines. The period saw the emergence of cinema and broadcasting as mass media and the development of a modern commercialized consumer culture in which art and entertainment were commodities like any other to be mass produced, bought and sold. People responded to these developments in a variety of ways which ranged from eager acceptance to horrified anxiety and 'culture' became another battleground on which the struggle for the soul of the nation was played out.

All this was to some extent facilitated and encouraged by a sense of Germany as a 'cultural nation' in which the state (or at least regional and local authorities) had a role to play in subsidizing the arts and culture, but with that came certain limits on what was acceptable and increasing calls for the regulation of cultural expression, and of popular culture in particular. This led to the rolling back of some of the freedoms gained in the November Revolution and the development of new systems of censorship. At the same time, the wider struggle for values of which critiques of Weimar culture were only one front, took on a new urgency and militancy as Germany entered a new period of crisis after 1929.

6

CRISIS AND COLLAPSE, 1929–33

The apparent calm and relative stability of Weimar's middle period was shattered by the onset of a new economic crisis in 1929. As unemployment rose the social tensions and anxieties which had simmered beneath the surface throughout the 'Golden Twenties' came to the fore, disagreements over how to cope with the Depression broke the fragile political consensus that had emerged since 1925 and once more exposed the deep divisions in German political culture. For those who desired a reconfiguration of German politics this new crisis presented opportunities to challenge the political order established in 1919. Faced by loss of livelihood and self-respect, many Germans turned to the political extremes in search of salvation, while traditional elites attempted to maintain their hold on power and reshape the republic into a political system more in keeping with their ideals by trying to harness the rising tide of right-wing radicalism. This proved to be a serious miscalculation on their part which ultimately led not to a military dictatorship or restoration of the monarchy, but instead delivered Germany into the hands of Adolf Hitler and his followers.

THE GREAT DEPRESSION

To a very great extent, economics is all about confidence. While people believe that the money in their pockets is worth a certain amount, or that the money in their bank accounts is secure, all is well. But once that faith is shaken, panic often turns fears into reality. German share prices experienced a dramatic collapse on 13 May 1927 (two years before the

Wall Street Crash) and German stocks had remained sluggish even as the American market boomed.[1] The first signs of recession were seen in 1928 and to make matters worse, Germany was also gripped by a banking crisis in April–May 1929 amidst fears that negotiations over reducing reparations payments that ultimately led to the Young Plan, would fail. Savers rushed to withdraw their money in large numbers, leading to the calling in of credit and frantic appeals from German banks to international partners for support. As supplies of available credit ran dry smaller banks went bust and the larger ones limited their opening hours.

The panic in the spring of 1929 was merely a prelude, not only to a more serious run on the banks in 1931, but also a major international economic shock which began in the autumn. On 24 October 1929, 'Black Thursday', the nine-year speculative boom of the American stock market came to a sudden and dramatic end. The United States' stock exchange dropped by 11 points in a single day and panic gripped investors who frantically sought to offload increasingly worthless stocks. Billions of dollars were lost, fortunes evaporated overnight and with them much of the short-term investment that had driven Germany's economic recovery after 1924. Heavily reliant on injections of foreign cash, many German businesses responded by attempting to cut costs, usually by laying off staff. As the effects of the crash began to be felt on international markets, world trade slumped, cutting German exports by half, and putting even more pressure on manufacturers. Production slumped to 58 per cent of 1928 levels and a drop in agricultural prices caused a debt crisis in rural areas which led to widespread bankruptcies and foreclosures. As belts were tightened and demand slackened in both home and international markets further cuts were made, resulting in yet more unemployment, while without foreign investment many businesses could no longer compete and went under completely, leaving more people out of work.

By the winter of 1929–30, 2 million Germans were already out of work. The figure reached 3 million in 1931 and was at 5.1 million by September 1932. The peak came in early 1933 when over 6.1 million Germans were out of work. Yet even these figures fail to give a true impression of the level of unemployment in the early 1930s as official statistics tended only to count the main earner in a household. Although those in the lowest socio-economic positions suffered worst, 'the depression also dragged down the middle class. From the small-scale shopkeepers to the graduate professionals in law and medicine, people struggled to survive in a world where their goods and services were decreasingly in demand'.[2] As had happened during the period of food shortages during the First World War, people from towns and cities were forced out into the countryside to forage for food, while others packed up their belongings and migrated from city to city in search of work. One commentator wrote of 'An almost unbroken chain of homeless men' young and old, skilled craftsmen and unskilled workers, moving in both directions 'along the whole length of the [200 miles of the] Hamburg-Berlin highway'.[3] By 1933 half of those registered had used up all their unemployment insurance and were reduced to relying on means-tested local government benefits which provided a minimum level of subsistence.

As terrible as the material effects of the Depression were, the psychological impact was in some ways worse. For many people, from skilled workers to middle-class professionals, unemployment meant not only material hardship, but also a loss of identity, pride and 'respectability'. Matters were made worse by the fact that the process of claiming unemployment benefits was regarded as being a humiliating and, for many men whose status and identity was rooted in providing for their families, emasculating experience. The Depression created a generation of young adults 'who had never had a job and never expected to have one',[4] and older workers struggled to find meaning and direction in a life bereft of the routine and stability provided by regular employment. As the crisis went on boredom and hopelessness turned to anger and a search for someone to blame, fuelling verbal and physical attacks on traditional scapegoats such as Jews, but also rival political groups and 'the system' itself. Coming only six years after the Great Inflation of 1923, for some the new economic crisis finally killed any faith that they had in the economic and political system of the Weimar Republic and led them to look for radical alternatives.

DEMOCRACY IN CRISIS

In this atmosphere, the economic crisis soon led to a political crisis. The range of interests represented in Hermann Müller's Grand Coalition (1928–30) had never been easy to reconcile and there had already been clashes within the government over defence and foreign policy. But it was the pressures placed on the coalition by the public's demand for action in the face of economic hardship that really exposed the stark ideological differences between the coalition partners. With so many out of work and bankruptcies soaring, the German government found themselves caught between falling tax revenue and rising expenditure on unemployment benefit. Social welfare provision amounted to 40.3 per cent of government expenditure in 1929–30 and it was assumed that this figure would go on rising for as long as the Depression lasted. In August 1930 15.7 per cent of those registered as unemployed were dependent on welfare support and this figure rose to 26.8 per cent in 1931 and 38.9 per cent in 1932. This was an intolerable situation, and the parties of the centre-right, already under pressure from middle-class voters to take a more conservative stand, demanded that the government take matters in hand to balance the budget and provide some relief for business. In contrast, the SPD feared losing ground to the Communists if they did not insulate their working-class constituents from the worst ravages of the slump and wanted to see unemployment benefit increased, not cut. Facing deadlock in the Reichstag, Müller asked the president for Emergency Powers under Article 48 of the constitution. Hindenburg, who had no love for the SPD, refused, and on 27 March 1930 the coalition collapsed. The Social Democrats withdrew from the government and Hindenburg asked the Centre Party politician Heinrich Brüning to form a 'presidential cabinet of experts' above party interest to deal with the crisis.

Brüning came to office declaring that his prime objective remained the same as that of the previous government, namely 'to secure parliamentary approval for a genuinely balanced budget ... so that the Reich would not suffer a disastrous cash-flow crisis'.[5] In April a 'Five Year Plan' to 'bolster the economy through lower production costs and large-scale public works' was announced and 1.5 billion marks were allocated for the construction of roads, canals and public housing,[6] but these plans had to be shelved after negotiations between business and the unions broke down. This left the government with no choice but to introduce drastic cuts in government spending and tax rises which only increased the numbers of people out of work. At the same time the failure to reach a broad-based solution to the economic crisis made a confrontation between the Chancellor and parliament inevitable when the Reichstag voted against the budget.

When Brüning attempted to force his austerity measures through by use of Article 48 the Reichstag voted to overturn the emergency decree, giving him no option but to ask Hindenburg to dissolve parliament and call new elections in the hope of securing a popular mandate for the cuts.

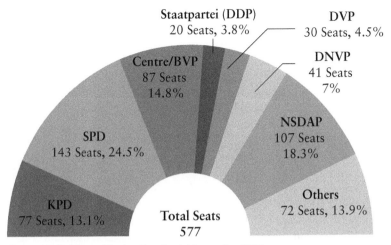

Figure 6.1 Reichstag Election Results, 14 September 1930.

This seriously backfired when the electorate sent a clear message of their discontent and lack of faith in the ability of the existing system to deal with the economic crisis by rejecting the moderate parties and turning to the political extremes. Although the share of the vote of both the SPD and the government's chief supporters, the Centre Party, remained stable (the former losing ten seats while the latter gained six), both the DVP and DNVP saw their share of the vote halved, while the Communists gained 23 seats. The big winners, though, were the previously negligible NSDAP whose share of the vote rocketed from 2.6 to 18.3 per cent, giving them 107 seats and making them the second largest party in the Reichstag after the Social Democrats.

Deeply alarmed by this development the leadership of the SPD was prepared to tolerate the Brüning administration as the lesser of two evils and decided to enter into 'objective co-operation' (*Sachliche Zusammenarbeit*) with the government. Although this meant that the Chancellor was able to survive confidence votes in parliament, it simultaneously helped to undermine his position with Germany's true powerbrokers. Hindenburg and his powerful clique of advisors – his son Oskar, State Secretary Meissner and General Groener's wartime protégé the head of the *Ministeramt* (political office) of the Reichswehr Kurt von Schleicher – continued to regard the SPD as the main threat to Germany and were determined to neutralize them as a political force and bring about an authoritarian reconfiguration of German politics. Initially it had been thought that Brüning, a former officer and staunch Catholic who had dedicated his life to public service, would be the man to bring this plan to fruition, but as time went on it became clear that he had a strong commitment to democracy and was determined to govern in accordance with the constitution as far as possible. Although he undoubtedly presided over a 'drift towards authoritarianism'[7] in which normal democratic procedure was increasingly sidelined – Article 48 was used five times in 1930, rising to 44 times in 1931 and 60 in 1932, while sittings of the Reichstag declined from 94 in 1930, to 41 in 1931, to a mere 13 in 1932 – Brüning's willingness to work with the SPD and resistance to calls to dissolve the Reichstag indefinitely and abandon constitutional government altogether, ultimately led Schleicher to conclude that while he made an excellent foreign minister he was not the 'strong man with the military spirit' that was required to lead Germany.[8]

FOREIGN POLICY

On 3 October 1929 Gustav Stresemann, the man who had overseen the stabilization of the currency after the Great Inflation and done more than anyone else to restore Germany's presence on the international stage, suffered a stroke that left him paralysed and unable to speak. A few days later he died, aged only 51. In London *The Times* paid tribute to him as an 'intelligent and practical patriot' who 'did inestimable service to the German Republic' and whose 'work for Europe as a whole was almost as great',[9] while Count Harry Kessler noted that in Paris public grief was 'so general and sincere' that it was 'almost as if an outstanding French statesman had died'.[10] In Germany, though, the response was more muted. Stresemann had always been a divisive figure and his domestic opponents on the right saw him as little more than a traitor who had sold out Germany to the West.

Despite Stresemann's achievements of the previous five years, Germany's chief foreign policy aims – an end to reparations, the retrieval of territory in the east, and equality in armaments – remained unfulfilled.

And after his death it fell to his DVP colleague, Julius Curtius, and then to Chancellor Brüning to try to find a more lasting solution to the running sore of reparations. This became even more imperative now that the economic crisis had begun to bite. When he came to power Brüning was politically committed to neither a conciliatory nor a confrontational programme and as a result his policy often seemed to fall between two stools: being 'either too uncompromising or not "national" enough' for his domestic critics.[11] Yet keenly aware that success abroad could strengthen his position at home, the new Chancellor was determined to pursue a more assertive foreign policy in the hope that rapid gains would shore up Germany's precarious economic and political situation. Essentially, the polarization of domestic politics and the renewed economic crisis after 1929 meant that Brüning could not afford to wait for his policy to bear fruit as Stresemann had done: he needed results and he needed them quickly.

Brüning is often accused of pursuing a ruinous economic policy in the hope of persuading the Allies to cancel reparations which he regarded as the true cause of Germany's economic crisis.[12] However, 'he had never intended for Germany to have the highest unemployment rate in Europe' and the hardships that entailed.[13] Indeed, this would have been completely against his paternalist attitude towards the less fortunate in society. Instead, the Chancellor's original intention had been to put pressure on Britain and France to revise the Young Plan by allowing a trade surplus to build, thereby creating jobs in export industries while undermining the international case for reparations. But it soon became clear that while the trade surplus did grow from 1.6 million in 1930 to 2.9 million in 1932 exports were not growing, merely shrinking more slowly than imports. This realization, together with growing pressure from the extreme right, pushed the government into a new course and they embarked upon a more active and assertive foreign policy. In January 1931 the Council of the League of Nations tacitly approved Germany's view that Polish minority policy was discriminatory and the source of friction along the frontier between the two countries. Shortly afterwards, German objections to British plans to incorporate what had, until 1918, been German East Africa into its neighbouring colonial possessions succeeded in pressuring the British into abandoning it. At the same time, the German government managed to win Russian and Italian (and to some extent British) support for its claim to equality in armaments with the other European powers.

In the meantime, Curtius pushed for the conclusion of a *Zollunion* (customs union) with Austria, a move 'intended primarily to address the deteriorating domestic political climate' by throwing a bone to pan-German nationalists.[14] At first Brüning was unenthusiastic, thinking that any such preliminary moves towards *Anschluss* could only be considered once reparations had been cancelled. But in February 1931 he dropped his objections after increasingly desperate appeals from Austrian business for closer economic ties to Germany. A draft treaty was prepared in secret and approved by the cabinet on 18 March before being announced to the world three days later. This created a diplomatic storm, with France and Britain (who feared that it would herald political union between the two states, much as the nineteenth-century *Zollverein* had presaged German unification) demanding that the matter be referred to the League of Nations. However, in the event, the plan was soon overtaken by events. The bankruptcy of Austria's biggest bank, the Credit-Anstalt, on 11 May and the subsequent Austro–German banking crisis (see below) killed the projected customs union as the Austrian government withdrew from the project to seek financial assistance from the Western Powers.

The customs union fiasco cost Curtius his job and the Chancellor took on the Foreign Ministry himself. Brüning has often been contrasted negatively with Stresemann, but he possessed advantages that even his famous predecessor lacked. His Catholicism formed a bond with the French who to some extent had remained wary of Stresemann as a Prussian protestant,[15] while Brüning's position as both Chancellor and foreign minister allowed him to speak with more authority on international issues. And he did have some notable successes, particularly regarding détente with France. In July 1931 he visited Paris, and in September a reciprocal visit by Pierre Laval was the first time a French statesman had visited Berlin since 1878. This resulted in the establishment of a Franco–German Joint Commission to discuss economic cooperation. Although this proved the high point of Franco–German rapprochement, Brüning was also able to secure a moratorium on reparations by pointing to the uproar caused by his second emergency decree as evidence that only this could stave off the threat of revolution as well as economic collapse. This was perhaps the Chancellor's greatest achievement, the foreign policy breakthrough that he had been seeking since coming to office. Unfortunately, it was not enough to save him from the intrigues of the powerbrokers around the president who were growing impatient at Brüning's failure to steer Germany in a more right-wing direction.

THE RISE OF THE NAZIS

This reconfiguration of politics seemed even more pressing as the parties of the political extremes picked up support and the pillars of the existing order seemed to be crumbling. As the effects of the Depression began to be felt voters increasingly abandoned the moderate parties of the centre who had been the champions of Weimar democracy in favour of groups that offered radical solutions to Germany's problems. This led to an increase in electoral support for the Communists, who were particularly well placed to appeal to disillusioned workers at a time when it appeared that the very foundations of capitalism were crumbling. The national membership of the KPD tripled between 1928 and November 1932 and the Party nearly doubled their representation in the Reichstag. The KPD's share of the overall vote rose from 10.6 to 19.9 per cent. Support for the Communists rose even in Catholic and conservative Bavaria, where membership of the local branch of the KPD increased fivefold between 1928 and 1932.[16]

For those who remembered the upheavals of 1918–19 the surge in support for the Communists re-awakened fears of revolution that had lain dormant for a decade. This in turn drove voters into the arms of the Nazis. Even before the Wall Street Crash, the NSDAP had a network of over 3,000 branches throughout Germany with more members than either the DDP or DVP by 1928. In many ways, the swing towards the Nazis in 1930 can be seen as the culmination of a trend in which the established middle-class parties had gradually seen 'their organizations disintegrate, their local authority collapse, and their voter base erode'.[17] Ever since the collapse of the DDP's share of the vote in 1920 middle-class voters had been migrating to the right and by 1930 even the conservative-nationalist DNVP was deemed too staid and mired in the existing political system to be an effective representative of their desires. This suggests that for many middle-class voters at least turning to the extreme right was not merely a response to the Great Depression but also a sign of a deeper-seated dissatisfaction with the democratic system.[18]

Nevertheless, the Nazi network of activists did not necessarily translate into electoral success. In 1928 the NSDAP polled only 2.6 per cent of the vote, less than either the BVP or the Business Party, and secured a mere 12 seats in parliament. Their profile was raised by their participation in the campaign against the Young Plan in 1929 during which they were able to make use of the media empire controlled by the DNVP leader Alfred

Hugenburg to present themselves as a radical nationalist alternative not only to the left-wing and republican parties, but also the traditional right. But it was the Depression that really transformed their fortunes. 'Crisis was Hitler's oxygen'[19] and the renewed descent into economic turmoil revitalized the NSDAP's fortunes. At the same time, the Nazis fanned the flames of the political crisis by taking their struggle against democracy and 'Marxism' to the streets.

Political violence had long been a feature of Weimar politics, but during the republic's middle period it had retreated into the background. With the onset of the Great Depression the violence stepped up dramatically as unemployed and disaffected young men flocked to join the various paramilitary wings of rival political factions. According to statistics gathered by the parties, 30 Nazis had been killed by the Communists between 1924 and 1929, while the KPD recorded 92 deaths and 239 injuries between 1924 and 1930. Thereafter the figures rose sharply. One hundred and seventy-one Communists were killed and over 18,000 injured in clashes with 'fascists' between 1930 and 1932, while the NSDAP reported that 143 of their members were killed and a staggering 18,515 were wounded in the same period. In Prussia alone 155 people were killed and 426 injured in clashes between 1929 and 1931, most of them Communists and Nazis, indicating that the struggle for control of the streets was largely a two-way conflict between the forces of the political extremes. Even so, not all the victims of this violence were Nazis or Communists. Nearly three times as many members of the SPD were victims of political violence in the period between 1929 and 1933 than had been the case between 1924 and 1929. Yet even as they helped to spread violence and uncertainty throughout Germany the Nazis presented themselves as a 'reserve force for order', who fought to preserve private property from the unruly masses of the Communists.[20]

In 1932 the SPD politician Kurt Schumacher denounced National Socialism as the 'constant appeal to the inner bastard' in us all.[21] This was true in the sense that the Nazi message played on the negative emotions – and especially the fears – of their audience. In the difficult times caused by the Depression many people were more open to the racist, nationalist and anti-democratic ideas of the NSDAP than they would have been at other times, and 'there can be little doubt that Nazi ideology did successfully identify itself with certain populist fears and desires which had already found expression in the intellectual and cultural history of Germany over the previous century'.[22] But who actually voted for the Nazis?

Despite the fact that the party originated and was based in Catholic Bavaria, support for the NSDAP tended to be highest in the protestant north and east of Germany. This indicated two key factors in support (or lack of it) for the National Socialists: religion and urbanization. Despite picking up votes from some blue-collar workers, the working-class vote still tended to be divided between the SPD and KPD. Similarly, while the party won an increasing percentage of the Catholic vote after 1928, 'the NSDAP was never able to undermine the solid foundation of Catholic support for the Zentrum. Backed by the Church, the Zentrum, like the Marxist parties, offered its followers a well-defined belief system vigorously reinforced by an extensive network of political, social, and cultural organizations.'[23] The Nazi vote was therefore lowest in the big cities of western Germany, such as Cologne and Düsseldorf, and highest in rural Pomerania. At the same time, the party tended to elicit a higher proportion of support from farmers and peasants, the lower middle classes (shopkeepers, artisans, etc.) and white-collar workers who feared a catastrophic loss of status unless drastic action was taken to uphold their social position, than it did from the urban working class who mostly continued to support the Social Democrats. All this led to the traditional view that the Nazis were supported by the middle classes, who turned to them when faced with economic hardship and the loss of their social position at the onset of the Great Depression.

However, more recent research has shown that patterns of support for the extreme right were more complex than was once thought. It has been argued that 'the Nazi/white-collar relationship remained far weaker than traditionally assumed, even after the onset of the depression' and although they were denounced by the trade unions and the parties of the left, the Nazis picked up support from a 'sizeable body of workers in handicrafts and small-scale manufacturing'.[24] In particular there are interesting discrepancies between party membership and electoral support: while peasants tended to vote for the Nazis in higher numbers than other social groups, they were less likely to join the party. Similarly, while electoral support for the NSDAP tended to be lower among the urban workers, they still made up 31.5 per cent of party members, while 63 per cent of the SA were from working-class backgrounds. In 1930, 13 per cent of all workers voted Nazi, a figure that rose to 27 and 28 per cent in the 1932 elections. By the summer of 1932 one in ten Nazi voters had defected from the Social Democrats.[25] It was a similar story with the young: disillusioned by Weimar politics and with little prospect of getting a job during the Depression, young people joined the party and its organizations in large numbers. In 1933, 61 per cent of Nazi Party members were aged between 20 and 30.

The figures cited above indicate that the traditional class-based explanation for the rise of German fascism is inadequate and begs the question, how were the National Socialists able to appeal to such a wide cross section of German society? Part of the answer is their skilful use of propaganda. Hitler had demonstrated an uncanny and cynical awareness of the power of propaganda from his earliest days in politics, and from April 1930 Josef Goebbels was placed in charge of the party's propaganda. Together they set up a highly efficient propaganda machine that allowed them to centrally control how the Nazi message was presented to the public, targeting money and efforts in key electoral districts or at key social groups. Furthermore, feedback was encouraged from grass-roots level, so that the effectiveness of their efforts could be judged, and successful campaigns and messages reproduced elsewhere. Goebbels practised mass politics on a grand scale, deluging the German people with leaflets, posters, etc., but at the same time producing specific material aimed directly at different social groups which played on their fears and concerns. In this way, the Nazis sought to be all things to all people and to some measure succeeded in convincing vastly different groups that they had their interests at heart. Furthermore, the Nazis made skilful use of modern technology, such as loudspeakers, film, and radio, as well as publicity stunts such as Hitler's 'Flight over Germany' during the 1932 presidential election campaign, to get the Nazi message across.

Through these methods the Nazis managed to present themselves as anti-Marxist, while at the same time being untainted by association with big business (unlike the DVP and DNVP) or collaboration with the Social Democrats (unlike the Centre or DDP). The SPD's toleration of the Brüning administration meant that between October 1930 and May 1932 the NSDAP could present themselves both as the only true opposition party aside from the KPD and as an anti-Marxist movement representing the 'national' interest. 'Moreover, because the NSDAP was not saddled with government responsibility before 1933, the party could make extravagant and often blatantly contradictory appeals to mutually hostile groups without having to reconcile those promises.'[26] At the same time, the Nazis 'mobilized unfulfilled reformist expectations' and held out the prospect of radical change that both broke with older traditions tainted by association with 'the politics of failure'.[27] The Nazi party became a unique phenomenon in German politics: 'a catch-all party of social protest' that 'managed to project an image of dynamism, energy and youth that wholly eluded the propaganda efforts of the other parties'.[28] However, this meant that its appeal was wide but not deep and by 1932 their support had already begun to fragment. Although by the beginning of 1933 they were the only party able to claim to be a broad-based *Volkspartei* whose appeal transcended traditional class and gender barriers, it seems unlikely that the Nazis would have been able to maintain their electoral appeal as economic conditions improved and it is therefore a tragic irony that Hitler was installed as Chancellor just at the moment that their fortunes had begun to wane.

HITLER VERSUS HINDENBURG

By the autumn of 1931 it looked increasingly as though Brüning's days were numbered. Over the summer Germany's mounting political crisis led to another run on the banks. On 12 June 200 million marks were withdrawn in a single day, and despite desperate attempts by the government and the Reichsbank to stabilize the situation the panic spread. On 13 July 1931 Germany's second largest bank, the Darmstädter und Nationalbank (Danat-Bank), went bankrupt, further undermining consumer confidence and pitching the international foreign exchange markets 'into complete chaos'.[29] In response a limit on the amount that customers were allowed to withdraw was imposed in Berlin and banks in Hamburg and Cologne stopped issuing withdrawals altogether. The government made Tuesday 14 and Wednesday 15 July emergency bank holidays and were able to contain the crisis but only at the expense of vast levels of public spending to prop up the banking system.[30] At the same time the right-wing cabal surrounding the president were becoming increasingly impatient and were urging Brüning to shift his government even further to the right. Feeling that their chance for power was imminent, the forces of the 'national opposition' (the DNVP, the Nazis and the *Stahlhelm*) met at the resort of Bad Harzburg on 11 October 1931 and proclaimed a united front against the government and the republic. Yet this show of right-wing unity was short-lived. Amidst an atmosphere of mutual distrust and antagonism the 'Harzburg Front' rapidly evaporated after Brüning managed to survive a vote of no-confidence on 13 October and the 'national opposition' proved unable to agree on a common candidate to challenge Hindenburg for the presidency.[31]

Georg Pahl, The German Banking Crisis, 1931: Crowds of savers rush to withdraw their money from the municipal saving bank, Berlin, 13 July 1931 (Bundesarchiv, Bild 102-12023/Georg Pahl/CC-BY-SA 3.0).

The presidential elections of 1932 witnessed a dramatic reversal of the groups that had backed Hindenburg in 1925. With the forces of the political extremes each making their own bids for the presidency all the moderate parties, including the SPD, lined up behind the Chancellor to support the re-election of the aged Hindenburg. With some irony, only the nationalist DNVP refused to support the incumbent and fielded their own candidate, the deputy leader of the *Stahlhelm*, Theodor Duesterberg. Unlike previous polls in which the candidates had made rational appeals to the electorate based on economic self-interest, the two principal candidates in the 1932 presidential campaign were 'men who relied first and foremost on their personal charisma to legitimate their claim to the leadership of the German nation'. Both Hitler and Hindenburg were presented to voters as 'mythical figures endowed with almost supernatural powers' who were uniquely able to satisfy the popular desire for unity and stability in uncertain times.[32] In doing so they drew on populist notions of *Führertum* (leadership) which had been present throughout the Weimar period, on the democratic left as much as on the nationalist right,[33] bringing about 'a decisive moment in the transformation of Weimar political culture' and an important step

Table 6.1: Results of the Presidential Elections, 1932

	First Round (13 March 1932)	Second Round (10 April 1932)
Turnout	86.2%	83.5%
Duesterberg (DNVP)	2,557,729 6.8%	–
Hindenburg (Independent)	18,651,791 49.6%	19,359,983 53%
Hitler (NSDAP)	11,339,446 30.1%	13,418,547 36.8%
Thälmann (KPD)	4,983,341 13.2%	3,706,759 10.2%

Note: Figures for each candidate indicate number of votes polled and percentage of total votes cast.

Source: Anna von der Goltz, *Hindenburg: Power, Myth and the Rise of the Nazis* (Oxford: Oxford University Press, 2009), 145.

towards the embrace of a system of politics based on the charismatic authority of a messianic leader.[34]

Amidst violence on the streets and ferocious rhetoric on the hustings, the first round of voting took place on 13 March. The initial vote knocked Duesterberg out of the race but was so close as to necessitate a run-off poll on 10 April in which Hindenburg secured a majority of 19.4 million votes (53 per cent), to Hitler's 13.4 million (36.8 per cent), and the Communist Thälmann's 3.8 million (10.2 per cent).[35] This was a big disappointment to Hitler, who had poured massive amounts of cash and energy into his campaign, and he now had no option but to set his sights on the Chancellorship instead.

FROM BRÜNING TO HITLER

Political violence had been on the increase since 1929, but it rose exponentially during the election campaigns of 1932. The Nazis claimed that 10,000 of their rank-and-file members had been wounded in clashes with the Communists, while the KPD reported 75 deaths at the hands of the Nazis in the first six months of 1932 alone.[36] A ban on the wearing of uniforms had already been imposed in December 1931 but this had little effect as the paramilitaries merely continued their marches and punch-ups in plain clothes. However, with the supposed threat of a Communist coup receding and under heavy pressure from the SPD and the governments of the *Länder*, Brüning managed to overcome the opposition of the Reichswehr (as represented by Schleicher) and persuade Hindenburg to sign an emergency decree prohibiting the SA on 13 April 1932. Nazi hostels were closed down, party offices raided by the police and arms, equipment and uniforms were confiscated.

However, although this to some extent curbed the violent excesses of the Nazis – or at least drove them off the streets and into pubs and meeting halls[37] – it could not save the administration. Despite all Brüning's efforts on his behalf during the recent election campaign, Hindenburg was deeply displeased that he had faced such concerted opposition in the polls and particularly that the Nationalists had run against him. Schleicher, who increasingly hoped to harness the mass appeal of the Nazis, capitalized on this, and conspired to bring down both the Chancellor and his former mentor, the Interior Minister Groener. Worn down by ill-health and a whispering campaign against him orchestrated by Schleicher, Groener was compelled to resign from the government on 10 May. With the loss of his greatest champion in the president's inner circle, Brüning's days were numbered. Under increasing pressure to bring more right-wingers into the cabinet and to form a Centre–NSDAP coalition in Prussia (where the SPD and State Party vote had collapsed in the recent *Landtag* elections and the Nazis had polled 36 per cent of the vote), Brüning's position became untenable, and he was forced to resign on 30 May 1932.

After a weekend of confusion during which both Schleicher's and Hindenburg's favoured candidates ruled themselves out, the Westphalian aristocrat Franz von Papen was named Chancellor. A former cavalry officer and conservative Catholic, Papen was a little-known member of the Prussian *Landtag* who had never held a government post. But he had impeccable contacts and was seen as the ideal frontman for the real power behind the throne, Schleicher.[38] Schleicher apparently believed that Papen's appointment would be enough to secure the continued support of the Centre Party, but in this he miscalculated. Offended by the intrigues which had ousted Brüning and anxious to avoid being linked to the forces of reaction, the Centre withdrew its support and Papen only managed to avoid being expelled from the party by resigning first.[39] Papen's government was therefore a 'cabinet of barons' drawn largely from the ranks of the DNVP, seven of whom were noblemen with little or no experience of practical politics. In return for the NSDAP's tolerance

Georg Pahl, Campaigners outside a Berlin polling station during the Reichstag elections, 31 July 1932 (Bundesarchiv, Bild 102-03497A/CC-BY-SA 3.0).

of the new government Hitler was promised the repeal of the SA ban and new elections, and the Reichstag was dissolved on 4 June.

Never widely supported in either parliament or the country, the new administration's popularity plummeted when it issued its first emergency decree on 14 June implementing swinging austerity measures that 'virtually abolished the system of unemployment insurance'.[40] The following day the ban on the SA was lifted, plunging Germany into a new orgy of paramilitary violence, culminating in a riot in Hamburg on 17 July that left 15 people dead and 50 injured. Of the 155 deaths in Prussia from political violence in 1932, 105 took place during the election campaign of June–July, while the police recorded 461 riots causing 82 deaths and 400 injuries during the first seven weeks of the campaign alone.[41] The public outcry that followed led to a new ban on political demonstrations but also provided the pretext for the unconstitutional dissolution of the SPD-Centre coalition in Prussia on 20 July and Papen's assumption of dictatorial powers in Germany's largest state. This *Preussenschalg* (Prussian coup) was designed to simultaneously weaken the SPD, 'placate Hitler … and advance the government's plan of centralising political authority',[42] but in actual fact all it achieved was to bring about a revival

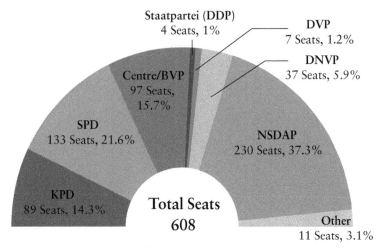

Figure 6.2 Reichstag Election Results, 31 July 1932.

of popular support for the KPD and SPD and provide the Nazis with a precedent for their unconstitutional actions after 1933.

Meanwhile, the National Socialists had reached the high-water mark of their electoral success. The DDP, DVP and *Wirtschaftpartei*'s share of the vote collapsed, but despite some losses support for the Centre, SPD and DNVP remained reasonably consistent. Even so, from July 1932 the KPD and NSDAP together outnumbered all other parties in the Reichstag. The Nazis had consolidated their gains in 1930, polling 37.3 per cent of the popular vote and securing 230 seats in the Reichstag, making them the largest single party. This removed any hope that Hitler would pursue a policy of 'objective co-operation' to Papen's government as the SPD had for Brüning. In an attempt to harness the popularity of the Nazis Hitler was offered the post of Vice-Chancellor in a 'government of national concentration', but the Nazi leader refused anything other than the Chancellorship. When the Reichstag reconvened on 12 September it was immediately prorogued when the Communists and Nazis joined together to defeat the government in a confidence vote and new elections were called in the hope of gaining a working majority for the government.

The results of the election of November 1932 clearly showed that the Nazi's popularity had peaked in July, as they lost 34 seats and their share of the vote declined by 4 per cent. What is more, the cost of fighting three election campaigns in one year had left the party virtually bankrupt. Yet the electorate also decisively rejected Papen's government with nearly

Chancellor Franz von Papen with State Secretary Dr Otto Meissner on the steps of the Reichstag at the Constitution Day celebrations, 11 August 1932 (Bundesarchiv, Bild 102-13743/CC-BY-SA 3.0).

90 per cent of voters backing the opposition parties.[43] When a second attempt to bring the Nazis into the government failed, Papen proposed declaring martial law and establishing a presidential dictatorship, but by this time the Chancellor had lost the support of his former backers in the president's inner circle. Annoyed at Papen's growing self-confidence and jealous of his close relationship with Hindenburg, Schleicher took this opportunity to withdraw the support of the army, declaring at a cabinet meeting on 2 December that the Reichswehr was incapable of opposing the domestic anarchy and foreign invasion that would be the inevitable result of the Chancellor's proposals.[44] This led to Papen's fall and his replacement by the arch-intriguer Schleicher who now decided that it was time for him to emerge from the shadows and take the reins of power himself.

Schleicher has often been dismissed as an arch-reactionary who conspired to destroy the republic and replace it with a restored monarchy or a military dictatorship. But although he had no love for democracy and favoured a strong state in which the military played a leading role, he was a pragmatist who accepted the political realities of the day. Following Germany's defeat in 1918 he became convinced that the nation needed to pursue a conciliatory foreign policy in order to concentrate on 'streamlining the economy', centralizing the power of the state and building up its military power.[45] At the same time, he believed

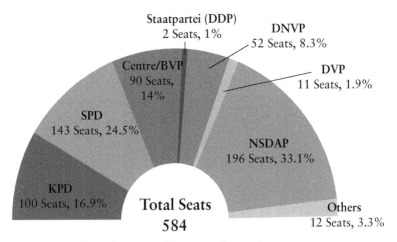

Figure 6.3 Reichstag Election Results, 6 November 1932.

that attempting to repress mass political movements (except those that openly espoused a violent transformation of the political and economic order) was counterproductive and that instead the political parties and paramilitaries should be harnessed to the state. To this end, Schleicher made overtures to the Nazis in the hope of simultaneously 'taming' them and bringing their popularity behind his government. When these efforts failed, he had no choice but to make the same appeal to Hindenburg to allow him to rule without parliament which his predecessor had done, an appeal that Hindenburg rejected using Schleicher's own arguments that such a move would lead to civil war.

Meanwhile, feeling betrayed, Papen had been intriguing against the new Chancellor and began secret negotiations with the Nazis, big business and the large landowners designed to bring about his return to power with majority support in the Reichstag. Fearful that the on-going economic crisis would bring about a Communist revolution, and underwhelmed by Schleicher's performance as Chancellor, the conservative elements within German society swung their support behind Papen who persuaded Hindenburg to dismiss Schleicher and appoint Hitler as Chancellor on the basis that as Vice-Chancellor he could control the Nazi leader. Wearied by the constant political upheaval of the past two years, Hindenburg allowed himself to be convinced and duly appointed Hitler as Chancellor on 30 January 1933.

THE END OF THE REPUBLIC

The massed ranks of the SA celebrated Hitler's appointment with a torchlit procession through the streets of Berlin, but in purely constitutional terms Hitler's position was not strong. He was one of only three Nazis in a Cabinet of 12 (Wilhelm Frick was Minister of the Interior and Hermann Göring was Minister without Portfolio); the NSDAP–DNVP Coalition did not have an unassailable majority in the Reichstag so any legislation that it tried to introduce could easily be blocked if the other parties were prepared to work in concert; and the Chancellor could only govern effectively if he retained the confidence of the president. This posed a problem for Hitler because it was well-known that Hindenburg had nothing but contempt for him. Nevertheless, Hitler had several advantages – firstly he was the leader of the largest single party in Germany and the ineffectual Papen and Schleicher governments had proven that the conservatives could not govern effectively without his support. Furthermore, there was a widespread fear amongst German conservatives that the only alternative to a Nazi government was civil war or a Communist coup. More importantly, Hitler's appointment as Chancellor gave the Nazi Party access to the full resources of the state. This came into its own during the Reichstag elections of March 1933.

On 31 January 1933 Hitler used his position as head of government to issue an 'Appeal to the German People' in which he blamed the prevailing conditions (including, ironically enough, the atmosphere of violence and intimidation in which the election campaign was taking place) on the democratic system and the terrorist activities of the Communists, while presenting his government as a 'national uprising' which would restore Germany's pride and unity. At the same time, as Prussian Minister of the Interior, Göring controlled the police force of Germany's largest state and was able to enrol 50,000 extra officers, most of them recruited from the ranks of the SA. Socialist and Communist rallies and meetings were routinely broken up by the police or Nazi thugs and 69 people were killed during the five-week election campaign. Then, on 27 February the Reichstag burned down. Although there was no evidence that the fire was the work of anything other than a single mentally disturbed arsonist, the Nazis presented it as evidence of a wide-ranging Communist conspiracy and persuaded the president to issue the 'Decree for the Protection of the People and the State' which effectively suspended civil liberties in Germany and increased the power of central government over state authorities.

Despite all this, when Germany went to the polls on 5 March 1933 the Nazi gains were quite limited. Their share of the vote only increased by just over 10 per cent giving them 288 seats in the Reichstag, meaning that they could only secure a majority with the aid of the 52 Nationalist deputies. This was a severe political blow to Hitler's plans because a clear two-thirds majority was necessary to make changes to the constitution. Nevertheless, this was merely a set-back and not a defeat. Without the majority necessary to alter the constitution, Hitler proposed the passage of an Enabling Bill that would 'effectively do away with parliamentary procedure and legislation and which would instead transfer full powers to the Chancellor and his government for the next four years. In this way the dictatorship would be grounded in legality'.[46] Correctly assuming that the Communists (or at least those not in prison) and the SPD would vote against such a measure, Hitler therefore had to reach out to the Centre Party in order to have any chance of securing the passage of the law.

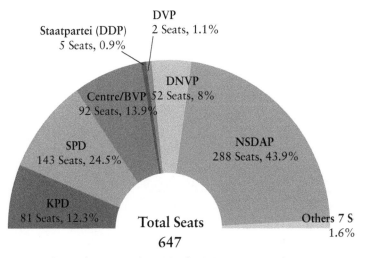

Figure 6.4 Reichstag Election Results, 5 March 1933.

But it was just at this moment that the delicate alliance between the Nazis and the forces of traditional conservatism threatened to be upset. The election campaign had built up a momentum within the lower ranks of the NSDAP that Hitler and the rest of the National Socialist leadership were finding difficult to contain. These elements scorned the legal route to power and pressed for the immediate creation of a Nazi dictatorship which would introduce radical measures, by violence if necessary. This threatened to alienate the conservatives and Nationalists and risked the army stepping in. Hitler therefore organized a great ceremonial act of reassurance, the so-called 'Day of Potsdam', where, in the presence of Hindenburg, the former crown prince and many of the highest-ranking officers in the Reichswehr, Hitler explicitly aligned National Socialism with the forces of traditional Prussian–German conservatism.

Two days later, on 23 March 1933, the Reichstag was opened in the new venue of the Kroll Opera House. The few remaining Communist deputies were refused admittance, while the SPD members were subjected to a barrage of intimidation from the armed ranks of the SA who surrounded the building. In his speech to the assembled Reichstag Hitler announced that he would respect the rights of the Catholic Church and uphold religious and moral values, false promises that the Centre Party deputies chose to believe. When the vote on the Enabling Act was

Theo Eisenhart, The Day of Potsdam, 21 March 1933. Reich Chancellor Adolf Hitler shakes hands with President Paul von Hindenburg. (Bundesarchiv, Bild 183-S38324/ CC-BY-SA 3.0).

taken it was passed by 444 votes to 94. From that point on Hitler was able to enact legislation, including amendments to the constitution, without having to subject them to the approval of either parliament or the president. This freed him from the necessity of ruling by presidential decree as his predecessors had done and gave all the Nazis' subsequent actions a veneer of legality. Over the next 12 months they centralized political power in Germany, broke the power of the trade unions and dealt ruthlessly with opposition from both within and without their own party. By the end of 1934 Germany was a one-party state, the army had sworn an oath to serve not the state but Hitler himself, and the Nazi leader had assumed the powers of both Chancellor and head of state.

CONCLUSION: DID WEIMAR FAIL?

Generations of students have answered essay and exam questions that are variations on the theme of 'why did the Weimar Republic fail?' For a long time seeking to understand how and why the Germans had succumbed to Nazism was the conundrum at the heart of scholarly interest in the republic. Yet as Weimar studies took a more 'cultural turn', historians ceased to see the republic as little more than a prelude to the Third Reich and focused more and more attention on all aspects of German society and culture in the 1920s. This has led to an interdisciplinary reshaping of the debate on the history of Weimar Germany in which the lines that once delineated political, cultural and social history have been broken or at least blurred. As this has happened, historians have increasingly challenged the old narrative of the inevitable collapse of democracy and stressed 'the contingency of the Weimar Republic'.[1] At the same time, we should be cautious of using the formula of 'failure' in discussing the fall of republic, implying, as it does, that the fault lay with the Weimar state itself. Instead, we should look at the problems that the German state and society faced, and the decisions that groups and individuals took, to assess just why the republic was unable to endure.

Born out of military defeat and violent revolution, the Weimar Republic inherited a bitter legacy of political and social division. Germany's long history of political disunity coupled with the deep social and cultural cleavages created by the experience of industrial modernity made the republic a fractured commonwealth riven by ideological conflict and social anxiety. These divisions were widened and deepened by the early tumultuous years of democracy when the new state faced violent challenges from both left and right at the same time as it struggled to deal with international and economic crises.

Against the odds German democracy survived the upheavals of the early 1920s (unlike some of its European neighbours) and entered a period of relative stability after 1924. However, the old social divisions between rich and poor still existed and although the state did much to help the less fortunate in society, the economic upheavals of the post-war years left a bitter legacy. The stabilization of the currency left middle-class Germans feeling that they had been unfairly treated while the working classes faced a precarious existence. In time, both groups came to feel that the promises of a better life inherent in the republic's 'welfare democracy' had not been realized. At the same time, reliance on foreign capital and the continuing burden of reparations payments left Germany dangerously exposed to fluctuations in the international economy and when the American stock market crashed in October 1929 Germany was particularly badly hit by the subsequent global economic downturn.

With the onset of the Great Depression German businesses began to go bust and unemployment rose rapidly. By 1932 one in three German workers was unemployed, and it appeared that capitalism had entered a period of terminal decline. The effects of the Depression were all-pervasive and reawakened memories of the uncertainty and hardships of the inflation era. Yearning for stability and security, German voters (many of whom had already begun to desert the moderate pro-republican parties of the political centre) abandoned the democratic parties in search of radical solutions to Germany's ills on the political extremes. At the same time, the Depression highlighted and exacerbated the ideological fissures between the political parties and made the compromise necessary for the political system to function almost impossible to achieve. Unable to command a majority in the Reichstag, from the summer of 1930 successive governments were forced to rely on presidential emergency powers to pass legislation and parliamentary democracy effectively ceased to function. From this point onwards the political initiative lay not so much with the people or the representatives of Weimar's political class as with the aging president Hindenburg and the coterie of aristocrats and army officers who made up his advisors. Never particularly enamoured with democracy, these men had long desired an authoritarian reconfiguration of German politics, but they ultimately shied away from abandoning parliamentary politics altogether. In the final months of the republic the desire to give 'presidential government' a sheen of legitimacy by harnessing the popularity of the Nazis and intrigues within the president's inner circle ultimately led to Hitler's appointment as Chancellor at the end of January 1933.

However, the history of the Weimar Republic is more than a mere litany of bad luck and poor decisions. The republic was far from the weak democracy or 'failed state' that it has sometimes been painted as. It may have come into being almost by accident and faced concerted opposition throughout its lifetime, but the republic was still able to mobilize mass support at least until 1929. Elections in 1919 and 1920 demonstrated that there was overwhelming popular support for the new democracy and the parties that supported it, and although the electorate moved to the right throughout the 1920s it was only after the onset of the Great Depression and the emasculation of the Reichstag in 1930 that the opponents of the Weimar state could claim a mass following. Under the republic 'Germans lived in the most democratic setting they had ever experienced, with a raucous free press and an intense, lively, streetscape of political theatre'.[2] Political participation remained consistently high and there was a greater degree of consensus amongst Weimar's political class (at least in the middle years of the republic) than some historians have suggested. Many of the supposed flaws within the constitution were not flaws in themselves, but only became so when they combined with other factors such as the pressures placed upon the system by economic and political crisis, or a president determined to uphold the letter of the constitution but at best ambivalent towards the spirit that lay behind it. As has recently been observed, 'Aside from *a specific crisis* in 1930–32, the Weimar Republic was a stable democracy'. The chief lesson that we can learn from Weimar is 'that democracies are fragile. They can fall fast'.[3]

Weimar Germany's legacy is more positive than has often been appreciated. Weimar 'established political liberties, opened up new avenues of representation' and 'enabled many people to live more freely chosen, more emancipated lives' than had been possible before 1918.[4] It led the world in social legislation, cultural experimentation and sexual tolerance and blazed a trail that many societies would later follow. Perhaps the greatest and most enduring legacy of Weimar Germany is the great flowering of art and literature, science and learning that it engendered. The republic 'produced an entire generation of probing, searching artists and intellectuals'[5] and 'one can barely count the bristling and bracing paintings, novels, poems, philosophical treatises, theatrical stagings, and films' produced during the Weimar era 'that still, almost one hundred years later, move and engage us on every conceivable level – intellectually, aesthetically, emotionally, erotically'.[6] German scientists of the Weimar period laid the foundations of theoretical physics, German composers transformed music and German philosophers and sociologists profoundly changed the way people thought about themselves and the world around them. At the same time, the eight-hour working day and the welfare state improved the lives of millions of Germans and provided models of social intervention that would be widely imitated after the Second World War. Women gained not only the vote but also more options and greater freedom to decide for themselves how they would live, work and dress, in some ways preparing them for even greater moves towards equality and emancipation in the wake of the Second World War, while Weimar's open discussions of sex and sexuality and liberal attitudes towards homosexuality prefigured the 'sexual revolution' of the 1960s. These successes are often forgotten, or at least dismissed as temporary achievements invalidated by their rollback under the Third Reich, but it was these very accomplishments that made the republic so contested and mobilized such vociferous opposition from the forces of the radical right.

At the same time, the circumstances of its birth meant that the fortunes of the republic were inextricably linked to developments on the international stage. To some extent the success or failure of the republic was from the beginning dependent on the actions of other nations and the vagaries of the global marketplace. The Treaty of Versailles, reparations and an economy reliant on foreign investment and export revenue meant that Weimar's political class could not remain aloof from international affairs even if they had wanted to; and the desire to wipe away the stain on their national honour left by defeat and the humiliating terms of the peace settlement meant that revisionism, either through peaceful negotiation or through confrontation, remained the abiding theme of German foreign policy throughout the interwar period. Although some of its key aims – recovery of the Polish Corridor, equality of armaments, etc. – remained out of reach, it is doubtless one of the great achievements of the republic that within seven years of the humiliating peace treaty Germany had recovered much of its pre-war international standing. Through the untiring efforts of Gustav Stresemann, Weimar Germany was able to overcome the suspicion of its former enemies and rejoin the community of nations as an equal in 1926. This was followed by the withdrawal of occupying troops ahead of schedule in 1930 and finally a moratorium on reparations payments in 1932. That these goals were achieved peacefully, although sometimes at the cost of domestic political harmony, is testament not only to the political skill of Stresemann, but also to the levels of consensus that could be achieved under the republic.

Moreover, when one begins to look at Weimar Germany from a comparative international perspective then its achievements become even more striking. The contention of those historians who espoused a *Sonderweg* view of German history was, simply put, that Weimar democracy failed because Germany was not Britain or France. But this is to 'assign Germany the part of the twentieth-century delinquent whose role is to certify the basic political virtue of France, Britain and the United States'.[7] Although it did ultimately succumb to dictatorship, the Weimar Republic held out against the forces ranged against it longer and left a more lasting legacy than many of its near neighbours. Of the 'new democracies' that emerged from the First World War, Germany preserved its parliamentary democracy longer than any other save Austria and Czechoslovakia. Germany's experience of revolution and counter-revolution, political violence and economic dislocation in the first half of the 1920s was far from unique and is mirrored by developments throughout Central and Eastern Europe and even in the British Isles. The shift to the right at the end of the 1920s and the ultimate abandonment of democracy when parliamentary politics seemed unable to adequately cope with renewed economic crisis with the onset of the Great Depression was a Europe-wide phenomenon in which Germany was not the first, nor the last, state to abandon democracy in favour of a more authoritarian or fascist alternative.

Considering what came after it, the fact that Weimar democracy did not endure was a tragedy not just for Germany but also for Europe and the wider world. Yet this should not detract from the myriad achievements of the republic's 15 years of existence. In trying to understand how and why the Weimar Republic collapsed we should not lose sight of the positive features of its history. The story of the republic is one of creation as well as destruction, whether that be the formation of democratic institutions, the building of a modern urban consumer society or the manufacture of great works of art, and it deserves to be remembered as such. It was a remarkable period in German history that demonstrates both the best and worst features of democratic politics and what can happen to modern industrial societies when they face extreme conditions. Indeed, given the pressures placed upon it and the consistent opposition it faced from large sections of German society, that Weimar democracy endured as long as it did is a remarkable achievement in itself.

Appendices

Appendix 1: German Political Parties, 1919–1933

Party	Abbreviation	Core Constituency	Notes
Bayerische Volkspartei (Bavarian People's Party)	BVP	Catholic Bavarians	A regional offshoot of the Centre Party that seceded over the Centre's support for centralized government. It remained essentially the Bavarian wing of the Centre Party, but its refusal to work with the SPD in the Bavarian *Landtag* led to it making alliances with the anti-democratic parties of the right.
Deutsche Demokratische Partei (German Democratic Party)	DDP	Supporters from a broad spectrum of German society from trade unionists to bankers, but rooted in the middle classes.	The DDP emerged out of an attempt to create a single liberal party in 1918 and was made up of a merger of the former Progressive Party with the left-wing of the old National Liberals. Its leaders were largely liberal intellectuals (leading to it being dubbed the 'Professor's Party') and its members made an important contribution to drafting the Weimar constitution. Like the other centrist parties it shifted to the right in the late 1920s and was renamed the *Deutsche Staatspartei* (German State Party) in 1930.
Deutsche Volkspartei (German People's Party)	DVP	The upper middle-classes. In 1930 a third of its Reichstag deputies were leading businessmen.	Made up of those National Liberals who felt excluded from the DDP due to their annexationist views, it attempted to strike a balance between liberalism and nationalism. They favoured increased centralization and a strong presidency. If not actively anti-republican it had strong reservations about the Weimar system.

| Deutsche Zentrums Partei (Centre Party) | ZP | Roman Catholics. Encompassed all areas of German society from aristocrats to workers, but most were active churchgoers. | Established in 1870 to represent the interests of German Catholics in the newly united Germany, attempts to rebrand itself as a non-denominational Christian People's Party in 1918 came to nothing. It moved to the left during the First World War and worked together with the SPD and liberals to help found the new republic. One of the most stable political forces during the Weimar period it participated in almost every coalition government between 1919 and 1933. It shifted to the right again in the late 1920s and voluntary disbanded after Hitler's rise to power. |
| Deutschenationale Volkspartei (German National People's Party) | DNVP | Conservative aristocrats and industrialists, civil servants and the lower middle-classes. | The political focal point of conservative anti-republicans, it was formed when the old German Conservative Party and the Free Conservatives merged with other right-wing interest groups in November 1918. An alliance of big business and the landed interest it was conservative and monarchist, but worked in coalition with the parties of the centre in the mid-1920s. Under pressure from the 'New Right' in the late 1920s it lurched to the right and ended by supporting Hitler. |

Party	Abbr.	Support	Description
Kommunistische Partei Deutschlands (Communist Party of Germany)	KPD	The radical working class, the unemployed, young workers.	Formed by an alliance of radical left-wing forces (the Spartacists, the Left Radicals and the Revolutionary Shop Stewards) at the end of 1918, the KPD opposed Western-style democracy and favoured a revolutionary overthrow of the republic and the establishment of a worker's state modelled on the USSR. After 1920 it increasingly came under the direction of Moscow and participated in a number of armed uprisings against the state. Its support was bolstered by the defection of USPD members in 1920 and by the economic crisis after 1929, but it never enjoyed mass support amongst the working class.
Nationalsozialistische Deutsche Arbeiterpartei (National Socialist German Workers Party)	NSDAP	Core support came from the lower middle-classes, peasants, the unemployed and female voters, but the NSDAP aspired to be a true *Volkspartei* attracting mass support from across German society.	Founded in 1919 as the German Worker's Party (DAP), the NSDAP was an anti-republican ultra-right-wing nationalist party whose programme included 'socialist' economic and social elements but was mainly virulently nationalistic and anti-Semitic. Led from 1921 by Adolf Hitler it attempted to seize power in an armed *coup d'état* in November 1923. Re-founded in 1925 after Hitler's release from prison it from then on pursued a policy of gaining power through legal means, even though it remained fundamentally opposed to the republic. Although its support was limited in the early years of the Weimar period it became the largest single party in the Reichstag in 1932.

Socialdemokratische Partei Deutschlands (German Social Democratic Party)	SPD	The 'aristocracy of labour': the skilled working class and trade unionists. SPD voters tended to be older, in work and owning property. Four-fifths of their support came from the working class and the party did little to reach beyond this core support.	A moderate socialist party, the SPD strongly supported parliamentary democracy. As the mainstay of the 'Weimar Coalition' it worked together with the moderate 'bourgeois' parties to uphold the republic in the face of opposition from both left and right. Boasting a well-established membership (1 million in 1919) and social organizations, it was the largest single party in the Reichstag between 1912 and 1932.
Unabhängige Socialdemokratische Partei Deutschlands (Independent German Social Democratic Party)	USPD	Radical elements of the German labour movement.	The USPD broke away from the SPD in 1917 over the issue of continuing support for the German war effort. It favoured radical social and economic change during the November Revolution, and it split in 1920, the majority of its members joining the KPD. The remainder rejoined the SPD in 1922.

Appendix 2: Reichstag Election Results, 1919–33

	19 January 1919	6 June 1920	4 May 1924	7 December 1924	20 May 1928	14 September 1930	31 July 1932	6 November 1932	5 March 1933
Turnout (%)	83	79.2	77.4	78.8	75.6	82	84	80.6	88.7
BVP	–	1.173	0.946	1.134	0.945	1.005	1.192	1.095	1.074
		4.1%	3.2%	3.7%	3.1%	3.0%	3.2%	3.2%	2.7%
		20	16	19	17	19	22	20	19
Centre Party	5.980	3.845	3.914	4.119	3.712	4.127	4.589	4.230	4.425
	19.7%	13.6%	13.4%	13.6%	12.1%	11.8%	12.5%	11.9%	11.2%
	91	64	65	69	61	68	75	70	73
DDP (After 1930 as German State Party)	5.641	2.333	1.655	1.920	1.505	1.322	0.371	0.336	0.334
	18.5%	8.3%	5.7%	6.3%	4.9%	3.8%	1%	1%	0.9%
	75	39	28	32	25	20	4	2	5
DNVP	3.121	4.249	5.696	6.206	4.381	2.458	2.177	2.959	3.136
	10.3%	15.1%	19.5%	20.5%	14.2%	7%	5.9%	8.3%	8%
	44	71	95	103	73	41	37	51	52
DVP	1.345	3.919	2.694	3.049	2.679	1.578	0.436	0.661	0.432
	4.4%	13.9%	9.2%	10.1%	8.7%	4.5%	1.2%	1.9%	1.1%
	19	65	45	51	45	30	7	11	2
KPD	–	0.589	3.693	2.709	3.264	4.592	5.283	5.980	4.848
		2.1%	12.6%	8.9%	10.6%	13.1%	14.3%	16.9%	12.3%
		4	62	45	54	77	89	100	81

	19 January 1919	6 June 1920	4 May 1924	7 December 1924	20 May 1928	14 September 1930	31 July 1932	6 November 1932	5 March 1933
NSDAP (in 1924 as National Socialist Freedom Movement)	–	–	1.918 6.5% 32	0.907 3% 14	0.810 2.6% 12	6.409 18.3% 107	13.745 37.3% 230	11.737 33.1% 196	17.277 43.9% 288
SPD	11.509 37.86% 163	6.179 21.9% 103	6.008 20.5% 100	7.881 26% 131	9.153 29.8% 153	8.577 24.5% 143	7.959 21.6% 133	7.248 20.4% 121	7.181 18.3% 120
USPD	2.317 7.6% 22	4.971 17.6% 83	0.235 0.8% –	0.099 0.3% –	0.021 0.1% –	–	–	–	–
Wirtschaftpartei	–	–	0.694 1.7% 7	1.005 2.2% 12	1.397 4.5% 23	1.361 3.9% 23	0.137 0.4% 2	0.110 0.3% 1	–
Others	0.208 0.68% 3	0.651 2.3% 6	1.824 6.2% 19	1.36 4.5% 12	3.1 10.8% 31	3.459 10% 49	0.98 2.7% 9	1.066 3% 11	0.629 1.6% 7

Figures indicate number of votes polled (in millions), percentage share of the vote and number of seats at the beginning of each parliamentary session.

Source: *Wahlen in der Weimarer Republik*, http://www.gonschior.de/weimar

Appendix 3: Governments of the Weimar Republic, 1918–1933

Term in Office	Days in Office	Chancellor	Coalition	Foreign Minister	Interior Minister	Defence Minister	Economics Minister	Finance Minister
13 Feb.–20 June 1919	130	Philipp Scheidemann (SPD)	SPD-DDP-Centre	Ulrich von Brockdorff-Rantzow (Independent)	Hugo Preuß (DDP)	Gustav Noske (SPD)	Rudolf Wissell (SPD)	Eugen Schiffer (DDP); Bernhard Dernberg (DDP)
21 June 1919–26 March 1920	277	Gustav Bauer (SPD)	SPD-DDP-Centre	Hermann Müller (SPD)	Eduard David (SPD); Erich Koch (DDP)	Gustav Noske (SPD)	Rudolf Wissell (SPD)	Mattias Erzberger (Centre)
27 March–20 June 1920	72	Hermann Müller (SPD)	SPD-DDP-Centre	Adolf Köster (SPD)	Erich Koch (DDP)	Otto Gessler (DDP)	Robert Schmidt (SPD)	Josef Wirth (Centre)
21 June 1920–4 May 1921	317	Konstantin Fehrenbach (Centre)	Centre-DDP-DVP	Walter Simons (Independent)	Erich Koch (DDP)	Otto Gessler (DDP)	Ernst Scholz (DVP)	Josef Wirth (Centre)
10 May 1921–14 Nov. 1922	553	Josef Wirth (Centre)	1st & 2nd: Centre-SPD-DDP	Friedrich von Rosenberg (Independent); Walther Rathenau (DDP)	Georg Gradnauer (SPD); Adolf Köster (SPD)	Otto Gessler (DDP)	Robert Schmidt (SPD)	Heinrich Brauns (Centre)
22 Nov. 1922–12 Aug. 1923	263	Wilhelm Cuno (Independent)	DVP-DDP-Centre-BVP	Frederic von Rosenberg (Independent)	Rudolf Oeser (DDP)	Otto Gessler (DDP)	Johannes Becker (DVP)	Andreas Hermes (Centre)

Term in Office	Coalition	Days in Office	Chancellor	Foreign Minister	Interior Minister	Defence Minister	Economics Minister	Finance Minister
13 Aug.–30 Nov. 1923	1st & 2nd: DVP-SPD-DDP-Centre	103	Gustav Stresemann (DVP)	Gustav Stresemann (DVP)	Wilhelm Sollmann (SPD); Karl Jarres (DVP)	Otto Gessler (DDP)	Hans von Raumer (DVP); Joseph Koeth (Independent)	Rudolf Hilferding (SPD); Hans Luther (Independent)
30 Nov. 1923–15 Jan. 1925	Centre-DVP-DDP	412	Wilhelm Marx (Centre)	Gustav Stresemann (DVP)	Karl Jarres (DVP)	Otto Gessler (DDP)	Eduard Hamm (DDP)	Hans Luther (Independent)
15 Jan. 1925–12 May 1926	1st: DVP-DNVP-Centre-DDP-BVP 2nd: DVP-Centre-DDP-BVP	482	Hans Luther (DDP)	Gustav Stresemann (DVP)	Martin Schiele (DNVP); Otto Geßler (DDP); Wilhelm Külz (DDP)	Otto Gessler (DDP)	Albert Neuhaus (DNVP); Rudolf Krohne (DVP); Julius Curtius (DVP)	Otto von Schlieben (DNVP); Hans Luther (Independent); Peter Reinhold (DDP)
17 May 1926–12 June 1928	1st: Centre-DDP-DVP-BVP 2nd: Centre-DVP-DNVP-BVP	792	Wilhelm Marx (Centre)	Gustav Stresemann (DVP)	Wilhelm Külz (DDP); Walter von Keudell (DNVP)	Otto Gessler (DDP); Wilhelm Groener (Independent)	Julius Curtius (DVP)	Peter Reinhold (DDP); Heinrich Köhler (Centre)
28 June 1928–27 March 1930	SPD-DDP-DVP-Centre-BVP	637	Hermann Müller (SPD)	Gustav Stresemann (DVP); Julius Curtius (DVP)	Carl Severing (SPD)	Wilhelm Groener (Independent)	Julius Curtius (DVP); Robert Schmidt (SPD)	Rudolf Hilferding (SPD); Paul Moldenhauer (DVP)

Term in Office	Coalition	Days in Office	Chancellor	Foreign Minister	Interior Minister	Defence Minister	Economics Minister	Finance Minister
30 March 1930–30 May 1932	1st: Centre-BVP-DVP-DDP–Business-KVP 2nd: Centre-DDP-BVP-KVP	792	Heinrich Brüning (Centre)	Julius Curtius (DVP); Heinrich Brüning (Centre)	Josef Wirth (Centre); Wilhelm Groener (Independent)	Wilhelm Groener (Independent)	Hermann Dietrich (DDP); Hermann Warmbold (Independent)	Paul Moldenhauer (DVP); Hermann Dietrich (DDP)
1 June–17 Nov. 1932	DNVP	170	Franz von Papen (Independent)	Konstantin Freiherr von Neurath (Independent)	Wilhelm Freiherr von Gayl (DNVP)	Kurt von Schleicher (Independent)	Hermann Warmbold (Independent)	Ludwig Graf Schwerin von Krosigk (Independent)
3 Dec. 1932–28 Jan. 1933	DNVP	55	Kurt von Schleicher (Independent)	Konstantin Freiherr von Neurath (Independent)	Franz Bracht (Independent)	Kurt von Schleicher (Independent)	Hermann Warmbold (Independent)	Ludwig Graf Schwerin von Krosigk (Independent)

Source: *Die Reichsregierungen 1918–1933*, http://www.gonschior.de/weimar/Deutschland/Uebersicht_Reg.html

Notes

INTRODUCTION

1   Joel Kotkin, 'Is America About to Suffer its Weimar Moment?', *The Daily Beast*, 30 December 2020 https://www.thedailybeast.com/is-america-about-to-suffer-its-weimar-moment?ref=scroll (accessed 20/6/2022).
2   For a scholarly discussion of the history of drawing parallels between American and Weimar democracy, see Daniel Bessner, 'Ghosts of Weimar: The Weimar Analogy in American Thought', *Social Research*, 84, No. 2 (2017), 831–55.
3   Leopold von Ranke, *Geschichten der Romanischen und Germanischen Völker von 1494 bis 1514* (Leipzig: Duncker und Humblot, 1874), vii.
4   For an exploration of the use of the term 'crisis' in the historiography of the Weimar Republic see Rüdiger Graf, 'Either-Or: The Narrative of "Crisis" in Weimar Germany and its Historiography', *Central European History*, 43, No. 4 (2010), 592–615.

CHAPTER 1

1   The Austrian Chancellor Klemens von Metternich said that 'Italy is only a geographical expression' ('Le mot "Italie" is une denomination géographique'), but the same could be said of Germany prior to unification. Richard von Metternich (ed.), *Aus Metternich's Nachgelassenen Papieren*, Vol. 7 (Vienna: Wilhelm Braumüller, 1883), 388.
2   Gustav Landauer, 'The United Republics of Germany and Their Constitution' (1918) in Gabriel Kuhn (ed. and trans.), *All Power to the Councils! A Documentary History of the German Revolution of 1918–1919* (Oakland: PM Press, 2012), 199.

3 Edwin H. Zeydel (ed.), *Constitutions of the German Empire and German States* (Washington: Government Printing Office, 1919), 8.

4 Gordan A. Craig, *Germany 1866–1945* (Oxford: Clarendon Press, 1978), 186–7.

5 Alexander Watson, *Ring of Steel: Germany and Austria-Hungary at War, 1914–1918* (London: Penguin, 2014), 64.

6 See Eric D. Weitz, *Weimar Germany: Promise and Tragedy* (Princeton: Princeton University Press, 2007), 8–9; Nina Lübbren, 'Gela Forster's Radical New Sculpture: Feminism, War and Revolution', *Art History*, 42, No. 4 (2019), 710; Heather R. Perry, *Recycling the Disabled: Army, Medicine and Modernity in WWI Germany* (Manchester: Manchester University Press, 2014), 2; Sabine Kienitz, 'Fürs Vaterland? Körperpolitik, Invalidität und Geschlechterordnung nach dem Ersten Weltkrieg' in Gabriele Metzler and Dirk Schumann (eds.), *Geschlechter(un)ordnung und Politik in der Weimarer Republik* (Bonn: Dietz, 2016), 159.

7 David Stevenson, *With Our Backs to the Wall: Victory and Defeat in 1918* (London: Penguin, 2011), 287–8.

8 Ibid., 418–19.

9 Erich Ludendorff, *My War Memories, 1914–1918*, Vol. 2 (London: Hutchinson, 1919), 679.

10 'Erich Ludendorff Admits Defeat: Diary Entry by Albrecht von Thaer (October 1, 1918)' in Roger Chickering, Steven Chase Gummer and Seth Rotramel (eds.), *Wilhelmine Germany and the First World War (1890–1918)*, Vol. 5, *German History in Documents and Images*, German Historical Institute, Washington, DC (www.germanhistorydocs.ghi-dc.org) (accessed 15/6/2022).

11 Ernst Toller, *I Was a German: An Autobiography* (Edward Crankshaw, trans.) (London: John Lane, 1934), 132.

12 Count Harry Kessler, *The Diaries of a Cosmopolitan, 1918–1937* (Charles Kessler, trans.) (London: Phoenix Press, 2000), 5.

13 Robert Gerwarth, *November 1918: The German Revolution* (Oxford: Oxford University Press, 2020), 91.

14 Christopher Dillon, 'The German Revolution of 1918/19' in Nadine Rossol and Benjamin Ziemann (eds.), *The Oxford Handbook of the Weimar Republic* (Oxford: Oxford University Press, 2022), 31.

15 Gerwarth, *November 1918*, 161.

16 See Helen L. Boak, 'Women in the German Revolution' in Gaard Kets and James Muldoon (eds.), *The German Revolution and Political Theory* (Cham: Palgrave, 2019); Kathleen Canning, 'Gender and the Imaginary of Revolution in Germany' in Klaus Weinhauer, Anthony McElligott and Kirsten Heinsohn (eds.), *Germany 1916–23: A Revolution in Context* (Bielefeld: Transcript, 2015), 118–25; William A. Pelz, *A People's History of the German Revolution*

(London: Pluto Press, 2018), Chapter 7; Claudie Weil, 'Women in the German Revolution' in Christine Fauré (ed.), *Political and Historical Encyclopedia of Women* (London: Routledge, 2003).

17 Maximilian, Prince von Baden, *The Memoirs of Prince Max of Baden* (W. M. Calder and C. W. H. Sutton, trans.), Vol. II (London: Constable, 1928), 312.

18 Ibid., 323–5.

19 Ibid., 353. The Kaiser himself did not issue a formal abdication proclamation until 28 November 1918, by which time he was already in exile in the Netherlands.

20 Ibid., 354.

21 Evelyn, Princess Blücher, *An English Wife in Berlin: A Private Memoir of Events, Politics, and Daily Life in Germany throughout the War and the Social Revolution of 1918* (London: Constable, 1920), 280.

22 Philipp Scheidemann, *Memoirs of a Social Democrat* (J. E. Mitchell, trans.), Vol. 2 (London: Hodder & Stoughton, 1929), 582.

23 Ibid., 582.

24 Gerwarth, *November 1918*, 135.

25 For an idea of the older view of the Ebert–Groener Pact see Pelz, *A People's History of the German Revolution*, 81–2.

26 Dillon, 'The German Revolution of 1918/19', 31.

27 Gerwarth, *November 1918*, 134.

28 Conan Fischer, '"A Very German Revolution"? The Post-1918 Settlement Re-Evaluated', *Bulletin of the German Historical Institute*, 28, No. 2 (2006), 15.

29 Von Baden, *The Memoirs of Prince Max of Baden*, Vol. II, 312.

30 Alan Farmer and Andrina Stiles, *The Unification of Germany, 1815–1919 (Third Edition)* (London: Hodder Education, 2007), 201.

31 Nigel Jones, *A Brief History of the Birth of the Nazis* (London: Robinson, 2004), 48.

32 Richard Bessel, 'The Great War in German Memory: The Soldiers of the First World War, Demobilisation, and Weimar Political Culture', *German History*, 6, No. 1 (1988), 26.

33 Scott Stephenson, *The Final Battle: Soldiers of the Western Front and the German Revolution of 1918* (Cambridge: Cambridge University Press, 2009), 204–7.

34 Ernst von Salomon, *The Outlaws* (Ian F. D. Morrow, trans.) (London: Arktos Media, 2013), 57.

35 Robert Gerwarth, 'The Central European Counter-Revolution: Paramilitary Violence in Germany, Austria and Hungary After the Great War', *Past and Present*, 200, No. 1 (2008), 180–82.

36 For some comparative studies on paramilitary violence in the interwar period see the special issue of *Contemporary European History* (19, No. 3, 2010)

dedicated to the subject, as well as Robert Gerwarth and John Horne (eds.), *War in Peace: Paramilitary Violence in Europe after the Great War* (Oxford: Oxford University Press, 2012) and Ian Kershaw, 'War and Political Violence in the Twentieth Century', *Contemporary European History*, 14, No. 1 (2005), 107–23.

37 'A Call to Revolt by the Spartacists and Revolutionary Shop Stewards, 9 January 1919', Document 3.1 in Ben Fowkes (ed.), *The German Left and the Weimar Republic: A Selection of Documents* (Chicago: Haymarket Books, 2015), 79, 81.

38 'The Proclamation of the Bavarian Council Republic, 7 April 1919' in Ibid., 62.

39 Ibid., 63; Erich Mühsam, 'From Eisner to Leviné: The Emergence of the Bavarian Council Republic' in Kuhn (ed. and trans.), *All Power to the Councils!*, 253.

40 Toller, *I Was a German*, 155–57.

41 Victor Klemperer, *Munich 1919: Diary of a Revolution* (Jessica Spengler, trans.) (Cambridge: Polity Press, 2017), 101.

42 Volker Weidermann, *Dreamers: When the Writers Took Power – Germany, 1919* (Ruth Martin, trans.) (London: Pushkin Press, 2017), 249.

43 Jones, *A Brief History of the Birth of the Nazis*, 157.

44 See Thomas Mergel, 'Elections, Election Campaigns and Democracy' in Rossol and Ziemann (eds.), *The Oxford Handbook of the Weimar Republic*, 167; Gerwarth, *November 1918*, 162.

45 Anthony McElligott, 'Political Culture' in Anthony McElligott (ed.), *Weimar Germany* (Oxford: Oxford University Press, 2009), 30.

46 See Simon Unger-Alvi, '"Leaders not Lords": Führertum, Democracy and Nazism in the Weimar Republic', *German History*, 39, No. 4 (2021), 565–66.

47 'The Constitution of the German Republic' in Anton Kaes, Martin Jay and Edward Dimendberg (eds.), *The Weimar Republic Sourcebook* (Berkeley: University of California Press, 1994), 48.

48 Geoff Layton, *From Bismarck to Hitler: Germany 1890–1933* (London: Hodder & Stoughton, 1995), 79.

49 Fischer, '"A Very German Revolution"?', 19.

50 McElligott, 'Political Culture', 28.

51 Dillon, 'The German Revolution of 1918/19', 27.

CHAPTER 2

1 'German Constitution: Historic Event at Weimar', *The Manchester Guardian*, 2 August 1919, 8.

2 Ernst Troeltsch, 'The German Democracy (1918)' in Anton Kaes, Martin Jay and Edward Dimendberg (eds.), *The Weimar Republic Sourcebook* (Berkley: University of California Press, 1994), 89.

3 David Stevenson, *1914–1918* (London: Penguin, 2012), 512.

4 The Fourteen Points were the moral principles for which the United States entered the First World War, as outlined in a speech given to Congress by President Woodrow Wilson on 18 January 1918. They included freedom of the seas, free trade, the withdrawal of German and Austrian troops from all occupied territory, the creation of an independent Polish state, and an end to the system of secret treaties and alliances that had dominated pre-war diplomacy.

5 Margaret MacMillan, *Peacemakers* (London: John Murray, 2002), 470.

6 Ernst Troeltsch, 'The Dogma of Guilt' in Kaes, Jay and Dimendberg (eds.), *The Weimar Republic Sourcebook*, 12.

7 Count Harry Kessler, *The Diaries of a Cosmopolitan, 1918–1937* (Charles Kessler, trans.) (London: Phoenix Press, 2000), 101–2.

8 'Philipp Scheidemann's speech of 12 May 1919 Against the Versailles Treaty' in Ben Fowkes (ed.), *The German Left and the Weimar Republic: A Selection of Documents* (Chicago: Haymarket Books, 2015), 204.

9 Paul von Hindenburg, 'The Stab in the Back' in Kaes, Jay and Dimendberg (eds.), *The Weimar Republic Sourcebook*, 15.

10 'Ebert to the returning troops, December 10, 1918' in George S. Vascik and Mark R. Sadler (eds.), *The Stab-in-the-Back Myth and the Fall of the Weimar Republic: A History in Documents and Visual Sources* (London: Bloomsbury, 2016), 89.

11 Wolfgang Elz, 'Foreign Policy' in Anthony McElligott (ed.), *Weimar Germany* (Oxford: Oxford University Press, 2009), 53.

12 'President Wilson's Fourteen Points (1918)' https://www.archives.gov/milestone-documents/president-woodrow-wilsons-14-points (accessed 12/7/22).

13 Stevenson, *1914–1918*, 523.

14 For a discussion of racist notions of Poland and eastern Europe in Germany in this period, see Vejas Gabriel Liulevicius, *The German Myth of the East: 1800 to the Present* (Oxford: Oxford University Press, 2009), 130–70.

15 Stevenson, *1914–1918*, 517; MacMillan, *Peacemakers*, 192; Conan Fischer, *The Ruhr Crisis, 1923–1924* (Oxford: Oxford University Press, 2003), 7–12.

16 'Lloyd George's Speech to the London Conference, 3 March 1921' in R. Butler and J. Bury (eds.), *Documents in British Foreign Policy (First Series)*, Vol. XV (London: HMSO, 1954), 258–9.

17 Alan Sharp, *Consequences of the Peace – The Versailles Settlement: Aftermath and Legacy, 1919–2010* (London: Haus Publishing, 2010), 6.

18 Conan Fischer, 'Continuity and Change in Post-Wilhelmine Germany: From the 1918 Revolution to the Ruhr Crisis' in Geoff Eley and James Retallack (eds.), *Wilhelminism and its Legacies: German Modernities, Imperialism, and the Meanings of Reform, 1890–1930* (Oxford: Berghahn Books, 2003), 205.

19 Walther Rathenau, *Gesammelte Reden* (Berlin: S. Fischer, 1924), 264.

20 Richard Bessel, *Germany After the First World War* (Oxford: Clarendon Press, 1993), 92.

21 Martin H. Geyer, 'The Period of Inflation, 1919–1923' in Nadine Rossol and Benjamin Ziemann (eds.), *The Oxford Handbook of the Weimar Republic* (Oxford: Oxford University Press, 2020), 53. For the debate over the causes of Germany's hyperinflation and the role of government policy, see Harold James, 'The Weimar Economy' in Anthony McElligott (ed.), *Weimar Germany* (Oxford: Oxford University Press, 2009), 108–12, Niall Ferguson, 'The German Inter-War Economy: Political Choice Versus Economic Determinism' in Mary Fulbrook (ed.), *German History Since 1800* (London: Arnold, 1997), 270–1, and Gerald D. Feldman, 'The Reparations Debate', *Diplomacy and Statecraft*, 16, No. 3 (2005), 487–98.

22 Bessel, *Germany After the First World War*, 125.

23 'Decree establishing the Reich Office for Economic Demobilization (Demobilization Office)' *Reichsgesetzblatt* (Berlin: Reich Office of the Interior, 1918), 1304–5.

24 Bessel, *Germany After the First World War*, 110.

25 'The Agreement for Co-operation Made on 15 November 1918 Between 21 Employers' Associations and 7 Trade Unions' in Fowkes (ed.), *The German Left and the Weimar Republic*, 19.

26 Helen Boak, *Women in the Weimar Republic* (Manchester: Manchester University Press, 2013), 22.

27 Ibid., 135–7.

28 Quoted in Bessel, *Germany After the First World War*, 122.

29 'Friedrich Ebert's Address to the Opening Session of the Constituent National Assembly, 6 February 1919' in Fowkes (ed.), *The German Left and the Weimar Republic*, 27.

30 'The Government Programme of 13 February 1919, Presented to the National Assembly by the SPD Reich Chancellor, Philipp Scheidemann' in Ibid., 29–30.

31 Bessel, *Germany After the First World War*, 101.

32 Anthony McElligott, *Rethinking the Weimar Republic* (London: Bloomsbury, 2014), 70.

33 For more on the Weimar welfare state see Karl Christian Führer, 'Social Policy in the Weimar Republic' in Rossol and Zeimann (eds.), *The Oxford Handbook of the Weimar Republic* and Young-Sun Hong, 'The Weimar Welfare System' in McElligott (ed.), *Weimar Germany*.

34 William Mulligan, 'The Reichswehr and the Weimar Republic' in McElligott (ed.), *Weimar Germany*, 85.

35 William Mulligan, *The Creation of the Modern German Army: General Walther Reinhardt and the Weimar Republic, 1914–1930* (Oxford: Berghahn Books, 2005), 163.

36 'Appeal of the Social Democratic Party for a General Strike', in Kaes, Jay and Dimendberg (eds.), *The Weimar Republic Sourcebook*, 16.

37 Richard Bessel, 'Germany from War to Dictatorship' in Fulbrook (ed.), *German History Since 1800*, 245.

38 Elz, 'Foreign Policy', 23.

39 Peter Krüger, 'The European East and Weimar Germany' in Eduard Mühle (ed.), *Germany and the European East in the Twentieth Century* (Oxford: Berg, 2003), 12.

40 See, for example, Dirk Schumann, *Political Violence in the Weimar Republic, 1918–1933* (Thomas Dunlap, trans.) (New York: Beghahn Books, 2009), 24.

41 Conan Fischer, '"A Very German Revolution"? The Post-1918 Settlement Re-Evaluated', *Bulletin of the German Historical Institute*, 28, No. 2 (2006), 20–3.

42 See Nigel Jones, *A Brief History of the Birth of the Nazis* (London: Robinson, 2004), 216, and Robert Gerwarth, 'The Central European Counter-Revolution: Paramilitary Violence in Germany, Austria and Hungary After the Great War', *Past and Present*, 200, No. 1 (2008), 183–4.

43 Josef Wirth's speech to the Reichstag, 25 June 1922, quoted in Eric Weitz, *Weimar Germany: Promise and Tragedy* (Princeton: Princeton University Press, 2007), 100.

44 See Manuela Achilles, 'Reforming the Reich: Democratic Symbols and Rituals in the Weimar Republic' in Kathleen Canning, Kerstin Brandt and Kristin McGuire (eds.), *Weimar Publics/Weimar Subjects: Rethinking the Political Culture of Germany in the 1920s* (Oxford: Berghahn Books, 2010), 175–91; and Manuela Achilles, 'Nationalist Violence and Republican Identity in Weimar Germany: The Murder of Walter Rathenau' in Christian Emden and David Midgley (eds.), *German Literature, History and the Nation: Papers from the Conference 'The Fragile Tradition'*, Cambridge 2002, Vol. 2 (Bern: Peter Lang, 2004), 305–28.

45 See Gerald D. Feldman, *The Great Disorder: Politics, Economics and Society in the German Inflation, 1914–24* (New York: Oxford University Press, 1997), 837–9; and Niall Ferguson, *Paper and Iron: Hamburg Business and German Politics in the Era of Inflation* (Cambridge: Cambridge University Press, 1995), 408–19.

46 See Carl-Ludwig Holtfrerich, *The German Inflation 1914–1923: Causes and Effects in International Perspective* (Berlin: De Gruyter, 1986). Holtfrerich's thesis has been criticized for making an artificial distinction between 'good inflation' that stimulated growth until 1922 and hyperinflation which led to economic chaos thereafter, and for taking an overly narrow approach based purely on the economic data that ignores the social and psychological aspects of the inflation.

47 Bessel, 'Germany from War to Dictatorship', 238.

48 Ibid., 238.

49 Adam Ferguson, *When Money Dies: The Nightmare of the Weimar Hyper-Inflation* (London: Old Street Publishing, 2010), 180.

50 Fischer, 'Continuity and Change in Post-Wilhelmine Germany', 213.

51 Ferguson, *When Money Dies*, 109.

52 Erin Sullivan Maynes, 'Making Money: *Notgeld* and the Material Experience of Inflation in Weimar Germany', *Art History*, 42, No. 4 (2019), 681.

53 See Fischer, '"A Very German Revolution"?', 28.

54 Quoted in Ferguson, *Paper and Iron*, 342.

55 Matthew Stibbe, *Germany 1914–1933: Politics, Society and Culture* (Harlow: Pearson Education, 2010), 118.

56 Geoff Layton, *From Bismarck to Hitler: Germany 1890–1933* (London: Hodder & Stoughton, 1995), 94.

57 Eberhard Kolb, *The Weimar Republic (Second Edition)* (P. S. Falla and R. J. Park, trans.) (Abingdon: Routledge, 2005), 185.

58 Gordon A. Craig, *Germany 1866–1945* (Oxford: Clarendon Press, 1978), 450.

59 Ferguson, *When Money Dies*, 236.

60 For a discussion of the influence of memory, or perhaps the misremembering, of the inflation era on contemporary German attitudes, see Lukas Haffert, Nils Redeker and Tobias Rommel, 'Misremembering Weimar: Hyperinflation, the Great Depression, and German Collective Economic Memory', *Economics & Politics*, 33 (2021), 664–86.

61 Kolb, *The Weimar Republic*, 48.

62 David Clay Large, '"Out with the Ostjuden": The Scheunenviertel Riots in Berlin, November 1923' in Christhard Hoffmann, Werner Bergmann and Helmut Walser Smith (eds.), *Exclusionary Violence: Antisemitic Riots in Modern German History* (Ann Arbor: University of Michigan Press, 2002), 123.

63 Martin H. Geyer, 'The Period of Inflation, 1919–1923' in Rossol and Ziemann (eds.), *The Oxford Handbook of the Weimar Republic*, 63.

64 Emil Julius Gumbel, *Vier Jahre politischer Mord* (Berlin: Verlag der neuen Gesellschaft, 1922), 78–80.

CHAPTER 3

1 Matthew Stibbe, 'Coalition-Building and Political Fragmentation, 1924–1930' in Nadine Rossol and Benjamin Zeimann (eds.), *The Oxford Handbook of the Weimar Republic* (Oxford: Oxford University Press, 2022), 74.

2 Anna von der Goltz, *Hindenburg: Power, Myth, and the Rise of the Nazis* (Oxford: Oxford University Press, 2009), 84.

3 'The SPD's 1921 Görlitz Programme', Document 10.3 in Ben Fowkes (ed.), *The German Left and the Weimar Republic: A Selection of Documents* (Chicago: Haymarket Books, 2015), 288–89.

4 John Hiden, *The Weimar Republic (Second Edition)* (Harlow: Longman, 1996), 39.

5 Stephen E. Hanson, *Post-Imperial Democracies: Ideology and Party Formation in Third Republic France, Weimar Germany and Post-Soviet Russia* (Cambridge: Cambridge University Press, 2010), 144–45.

6 'German National People's Party Programme (1931)' in Anton Kaes, Martin Jay and Edward Dimendberg (eds.), *The Weimar Republic Sourcebook* (Berkeley: University of California Press, 1994), 349.

7 See Larry Eugene Jones, 'German Conservatism at the Crossroads: Count Kuno von Westarp and the Struggle for Control of the DNVP, 1928–30', *Contemporary European History*, 18, No. 2 (2009), 147–77.

8 Peter Fritzsche, 'The NSDAP 1919–1934: From Fringe Politics to the Seizure of Power' in Jane Caplan, *Nazi Germany* (Oxford: Oxford University Press, 2008), 54.

9 'The Twenty-five Points' in Kaes, Jay and Dimendberg (eds.), *The Weimar Republic Sourcebook*, 124–26.

10 For the Magdeburg libel trial and its consequences see Bernd Fulda, *Press and Politics in the Weimar Republic* (Oxford: Oxford University Press, 2009), 80–9, George S. Vascik and Mark R. Sadler (eds.), *The Stab-in-the-Back Myth and the Fall of the Weimar Republic: a History in Documents and Visual Sources* (London, 2016), Chapter 9 and Richard J. Evans, *The Hitler Conspiracies* (London: Bloomsbury, 2020), 67–8.

11 Von der Goltz, *Hindenburg*, 84.

12 Ibid., 84–93, 96–102.

13 Ibid., 126.

14 Eberhard Kolb, *The Weimar Republic (Second Edition)* (P. S. Falla and R. J. Park, trans.) (Abingdon: Routledge, 2005), 76.

15 Zara Steiner, *The Lights That Failed: European International History, 1919–1933* (Oxford: Oxford University Press, 2005), 387.

16 Jonathan Wright, 'Stresemann and Locarno', *Contemporary European History*, 4, No. 2 (1995), 121.

17 Jonathan Wright, *Gustav Stresemann: Weimar's Greatest Statesman* (Oxford: Oxford University Press, 2002), 270.

18 Wright, 'Stresemann and Locarno', 123–24.

19 See David Cameron and Anthony Heywood, 'Germany, Russia and Locarno: The German-Soviet Trade Treaty of 12 October 1925' in Gaynor Johnson (ed.), *Locarno Revisited: European Diplomacy 1920–29* (London: Routledge, 2004).

20 Steiner, *The Lights That Failed*, 573.

21 Siegfried Kracauer, *The Salaried Masses: Duty and Distraction in Weimar Germany* (Quintin Hoare, trans.) (London: Verso, 1998), 43.

22 Ibid., 25.

23 For more on Weimar 'organizationalism' and economic institutions and interest groups, see Harold James, 'The Weimar Economy' in Anthony McElligott (ed.), *Weimar Germany* (Oxford: Oxford University Press, 2009), 106, and Niall Ferguson, 'The German Inter-War Economy: Political Choice Versus Economic Determinism' in Mary Fulbrook (ed.), *Germany Since 1800* (London: Arnold, 1997), 269–70.

24 See Albrecht Ritschl, *Deutschlands Krise und Konjunktur 1924–1934: Binnenkonjunktur, Auslandsverschuldung und Reparationsproblem zweichen Dawes-Plan und Transferperre* (Berlin: De Gruyter, 2002).

25 Hanson, *Post-Imperial Democracies*, 128.

26 Anthony McElligott, 'Introduction' in McElligott (ed.), *Weimar Germany*, 2.

27 Count Harry Kessler, *The Diaries of a Cosmopolitan, 1918–1937* (Charles Kessler, trans.) (London: Phoenix Press, 2000), 184.

28 Anthony McElligott, 'Political Culture' in McElligott (ed.), *Weimar Germany*, 29.

29 See Eric D. Weitz, *Weimar Germany: Promise and Tragedy* (Princeton: Princeton University Press, 2007), 92–101 and Robert Gerwarth, 'The Past in Weimar History', *Contemporary European History*, 15, No. 1 (2006), 8–10.

30 Eric Bryden, 'Heroes and Martyrs of the Republic: Reichsbanner *Geschichtspolitik* in Weimar Germany', *Central European History*, 43, No. 4 (2010), 646, 663.

31 Nadine Rossol, *Performing the Nation in Interwar Germany: Sport, Spectacle and Political Symbolism, 1926–1936* (Basingstoke: Palgrave, 2010), 81.

32 For the history of Germany's national anthem and the controversies surrounding this and other national symbols, see Michael E. Geisler, 'In the Shadow of Exceptionalism: Germany's National Symbols and Public Memory after 1989' in Michael E. Geisler (ed.), *National Symbols, Fractured Identities: Contesting the National Narrative* (Lebanon: Middlebury College Press, 2005), 63–100.

33 Nadine Rossol, 'Performing the Nation: Sports, Spectacles, and Aesthetics in Germany, 1926–1936', *Central European History*, 43, No. 4 (2010), 630.

34 Manuela Achilles, 'With a Passion for Reason: Celebrating the Constitution in Weimar Germany', *Central European History*, 43, No. 4 (2010), 670.

35 Rossol, 'Performing the Nation', *Central European History*, 620.

36 Achilles, 'With a Passion for Reason', 684; Rossol, *Performing the Nation*, 66–71.

37 For a detailed discussion of this campaign, see Alexander Otto-Morris, *Rebellion in the Province: The Landvolkbewegung and the Rise of National Socialism in Schleswig-Holstein* (Frankfurt am Main: Peter Lang, 2013).

38 See Chris Bowlby, 'Blutmai 1929: Police, Parties and Proletarians in a Berlin Confrontation', *The Historical Journal*, 29, No. 1 (1986), 137–58.

39 Anthony McElligott, *Rethinking the Weimar Republic* (London: Bloomsbury, 2014), 77.

CHAPTER 4

1 Stephan Malinowsky, *Nazis and Nobles: The History of a Misalliance* (Oxford: Oxford University Press, 2020), 10.

2 For more on the identity and outlook of the *Junker* class, see Christopher Clark, *Iron Kingdom: The Rise and Downfall of Prussia, 1600–1947* (London: Allen Lane, 2006), 155–69 and Giles MacDonogh, *Prussia: The Perversion of an Idea* (London: Mandarin, 1995), 231–54.

3 Malinowsky, *Nazis and Nobles*, 333.

4 See Anthony McElligott, *Rethinking the Weimar Republic* (London: Bloomsbury, 2014), 160–64.

5 See Karl Demeter, *The German Officer-Corps in Society and State 1650–1945* (Angus Malcolm, trans.) (London: Weidenfeld & Nicolson, 1965), 47–58, Gordon A. Craig, *The Politics of the Prussian Army 1645–1945* (New York: Oxford University Press, 1964), 393–96, and David Stone, *Fighting for the Fatherland: The Story of the German Soldier from 1648 to the Present Day* (London: Conway, 2006), 308.

6 David B. Southern, 'The Impact of the Inflation: Inflation, the Courts and Revaluation' in Richard Bessel and E. J. Feuchtwanger (eds.), *Social Change and Political Development in Weimar Germany* (London: Routledge, 1981), 55.

7 See Bernd Widdig, 'Cultural Capital in Decline: Inflation and the Distress of Intellectuals' in Kathleen Canning, Kerstin Brandt and Kristin McGuire (eds.), *Weimar Publics/Weimar Subjects: Rethinking the Political Culture of Germany in the 1920s* (Oxford: Berghahn Books, 2010), 302–17.

8 Matthew Stibbe, *Germany 1914–33: Politics, Society and Culture* (Harlow: Pearson Education, 2010), 114.

9 See Siegfried Kracauer, *The Salaried Masses* (Quintin Hoare, trans.) (London: Verso, 1998).

10 Pamela E. Swett, 'The Industrial Working Class' in Nadine Rossol and Benjamin Ziemann (eds.), *The Oxford Handbook of the Weimar Republic* (Oxford: Oxford University Press, 2022), 476–79.

11 Stibbe, *Germany*, 112.

12 Paul Bookbinder, *Weimar Germany: The Republic of the Reasonable* (Manchester: Manchester University Press, 1996), 158.

13 'Constitution of the German Reich' in Howard Lee McBain and Lindsay Rogers (eds. and trans.), *The New Constitutions of Europe* (Garden City, NY: Doubleday, 1922), 199.

14 Laurie Marhoefer, 'Did Sex Bring Down the Weimar Republic?', *Bulletin of the German Historical Institute*, 65 (2019), 62.

15 Ibid.

16 Paul Ginsborg, *Family Politics: Domestic Life, Devastation and Survival, 1900–1950* (New Haven: Yale University Press, 2014), 336.

17 Ibid., 345.

18 Ute Planert, 'Weimar Bodies: Gender, Sexuality, and Reproduction' in Rossol and Ziemann (eds.), *The Oxford Handbook of the Weimar Republic*, 531; Vibeke Rützou Petersen, *Women and Modernity in Weimar Germany* (New York: Berghahn Books, 2001), 21.

19 Petersen, *Women and Modernity in Weimar Germany*, 21–2.

20 Planert, 'Weimar Bodies' in Rossol and Ziemann (eds.), *The Oxford Handbook of the Weimar Republic*, 528.

21 Eric Weitz, *Weimar Germany: Promise and Tragedy* (Princeton: Princeton University Press, 2007), 56.

22 See Julia Sneeringer, 'The Shopper as Voter: Women, Advertising and Politics in Post-Inflation Germany', *German Studies Review*, 27, No. 2 (2004), 476–501.

23 Tim Mason, 'Women in Germany, 1925–1940: Family, Welfare, Work', *History Workshop Journal*, 1 (1976), 78–80.

24 Dagmar Reese, *Growing Up Female in Nazi Germany* (Ann Arbor: University of Michigan Press, 2006), 48, 192.

25 For a comparative perspective on issues of gender and sexuality during this period, see Alys Eve Winterbaum, Lynn M. Thomas, Priti Ramamurthy, Uta G. Poger and Tani E. Barlow (eds.), *The Modern Girl Around the World: Consumption, Modernity and Globalization* (Durham, NC: Duke University Press, 2008).

26 See Laurie Marhofer, 'Degeneration, Sexual Freedom, and the Politics of the Weimar Republic', *German Studies Review*, 34, No. 3 (2011), 532.

27 For the campaign for abortion reform in Weimar Germany, see Anita Grossmann, *Reforming Sex: The German Movement for Birth Control and Abortion Reform, 1920–1950* (Oxford: Oxford University Press, 1995). For the decriminalization of prostitution see Julia Roos, *Weimar through the Lens of Gender: Prostitution Reform, Woman's Emancipation and German Democracy, 1919–33* (Ann Arbor: University of Michigan Press, 2010).

28 *Strafgesetzbuch für das Deutsche Reich* (1871) https://de.wikisource.org/wiki/Strafgesetzbuch_f%C3%BCr_das_Deutsche_Reich_(1871)#%C2%A7_175. (accessed 11/11/2022).

29 See Mel Gordon, *Voluptuous Panic: The Erotic World of Weimar Berlin* (Los Angeles: Feral House, 2001), 92–4.

30 See John Chancellor, *How to be Happy in Berlin* (London: Arrowsmith, 1929), 136–37. For more on British 'sex tourism' see Colin Storer, *Britain and the Weimar Republic: The History of a Cultural Relationship* (London: I B Tauris, 2010), Chapter 1.

31 Katie Sutton, 'Sexological Cases and the Prehistory of Transgender Identity Politics in Interwar Germany' in Joy Damousi, Birgit Lang and Katie Sutton (eds.), *Case Studies and the Dissemination of Knowledge* (Abingdon: Routledge, 2015), 85.

32 Quoted in Katie Sutton, '"We Too Deserve a Place in the Sun": The Politics of Transvestite Identity in Weimar Germany', *German Studies Review*, 35, No. 2 (2012), 338.

33 See Jasmine Bhinder and Prashant Upadhyaya, 'A Brief History of Gender Affirmation Medicine and Surgery' in Dmitry Nikolavsky and Stephen A. Blakey (eds.), *Urological Care for the Transgender Patient* (Cham: Palgrave, 2021), 251; Lili Elbe, *Man into Woman: A Comparative Scholarly Edition* (London: Bloomsbury, 2020); Sabine Meyer, '*Wie Lili zu einem richtigen Mädchen wurde*' – *Lili Elbe: Zur Konstruktion von Geschlecht und Identität zwischen Medialisierung, Regulierung und Subjektivierung* (Bielefeld: Transcript, 2015).

34 Sutton, '"We Too Deserve a Place in the Sun"', 344.

35 Marhoefer, 'Did Sex Bring Down the Weimar Republic?', 62.

36 See James Kollenbroich, *Our Hour Has Come: The Homosexual Rights Movement in the Weimar Republic* (Saarbrücken: VDM Verlag, 2007); Marhofer, 'Degeneration', 538–39.

37 Klaus J. Bade and Jochen Oltmer, 'Germany' in Klaus J. Bade, Pieter C. Emmer, Leo Lucassen and Jochen Oltmer (eds.), *The Encyclopedia of Migration and Minorities in Europe: From the Seventeenth Century to the Present*, 2nd edition (Cambridge: Cambridge University Press, 2013), 70.

38 Robbie Aitken and Eve Rosenhaft, *Black Germany: The Making and Unmaking of a Diaspora, 1884–1960* (Cambridge: Cambridge University Press, 2013), 2.

39 Annemarie Sammartino, 'Culture, Belonging and Law: Naturalisation in the Weimar Republic' in Geoff Eley and Jan Palmowski (eds.), *Citizenship and National Identity in Twentieth-Century Germany* (Stanford: Stanford University Press, 2008), 61.

40 Ibid.

41 Sharon Gillerman, 'German Jews in the Weimar Republic' in Rossol and Ziemann (eds.), *The Oxford Handbook of the Weimar Republic*, 567.

42 Anthony D. Kauders, 'Weimar Jewry' in Anthony McElligott (ed.), *Weimar Germany* (Oxford: Oxford University Press, 2009), 238.

43 Donald L. Niewyk, *The Jews in Weimar Germany* (New York: Routledge, 2017), 1.

44 Jan Rybak, 'Emancipation and Constitutional Patriotism: The Centralverein and the Weimar Republican Order', *German History*, 40, No. 4 (2022), 525.

45 Ibid., 521–2, 534.

46 Susanne Wein and Martin Ulmer, 'Antisemitism in the Weimar Republic' in Rossol and Ziemann (eds.), *The Oxford Handbook of the Weimar Republic*, 405.

47 Ibid., 416–17.

48 See Mischa Honeck, Martin Klimke, and Anne Kuhlmann (eds.), *Germany and the Black Diaspora: Points of Contact, 1250–1914* (New York: Berghahn Books, 2013).

49 Fatima El-Tayeb, 'Dangerous Liaisons: Race, Nation and German Identity' in Patricia Mazón and Reinhild Steingröver (eds.), *Not so Plain as Black and White: Afro-German Culture and History, 1890–2000* (Rochester: University of Rochester Press, 2005), 29.

50 For more on the so-called 'Black Horror on the Rhine', see Iris Wigger, *The 'Black Horror on the Rhine': Intersections of Race, Nation, Gender and Class in 1920s Germany* (London: Palgrave, 2017) and Peter Collar, *The Propaganda War in the Rhineland: Weimar Germany, Race and Occupation after World War I* (London: I B Tauris, 2014).

51 'Founding Articles of the African Welfare Association' (1918) https://blackcentraleurope.com/sources/1914-1945/founding-a-african-self-help-association-1918/ (accessed 15/12/2022).

52 John Bingham, 'The "Urban Republic"' in McElligott (ed.), *Weimar Germany*, 127.

53 Weitz, *Weimar Germany*, 41.

54 Franz Hessel, *Walking in Berlin* (Amanda DeMarco, trans.) (London: Scribe, 2016), 7.

55 Adelheid von Saldern, '"Neues Wohnen": Housing and Reform' in McElligott (ed.), *Weimar Germany*, 210.
56 Weitz, *Weimar Germany*, 43.
57 Sneeringer, 'The Shopper as Voter', 478.
58 Bingham, 'The "Urban Republic"', 129.
59 Giles MacDonough, *Berlin* (London: St. Martin's Press, 1997), 214.
60 Detlev Peukert, *The Weimar Republic* (London: Penguin, 1993), 150. See also Richard Wetzell, *Inventing the Criminal: A History of German Criminology, 1880–1945* (Chapel Hill: University of North Carolina Press, 2000), 109–20.
61 Victoria Harris, *Selling Sex in the Reich: Prostitutes in German Society, 1914–1945* (Oxford: Oxford University Press, 2010), 55.
62 Sace Elder, *Murder Scenes: Normality, Deviance and Criminal Violence in Weimar Berlin* (Ann Arbor: University of Michigan Press, 2010), 7.
63 Ibid., 3.
64 For a comparative perspective on Weimar crime and detection rates see James F. Richardson, 'Berlin Police in the Weimar Republic: A Comparison with Police Forces in Cities of the United States' in George L. Mosse (ed.), *Police Forces in History* (London: Sage, 1975), 82; Hsi-huey Liang, *The Berlin Police Force of the Weimar Republic* (Berkeley: University of California Press, 1970), Chapters 3 and 4.
65 Todd Herzog, *Crime Stories: Criminalistic Fantasy and the Culture of Crisis in Weimar Germany* (New York: Berghahn Books, 2009), 2–3.

CHAPTER 5

1 David Clay Large, *Berlin: A Modern History* (London: Allen Lane, 2001), 158.
2 Walter Laqueur, *Weimar: A Cultural History 1918–1933* (London: Phoenix Press, 2000), 183.
3 Eric Weitz, *Weimar Germany: Promise and Tragedy* (Princeton: Princeton University Press, 2007), 253.
4 Gustav Frank, 'Beyond the Republic? Post-Expressionist Complexity in the Arts' in Jochen Hung, Godela Weiss-Sussex and Geoff Wilkes (eds.), *Beyond Glitter and Doom: The Contingency of the Weimar Republic* (Munich: Iudicium, 2012), 48.
5 Karl Christian Führer, 'High Brow and Low Brow Culture' in Anthony McElligott (ed.), *Weimar Germany* (Oxford: Oxford University Press, 2009), 261.
6 Gustav Hartlaub in Paul Westheim, 'Ein Neue Naturalismus? Eine Rundfrage des Kunstblatts', *Der Kunstblatt*, No. 9 (1922), quoted in Matthew Gale and

Katy Wan, *Magic Realism: Art in Weimar Germany, 1919–1933* (London: Tate Publishing, 2018), 15.

7 Weitz, *Weimar Germany*, 293.

8 Laqueur, *Weimar*, 183.

9 Peter Watson, *The German Genius* (London: Simon & Schuster, 2010), 35.

10 See Tara Windsor, 'Extended Arm of Reich Foreign Policy? Literary Internationalisms, Cultural Diplomacies and the First German PEN Club in the Weimar Republic', *Contemporary European History*, 30, No. 2 (2021), 181–97; Elana Passman, 'Civic Activism and the Pursuit of Cooperation in the Locarno Era' in Carine Germond and Henning Turk (eds.), *A History of Franco-German Relations in Europe: From 'Hereditary Enemies' to Partners* (Basingstoke: Palgrave, 2008), and Conan Fischer, *A Vision of Europe: Franco-German Relations during the Great Depression, 1929–1932* (Oxford: Oxford University Press, 2017), 29–36.

11 Corey Ross, 'Cinema, Radio, and "Mass Culture" in the Weimar Republic: Between Shared Experience and Social Division' in John Alexander Williams (ed.), *Weimar Culture Revisited* (New York: Palgrave, 2011), 23.

12 Jochen Hung, 'Mass Culture' in Nadine Rossol and Benjamin Ziemann, *The Oxford Handbook of the Weimar Republic* (Oxford: Oxford University Press, 2020), 611.

13 Ross, 'Cinema, Radio, and "Mass Culture"', 25–6.

14 Ibid., 27.

15 Ibid., 35.

16 Karl Christian Führer, 'A Medium of Modernity? Broadcasting in Weimar Germany, 1923–1932', *The Journal of Modern History*, 69, No. 4 (1997), 731.

17 Ross, 'Cinema, Radio, and "Mass Culture"', 28.

18 Robert Nippoldt and Boris Pofalla, *Night Falls on the Berlin of the Roaring Twenties* (Cologne: Taschen, 2018), 336.

19 Frank Warschauer, 'Jazz: On Whiteman's Berlin Concerts' in Anton Kaes, Martin Jay and Edward Dwimendberg (eds.), *The Weimar Republic Sourcebook* (Berkeley: University of California Press, 1994), 571.

20 Jonathan O. Wipplinger, *Jazz Republic: Music, Race and American Culture in Weimar Germany* (Ann Arbor: University of Michigan Press, 2017), 2.

21 Warschauer, 'Jazz', 572.

22 Alice Gerstel, 'Jazz Band' in Kaes, Jay and Dwimendberg (eds.), *The Weimar Republic Sourcebook*, 554–55.

23 Kurt Tucholsky, *Jazz und Shimmy: Brevier der neuesten Tänzen* (1921) quoted in Rainer Metzger, *Berlin in the Twenties: Art and Culture, 1918–1933* (London: Thames & Hudson, 2007), 268.

24 See Michael H. Kater, 'The Jazz Experience in Weimar Germany', *German History*, 6, No. 2 (1988), 145–47.

25 Count Harry Kessler, *The Diaries of a Cosmopolitan, 1918–1937* (Charles Kessler, trans.) (London: Phoenix Press, 2000), 390.

26 Brendan Fay, *Classical Music in the Weimar Republic* (London: Bloomsbury, 2020), 55.

27 Joseph Roth, *What I Saw* (London: Granta, 2003), 41.

28 Siegfried Kracauer, *The Mass Ornament: Weimar Essays* (Cambridge, MA: Harvard University Press, 1995), 325.

29 Nippoldt and Pofalla, *Night Falls*, 10.

30 Rüdiger Graf, 'Anticipating the Future in the Present: "New Women" and Other Beings of the Future in Weimar Germany', *Central European History*, 42, No. 4 (2009), 650–51.

31 Conrad Felixmüller quoted in Rhys W. Williams, 'Conrad Felixmüller: The Literary and Cultural Milieu' in Shulamith Behr and Amanda Wadsley (eds.), *Conrad Felixmüller 1897–1977: Between Politics and the Studio* (Leicester: Leicestershire Museums Arts & Records Service, 1994), 28.

32 Richard Murphy, 'Expressionism' in David Bradshaw and Kevin J. H. Dettmar (eds.), *A Companion to Modernist Literature and Culture* (Chichester: Wiley-Blackwell, 2008), 200.

33 Peter Childs, *Modernism*, 3rd edition (London: Routledge, 2017), 126.

34 Laqueur, *Weimar*, 114.

35 Sergiusz Michalski, *New Objectivity: Painting, Graphic Art and Photography in Weimar Germany 1919–1933* (Michael Claridge, trans.) (Cologne: Taschen, 2003), 20, 16

36 Ibid., 18.

37 Dorothy C. Rowe, *After Dada: Marta Hegemann and the Cologne Avant-Garde* (Manchester: University of Manchester Press, 2013), 80. See also Helmut Lethen, *Cool Conduct: The Culture of Distance in Weimar Germany* (Berkeley: University of California Press, 2002).

38 See Matthew Jeffries, '*Lebensreform*: A Middle-Class Antidote to Wilhelminism?' in Geoff Eley and James Retallack (eds.), *Wilhelminism and its Legacies: German Modernities, Imperialism, and the Meanings of Reform, 1890–1930: Essays for Hartmut Pogge von Strandmann* (New York: Berghahn Books, 2008).

39 Berghard Schmidt, 'German Irrationalism during Weimar', *Telos*, 65 (1985), 88.

40 Quoted in Tom Neuhaus, 'How Can War be Holy? Weimar Attitudes Toward Eastern Spirituality' in Williams (ed.), *Weimar Culture Revisited*, 127.

41 See Corinna Treitel, *A Science for the Soul: Occultism and the Genesis of the German Modern* (Baltimore: Johns Hopkins University Press, 2004),

56–131; Nicholas Goodrick-Clarke, *The Occult Roots of Nazism* (London: I B Tauris, 2009), 123–204; Jay Lockenour, *Dragonslayer: The Legend of Erich Ludendorff in the Weimar Republic and Third Reich* (Ithaca: Cornell University Press, 2021), 118–24.

42 Neuhaus, 'How Can War be Holy?', 118–22.

43 See Heather Wolffram, 'Crime, Clairvoyance and the Weimar Police', *Journal of Contemporary History*, 44, No. 4 (2009), 581–601; Treitel, *A Science for the Soul*, Chapter 6 and Peter S. Fisher, *Weimar Controversies: Explorations in Popular Culture with Siegfried Kracauer* (Bielefeld: Transcript, 2020), Chapter 1.

44 Franz Roh, quoted in Rowe, *After Dada*, 149.

45 Joachim Fest, *Hitler* (London: Weidenfeld & Nicolson, 1996), 74. See also Siegfried Kracauer, *From Caligari to Hitler: A Psychological History of the German Film* (Princeton: Princeton University Press, 2004).

46 Laqueur, *Weimar*, 121–40.

47 Marsha Meskimmon, 'Domesticity and Dissent: The Dynamics of Women Realists in the Weimar Republic' in Amanda Wadsley (ed.), *Domesticity and Dissent: The Role of Women Artists in Germany 1918 to 1938* (Leicester: Leicestershire Museums Arts & Records Service, 1992), 24.

48 Helen Boak, *Women in the Weimar Republic* (Manchester: Manchester University Press, 2013), 255.

49 Elinor Beaven, 'Regional Women Artists and the Artist as Mother: Elsa Haensgen-Dingkuhn (1898–1991)', *Art History*, 42, No. 4 (2019), 729.

50 Ibid., 735.

51 Guenter Lewy, *Jews and Germans: Promise, Tragedy, and the Search for Normalcy* (Philadelphia: University of Nebraska Press, 2020), 174.

52 Michael Brenner, *The Renaissance of Jewish Culture in Weimar Germany* (New Haven and London: Yale University Press, 1996), 219.

53 Ibid., 54–5, 61.

54 Robert S. Abbott, 'My Trip Abroad VIII: The Negro in Berlin', *Chicago Defender*, 28 December 1929.

55 Tobias Nagl, 'Louis Brody and the Black Presence in German Film before 1945' in Patricia Mazon and Reinhild Steingrover (eds.), *Not So Plain as Black and White: Afro-German Culture and History, 1890–2000* (Rochester: University of Rochester Press, 2005), 109.

56 Robbie Aitken and Eve Rosenhaft, *Black Germany: The Making and Unmaking of a Diaspora Community, 1884–1960* (Cambridge: Cambridge University Press, 2013), 146.

57 Wipplinger, *Jazz Republic*, 34.

58 Aitken and Rosenhaft, *Black Germany*, 146.

59 Nagl, 'Louis Brody', 117.

60 Aitken and Rosenhaft, *Black Germany*, 152.

61 'The Constitution of the German Republic' in Kaes, Jay and Dimendberg (eds.), *The Weimar Republic Sourcebook*, 50.

62 Martin Loiperdinger, 'Film Censorship in Germany' in Daniel Biltereyst and Roel Vande Winkel (eds.), *Silencing Cinema* (Basingstoke: Palgrave, 2013), 82–6.

63 Margaret F. Stieg, 'The 1926 German Law to Protect Youth against Trash and Dirt: Moral Protectionism in a Democracy', *Central European History*, 23, No. 1 (1990), 55.

64 Hugh Ridley, 'The Culture of Weimar: Models of Decline' in Michael Laffan (ed.), *The Burden of German History, 1919–45* (London: Methuen, 1988), 11.

65 Kurt Sontheimer, 'Weimar Culture' in Laffan (ed.), *The Burden of German History, 1919–45*, 7–8.

CHAPTER 6

1 Theo Balderston, *Politics and Economics in the Weimar Republic* (Cambridge: Cambridge University Press, 2002), 82.

2 Geoff Layton, *From Bismarck to Hitler* (London: Hodder & Stoughton, 1995), 132.

3 Heinrich Hauser, 'The Unemployed' (1933) in Anton Kaes, Martin Jay and Edward Dimendberg (eds.), *The Weimar Republic Sourcebook* (Berkeley: University of California Press, 1994), 84.

4 Ibid.

5 William L. Patch, *Heinrich Brüning and the Dissolution of the Weimar Republic* (Cambridge: Cambridge University Press, 1998), 73.

6 Ibid., 83.

7 Matthew Stibbe, *Germany 1914–1933* (Harlow: Pearson Education, 2010), 172.

8 Patch, *Heinrich Brüning*, 221.

9 'Herr Stresemann', *The Times*, 4 October 1929, 15.

10 Count Harry Kessler, *The Diaries of a Cosmopolitan 1918–1937* (London: Phoenix Press, 2000), 368.

11 Wolfgang J. Helbich, 'Between Stresemann and Hitler: The Foreign Policy of the Brüning Government', *World Politics*, 12, No. 1 (1959), 26.

12 See Anthony McElligott, *Rethinking the Weimar Republic* (London: Bloomsbury, 2014), 88.

13 Patch, *Heinrich Brüning*, 151.

14 Conan Fischer, *A Vision of Europe: Franco-German Relations during the Great Depression, 1929–1932* (Oxford: Oxford University Press, 2017), 88.

15 Ibid., 106.

16 Hartmut Mehringer, 'Die KPD in Bayern 1919–1945' in Martin Broszat and Hartmut Mehringer (eds.), *Bayern in der NS-Zeit: Studien und Dokumentation. Vol. V: Die Partien KPD, SPD, BVP in Verfolgung und Widerstand* (Munich: De Gruyter, 1983), 27 (Table 3).

17 Peter Fritzsche, 'The NSDAP 1919–1934: From Fringe Politics to the Seizure of Power' in Jane Caplan, *Nazi Germany* (Oxford: Oxford University Press, 2008), 51.

18 Ibid., 60–6.

19 Ian Kershaw, *Hitler 1889–1936* (London: Allen Lane, 1998), 201.

20 Eve Rosenhaft, *Beating the Fascists? The German Communists and Political Violence, 1929–1933* (Cambridge: Cambridge University Press, 1983), 6; Dirk Schumann, *Political Violence in the Weimar Republic, 1918–1933* (Thomas Dunlap, trans.) (New York: Berghahn Books, 2009), 252, 223, 312.

21 The German phrase he used was 'ein dauernder Appell an den inneren Schweinehund im Menschen.' Document 19: 'The appeal to the inner bastard.' Speech on 23 February 1932 in the German Reichstag. Minutes of the Reichstag, 57th session of 23 February 1932, p. 2254f. Friedrich Ebert Stiftung https://www.fes.de/fulltext/historiker/00781a20.htm (accessed 19/12/2022).

22 Geoff Layton, *Germany: The Third Reich, 1933–1945* (Trowbridge: Hodder & Stoughton, 1992), 40.

23 Thomas Childers, *The Nazi Voter: The Social Foundations of Fascism in Germany 1919–1933* (Chapel Hill: University of North Carolina Press, 1983), 266.

24 Ibid., 264–5.

25 Jürgen Falter, *Hitler's Wähler* (Munich: C H Beck, 1991), 220–29.

26 Childers, *The Nazi Voter*, 268.

27 Peter Fritzsche, 'Did Weimar Fail?', *The Journal of Modern History*, 68, No. 3 (1996), 642.

28 Richard J. Evans, *The Coming of the Third Reich* (London: Penguin, 2003), 264–65.

29 'The Money Market', *The Economist*, 18 July 1931, 102.

30 For a recent discussion of the 1931 banking crisis and its impact, see Tobias Straumann, *1931: Debt, Crisis and the Rise of Hitler* (Oxford: Oxford University Press, 2021).

31 See Larry Eugene Jones, 'Nationalists, Nazis, and the Assault against Weimar: Revisiting the Harzburg Rally of October 1931', *German Studies Review*, 29, No. 3 (2006), 483–94.

32 Larry Eugene Jones, *Hitler Versus Hindenburg: The 1932 Presidential Elections and the End of the Weimar Republic* (Cambridge: Cambridge University Press, 2016), 359.

33 For a discussion of the different ways in which the concept of leadership was conceived and employed in Weimar political discourse see Simon Unger-Alvi,

'"Leaders not Lords": *Führertum*, Democracy and Nazism in the Weimar Republic', *German History*, 39, No. 4 (2021), 560–84.

34 Jones, *Hitler Versus Hindenburg*, 361.

35 See Anna von der Goltz, *Hindenburg: Power, Myth, and the Rise of the Nazis* (Oxford: Oxford University Press, 2009), 144–46 and Jürgen W. Falter, 'The Two Hindenburg Elections of 1925 and 1932: A Total Reversal of Voter Coalitions', *Central European History*, 23, No. 2–3 (1990), 225–41.

36 Evans, *The Coming of the Third Reich*, 270.

37 Schumann, *Political Violence*, 256.

38 Benjamin Carter Hett, *The Death of Democracy: Hitler's Rise to Power* (London: William Heinemann, 2018), 144–47.

39 Larry Eugene Jones, 'Franz von Papen, the German Centre Party, and the Failure of Catholic Conservatism in the Weimar Republic', *Central European History*, 38, No. 2 (2005), 206.

40 Patch, *Heinrich Brüning*, 276.

41 Evans, *The Coming of the Third Reich*, 270.

42 Gordon Craig, *The Politics of the Prussian Army 1650–1945* (New York: Oxford University Press, 1964), 456.

43 Henry Ashby Turner, *Hitler's Thirty Days to Power* (Reading: Addison-Wesley Publishing, 1996), 15–16.

44 Ibid., 19.

45 Peter Hayes, '"A Question Mark with Epaulettes"? Kurt von Schleicher and Weimar Politics', *The Journal of Modern History*, 52, No. 1 (1980), 37–8. See also Turner, *Hitler's Thirty Days to Power*, 20–1.

46 Layton, *Germany: The Third Reich*, 48.

CONCLUSION

1 See, for example, Jochen Hung, Godela Weiss-Sussex and Geoff Wilkes (eds.), *Beyond Glitter and Doom: The Contingency of the Weimar Republic* (Munich: Iudicum, 2012).

2 Eric D. Weitz, 'Weimar Germany and its Histories', *Central European History*, 43, No. 4 (2010), 582.

3 Laurie Marhoefer, 'Did Sex Bring Down the Weimar Republic?', *Bulletin of the German Historical Institute*, 65 (2019), 71.

4 Eric D. Weitz, *Weimar Germany: Promise and Tragedy* (Princeton: Princeton University Press, 2007), 364.

5 Ibid., 364.

6 Weitz, 'Weimar Germany and its Histories', 582.

7 Peter Fritzsche, 'Did Weimar Fail?', *The Journal of Modern History*, 68, No. 3 (1996), 630.

Further Reading

The literature on the Weimar Republic in English alone is huge and grows every year. What follows is therefore not intended to be an exhaustive list of all the books, articles and websites consulted in the writing of this book (references to many of which can be found in the notes), let alone of the literature in its entirety. Rather it is intended as a guide to further reading for Anglophone readers who wish to explore the subject in more depth.

Over the years, numerous single-volume histories of Weimar Germany have been published. Perhaps the most influential have been Detlev Peukert's (Richard Deveson, trans.), *The Weimar Republic: The Crisis of Classical Modernity* (London: Penguin, 1992) and Hans Mommsen's (Elborg Forster and Larry Eugene Jones, trans.) *The Rise and Fall of the Weimar Republic* (Chapel Hill: University of North Carolina Press, 1996). Although in some respects now a little dated, both continue to offer incisive thought-provoking analyses. Eric Weitz blends political and social/cultural history in his highly readable *Weimar Germany: Promise and Tragedy* (Princeton University Press, 2007), while Anthony McElligott's *Rethinking the Weimar Republic* (London: Bloomsbury, 2014) seeks to reassess the history of the period by looking at a range of subjects through the prism of 'authority'. Frank McDonough's *The Weimar Years: Rise and Fall, 1918–1933* (London: Apollo, 2023) provides an excellent illustrated, year-by-year narrative history of the republic. C. Paul Vincent's *A Historical Dictionary of Germany's Weimar Republic, 1918–1933* (Westport: Greenwood Press, 1997) is an invaluable work of reference, while the essays in Nadine Rossol and Benjamin Ziemann (eds.), *The Oxford Handbook of the Weimar Republic* (Oxford: OUP, 2022) and Anthony McElligott (ed.), *Weimar Germany* (Oxford: OUP, 2009) provide excellent introductions to individual topics.

For those who want to get back to the original documents, more and more primary source material has become available in English translation in recent years. Anton Kaes, Martin Jay and Edward Dimendberg (eds.), *The Weimar Republic Sourcebook* (Berkeley: University of California Press, 1994) provides an excellent range of sources on all aspects of the republic and should be the go-to volume for those who wish to read about the republic in the words of those who lived through it. For those interested in the history of the German left, during and after the revolution of 1918–19, Gabriel Kuhn (ed. and trans.), *All Power to the Councils! A Documentary History of the German Revolution of 1918–1919* (Oakland: PM Press, 2012) and Ben Fowkes (ed.), *The German Left and the Weimar Republic: A Selection of Documents* (Chicago: Haymarket Books, 2015) provide a good selection of documents. Count Harry Kessler (Charles Kessler, trans.), *The Diaries of a Cosmopolitan, 1918–1937* (London: Phoenix Press, 2000) is the day-by-day account of the life of the well-connected aristocratic diarist, as well as commentary on political and cultural developments that he witnessed. Josef Roth's (Michael Hofmann, trans.) *What I Saw* (London: Granta, 2003) is a good selection of the Austrian author's journalism written in and about Berlin between 1920 and 1933, while Franz Hessel, *Walking in Berlin* (Amanda DeMarco, trans.) (London: Scribe, 2016) gives the author's view of the German capital in the form of a 'walking tour' of the city. Both are accessible to general readers and give some sense of what life was like for 'ordinary people' during the Weimar years. *Billy Wilder on Assignment: Dispatches from Weimar Berlin and Interwar Vienna*, edited by Noah Isenberg (Princeton: Princeton University Press, 2021), is a selection of the Hollywood director's journalism and film reviews from his time as a journalist in Weimar Germany, while Siegfried Kracauer (Thomas Y. Levin, trans.), *The Mass Ornament: Weimar Essays* (Cambridge: Harvard University Press, 1995) collects some of the author's cultural criticism from his time working on the *Frankfurter Zeitung* in the 1920s. Determined students can also track down the memoirs of many of the key political and cultural figures of the time, though most are no longer in print.

A good way to get a 'feel' of any period of history is to read the fiction produced during it. This often, consciously or unconsciously gives a sense of some of the details of what it was like to live during the era as well as the issues that concerned people and (sometimes) commentary on political and social events. Works by most of the well-known authors of the Weimar period (Thomas Mann, Erich Maria Remarque, Erich Kästner, Alfred Döblin, Vicki Baum, Ernst Jünger, etc.) can be read in English translation. Particularly recommended are Irmgard Keun (Kathie von Ankum, trans.), *The Artificial Silk Girl* (London: Penguin, 2019) and Vick Baum (Basil Creighton and Margot Bettauer Dembo, trans.) *Grand Hotel* (New York: New York Review of Books, 2016). Most of the films mentioned in this book (and elsewhere) can also be found on YouTube or are available on Blu-ray or DVD (or to stream) via the BFI or the Eureka 'Masters of Cinema' range.

Roger Chickering's *Imperial Germany and the Great War, 1914–1918* (Third Edition) (Cambridge: Cambridge University Press, 2014) is perhaps the best concise history of Germany's experience of the conflict that gave birth to the republic, while Alexander Watson's *Ring of Steel: Germany and Austria-Hungary at War, 1914–1918*

(London: Penguin, 2014) provides a more in-depth, but still highly readable, account of the Central Powers in the First World War. The best history of the German Home Front in the First World War remains Belinda J. Davis, *Home Fires Burning: Food, Politics and Everyday Life in World War I Berlin* (Chapel Hill: University of North Carolina Press, 2000). The centenary of the November Revolution led to a rash of publications concerning that event. The best narrative history is Robert Gerwarth's *November 1918: The German Revolution* (Oxford: OUP, 2020). A spirited account from a left-wing perspective is William A. Peltz's, *A People's History of the German Revolution* (London: Pluto Press, 2018). While this is a little biased in terms of its political position, it is worth reading for the chapter on the role played by women in the November Revolution alone. Mark Jones's *Founding Weimar: Violence and the German Revolution of 1918–1919* (Cambridge: Cambridge University Press, 2016) examines the role of violence and political polarization and radicalization in the events of 1918–9 and how they shaped German political culture. The essays in Klaus Weinhauer, Anthony McElligott and Kirsten Heinsohn (eds.), *Germany 1916–23: A Revolution in Context* (Bielefeld: Transcript, 2015) delve into various aspects of the revolution and seek to place the event in a global context. Robert Gerwarth's *The Vanquished: Why the First World War Failed to End, 1917–1923* (London: Allen Lane, 2016) connects events in Germany with those in Central Europe and the Middle East in the same period and views the German Revolution in the context of war and Imperial collapse.

Perhaps the best book on the transition from war to peace in Germany remains Richard Bessel, *Germany after the First World War* (Oxford: OUP, 1993). Dirk Schumann (Thomas Dunlap, trans.), *Political Violence in the Weimar Republic, 1918–1933* (New York: Berghahn Books, 2009) and the essays contained in Kathleen Canning, Kerstin Brandt and Kristin McGuire (eds.), *Weimar Publics/ Weimar Subjects: Rethinking the Political Culture of Germany in the 1920s* (Oxford: Berghahn Books, 2010) give a good overview of aspects of the political culture of the Weimar Republic. Perhaps unsurprisingly, the German right has attracted a lot of historians of Weimar Germany. Larry Eugene Jones, *The German Right, 1918–1930: Political Parties, Organized Interests and Patriotic Associations in the Struggle Against Weimar Democracy* (Cambridge: Cambridge University Press, 2020) and the essays in Larry Eugene Jones (ed.), *The German Right in the Weimar Republic* (New York, Oxford: Berghahn Books, 2014) provide a sense of the latest research in this area. The essays in Ralf Hoffrogge and Norman Laporte (eds.), *Weimar Communism as a Mass Movement, 1918–1933* (London: Lawrence and Wishart, 2017) perform a similar function for the far-left. Larry Eugene Jones, *German Liberalism and the Dissolution of the Weimar Party System, 1918–1933* (Chapel Hill: University of North Carolina Press, 1988) is an important study of the decline of German liberalism.

The best introduction to Weimar's economic history is Theo Balderston, *Politics and Economics in the Weimar Republic* (Cambridge: University of Cambridge Press, 2002). Many books have been published on the period of hyperinflation, but the most accessible are perhaps Adam Ferguson, *When Money Dies: The Nightmare of the Weimar Hyper-Inflation* (London: Old Street Publishing, 2010) and Frederick Taylor, *The Downfall of Money: Germany's Hyperinflation and the Destruction of the Middle Class* (London: Bloomsbury, 2014). Both give a chilling sense of the social and cultural impacts of the inflation as well as its effect on the economic fortunes of the republic. Tobias Straumann, *1931: Debt, Crisis and the Rise of Hitler* (Oxford: OUP, 2021) gives a similarly incisive and impactful account of the role that the Great Depression and the German banking crisis of 1931 played in bringing about the collapse of the Weimar Republic.

There have been surprisingly few book-length studies of Weimar foreign policy in English and most of those that have been published are now several decades old. However, there are good overviews by Wolfgang Elz in Anthony McElligott (ed.), *Weimar Germany*, by Jonathan Wright in the *Oxford Handbook of the Weimar Republic* and by Immanuel Geiss in Panikos Panayi (ed.), *Weimar and Nazi Germany: Continuities and Discontinuities* (Abingdon: Routledge, 2014). The best overview of the Paris Peace Conference and the post-war order that emerged from it is perhaps Margaret MacMillan's *Peacemakers* (London: John Murray, 2002). Conan Fischer's *The Ruhr Crisis, 1923–1924* (Oxford: Oxford University Press, 2003) is a comprehensive account of what can be seen as a pivotal event in the early life of the republic; while *A Vision of Europe: Franco-German Relations during the Great Depression, 1929–1932* (Oxford: Oxford University Press, 2017) by the same author is an excellent exploration of Germany's relations with its western neighbour in the latter years of the republic.

Helen Boak's *Women in the Weimar Republic* (Manchester: University of Manchester Press, 2013) provides an excellent overview of all aspects of the female experience in Weimar Germany. I would also recommend Vibeke Rützou Petersen's *Women and Modernity in Weimar Germany* (New York: Berghahn Books, 2001) which looks at intersections between the realities of the female experience and fictional representations of it. Julia Sneeringer, *Winning Women's Votes: Propaganda and Politics in Weimar Germany* (Chapel Hill: University of Michigan Press, 2002) is an excellent study of the role played by newly enfranchised women in the political life of the republic. Cornelie Usborne's *The Politics of the Body in Weimar Germany: Women's Reproductive Rights and Duties* (Ann Arbor: University of Michigan Press, 1992), Anita Grossmann, *Reforming Sex: The German Movement for Birth Control and Abortion Reform, 1920–1950* (Oxford: Oxford University Press, 1995) and Julia Roos, *Weimar Through the Lens of Gender: Prostitution Reform, Women's Emancipation, and German Democracy, 1919–33* (Ann Arbor: University of Michigan Press, 2010) are all important studies of female sexuality and reproduction. The essays in Christine Schönfeld (ed.), *Practicing Modernity: Female Creativity in the Weimar Republic* (Würzburg: Königshausen and Neumann, 2005) give a good overview of aspects of *Frauenkultur*.

For readers who want to look in more depth at queerness and the gay rights movement of the period, John Clinton Whisnant, *Queer Identities and Politics in Germany: A History, 1880–1945* (New York: Harrington Park Press, 2016), Laurie Marhoefer, *Sex and the Weimar Republic: German Homosexual Emancipation and the Rise of the Nazis* (Toronto: University of Toronto Press, 2015) and James Kollenbroich, *Our Hour Has Come: The Homosexual Rights Movement in the Weimar Republic* (Saarbrücken: VDM Verlag, 2007) are good places to start.

Donald L. Niewyk's *The Jews in Weimar Germany* (New York: Routledge, 2017) is a comprehensive study of the Jewish community and its relations with wider German society. Part memoir, part history, Guenter Lewy's *Jews and Germans: Promise, Tragedy, and the Search for Normalcy* (Philadelphia: University of Nebraska Press, 2020) gives a personal account of Jewish life under the republic, with particularly good chapters on Jewish youth movements and Jewish nationalism. Michael Brenner, *The Renaissance of Jewish Culture in Weimar Germany* (New Haven and London: Yale University Press, 1996) gives an excellent overview of Jewish culture in the period and of some of the social and political pressures which led to the rediscovery of a distinct Jewish identity and culture under the republic.

After many years of being largely ignored by historians, the place of people of colour in modern German history has attracted more attention recently. Although there are still not many books on the subject available in English, Robbie Aitken and Eve Rosenhaft's *Black Germany: The Making and Unmaking of a Diaspora, 1884–1960* (Cambridge: Cambridge University Press, 2013) is a good starting point. The journal *German History* recently put together a special collection of articles dealing with race in modern German history which can be accessed on their website. A good range of articles and primary sources can also be found on the Black Central Europe website (https://blackcentraleurope.com/sources/1914-1945/).

Two classic texts, which were instrumental in introducing generations of British and American historians to the study of Weimar culture are Peter Gay, *Weimar Culture: The Outsider as Insider* (London: Penguin, 1992) and Walter Laqueur, *Weimar: A Cultural History 1918–1933* (London: Phoenix Press, 2000). These books began the 'cultural turn' in Weimar historiography and have been joined by a host of books, many richly illustrated, that seek to give modern readers a sense of what was so exciting and modern about Weimar culture. Rainer Metzger, *Berlin in the Twenties: Art and Culture, 1918–1933* (London: Thames and Hudson, 2007) and Robert Nippoldt and Boris Pofalla, *Night Falls on the Berlin of the Roaring Twenties* (Cologne: Taschen, 2018) are both good recent examples. Recent historiography has taken a more diverse view of Weimar culture than that provided by Gay and Laqueur. A good sense of this trend can be found in the essays in

John Alexander Williams (ed.), *Weimar Culture Revisited* (New York: Palgrave, 2011). Jonathan O. Wipplinger, *Jazz Republic: Music, Race and American Culture in Weimar Germany* (Ann Arbor: University of Michigan Press, 2017) and Brendan Fay, *Classical Music in the Weimar Republic* (London: Bloomsbury, 2020) look at different aspects of the musical culture of the time, while Bernhard Fulda, *Press and Politics in the Weimar Republic* (Oxford: OUP, 2009) examines the role of the press in Weimar culture and politics. Corey Ross, *Media and the Making of Modern Germany: Mass Communications, Society, and Politics from the Empire to the Third Reich* (Oxford: OUP, 2008) is an excellent and in-depth exploration of mass media in Weimar Germany, while the essays in Noah Isenberg (ed.), *Weimar Cinema: An Essential Guide to Classic Films of the Era* (New York: Columbia University Press, 2009) provide analyses of many of the most famous and important examples of Weimar cinema.

As has been mentioned previously, the final years of the republic and the conundrum of why Germany succumbed to the appeal of National Socialism have been subjects of enduring fascination to historians and general readers alike. The books on these subjects are too many to list, but for those interested in this subject Richard J. Evans, *The Coming of the Third Reich* (London: Penguin, 2003), Henry Ashby Turner, *Hitler's Thirty Days to Power* (Reading: Addison-Wesley Publishing, 1996), Larry Eugene Jones, *Hitler Versus Hindenburg: The 1932 Presidential Elections and the End of the Weimar Republic* (Cambridge: Cambridge University Press, 2016), Benjamin Carter Hett, *The Death of Democracy: Hitler's Rise to Power* (London: William Heinemann, 2018) and Peter Walther (Peter Lewis, trans.), *Darkness Falling: The Strange Death of the Weimar Republic, 1930–3* (London: Apollo, 2021) are all recommended.

The Weimar Republic, with its reputation for decadence in the shadow of dictatorship, has sparked the imaginations of novelists, artists and filmmakers ever since Christopher Isherwood's *Berlin Novels* (London: Vintage, 1999) in the 1930s. Recently, it has been especially attractive to writers of crime fiction. Volker Kutscher's series of novels beginning with *Babylon Berlin* (Dingwall: Sandstone Press, 2016) follow detective Gereon Rath through the Weimar Republic and beyond and have recently been adapted for German television in a series that for all its occasional historical inaccuracies is highly recommended. Polish author Marek Krajewski's series of thrillers featuring Breslau detective Eberhard Mock, starting with *The End of the World in Breslau* (London: Quercus, 2010), provide a slightly darker, weirder take on a similar theme and are notable for being set in Breslau, not Berlin. Philip Kerr's *Metropolis* (London: Quercus, 2019) sees his German private eye Bernie Gunther investigate a case from early in his career in the Berlin police. Outside of the crime genre, Jason Lutes's graphic novel *Berlin* (Montreal: Drawn and Quarterly, 2018) has rightfully attracted high praise as both a compelling historical novel and a work of history, telling the story of Weimar

Berlin through the eyes of a number of characters, some fictional, some drawn from real life. Brendan Nash's novels *The Landlady* (Berlin: Nollendorf Press, 2019) and *The Director* (Berlin: Baxter Jardine, 2022) centre on a cast of colourful characters living in and around Nollendorfstrasse in mid-1920s Berlin and channel the spirit of Isherwood and Armistad Maupin's *Tales of the City*. Finally, although to the best of my knowledge the Weimar Republic has not yet featured in the world of video games, the card based social deduction game, *Secret Hitler* (https://www.secrethitler.com/) has players take on the roles of different factions and enact 'liberal' or 'fascist' policies, while players of the tabletop roleplaying game *Call of Cthulhu* can battle creatures from H. P. Lovecraft's Cthulhu mythos in Weimar Germany in David Larkins, *Berlin: The Wicked City* (Ann Arbor: Chaosium, 2019).

Index

Bold page numbers indicate tables, *italic* numbers indicate figures.